CULTURE IN THE MARKETPLACE

OBJECTS / HISTORIES ◉ *Critical Perspectives on Art, Material Culture,*

and Representation ◉ a series edited by Nicholas Thomas

CULTURE IN THE MARKETPLACE

Gender, Art, and Value in the American Southwest

MOLLY H. MULLIN

DUKE UNIVERSITY PRESS Durham and London 2001

©2001 Duke University Press

All rights reserved

Printed in the United States of

America on acid-free paper ∞

Typeset in Dante by Keystone

Typesetting, Inc.

Library of Congress Cataloging-

in-Publication Data appear on the

last printed page of this book.

CONTENTS

PREFACE

 I first visited Santa Fe in 1989, when I presented a paper at the annual meeting of the American Ethnological Society. While passing through a crowd of fellow conventioneers, I overheard a remark I would often recall when I went back to live there the following year. Mingling outside the art galleries and boutiques lining San Francisco Street, a woman turned to her companions and observed, in a tone suggesting a combination of wry amusement and mild embarrassment, that in Santa Fe, "you can hardly tell the anthropologists from the tourists." It is still not entirely clear to me what particular commonalities were being remarked on, though at this point I could hazard a guess. A student at the time, I was working at the intersection of several academic disciplines (anthropology, history, literature), and it had never occurred to me that one might distinguish, on the basis of appearance, anthropologists from anyone else. But regardless of its ambiguity, the observation intrigued me in its suggestion of unusually blurred boundaries between anthropologists and other travelers, an academic discipline and a broader public, and the academy and the marketplace.

Apart from not wanting to be mistaken for tourists, there are a number of reasons why anthropologists might well be disconcerted by Santa Fe, a city where one is confronted with a striking degree of popular enthusiasm for ideas and sensibilities historically associated with anthropology and anthropologists. Santa Fe, marketed to tourists and convention-goers as "the City Different" and a "city of three cultures," is a place where art galleries specialize in the "tribal" and the "primitive" and advertise "ethnographic weekends" and "the art of ethnographic peoples." If, in other locales, where disdain for cultural difference of any kind remains alive and well, many anthropologists still imagine themselves rare specialists in the exotic, in Santa Fe they find themselves in plenty of company. If they have mixed feelings about this company, the reasons are more complicated than a fear of competition or loss of distinction, or even consternation at how words like "ethnographic" can be so distorted in their commercial deployment.

I returned to Santa Fe after that conference and was most intrigued by a disjunction: the increasing popularity of ideas and sensibilities historically associated with anthropology, such as one is likely to see in Santa Fe tourism, at a time when anthropologists and scholars in related fields have been subjecting those very same notions to sustained critique and revision. A particularly striking example of this disjunction, and one of the primary concerns of this book, is the concept of culture. Whereas it was once suggested that one could define an anthropologist as "someone who uses the word 'culture' habitually" (Wagner 1981:1), in recent years many anthropologists have become increasingly ill at ease with the concepts of culture most often associated with their discipline. Though long assumed to be a useful tool for characterizing differences among peoples in a non-hierarchical manner, over the past two decades the concept has been critiqued by scholars as misleading in important ways, as potentially perpetuating stereotypes, and as inadequately simplistic in a world of contested, shifting, and permeable boundaries (e.g., Gupta and Ferguson 1992). Discussing "cultures" as if they were static and homogeneous entities obscures power and change. In *Colonialism's Culture* Nicholas Thomas (1994) situates anthropological notions of "cultures" and their "language of typification" within the project of nineteenth-century colonialism, a project many contemporary anthropologists have sought to document and critique, rather than reproduce. As Mary Margaret Steedly has written, "like other such 'useful categories' as 'gender' or 'woman' or 'experience,' the concept of culture can be an instrument of dangerous utility" (1996:22). For James Clifford, culture is "a deeply compromised idea," but one that he "cannot yet do without" (1988:10). Lila Abu-Lughod has suggested that "the notion of culture (especially as it functions to distinguish 'cultures'), despite a long usefulness, may now have become something anthropologists would want to work against in their theories, their ethnographic practice, and their ethnographic writing" (1991:138). More straightforwardly, Joel Kahn has proposed that anthropologists might well consider abandoning the concept altogether (1989:21).[1]

Yet while anthropologists debate the relative merits of rehabilitating or abandoning the notions of culture once championed by their discipline, outside anthropology those same notions—or some semblance of them, anyway—enjoy greater popularity than ever. In response to this disjunction, this study examines some particular examples of the social history of concepts of culture, how notions of culture historically associated with anthropology have been put into practice outside the academy, and how the category of culture has been positioned in relation to other categories such as race, class, gender, and art.

As Virginia Dominguez (1994) has noted, the recent popularity of anthropological notions of culture can be considered part of a widespread "culturalization of difference"—a phenomenon in which human differences that could be and have been ordered in other ways (ways that are not necessarily any more accurate or politically preferable) are recategorized in terms of "culture" and "cultural difference." Following lines of thought pursued by Clifford (1988) and others, in her discussion of what gets included and excluded from the purview of national "cultural policies" Dominguez observes that what may appear to represent a progressive departure from hierarchical and Eurocentric perspectives of what culture is may not indicate any such departure after all. Much contemporary usage of the term *culture*, Dominguez notes, stops short of the more holistic notion of culture used by many anthropologists. In a holistic perspective, "culture" is no more about things like art or literature or music than it is about cusswords, prisons or laboratories, what to do with a telephone, what gets tossed in the garbage, or, in the words of a classic title in anthropology, "how to ask for a drink" (Frake 1972). As Dominguez puts it, "An anthropologically holistic definition of culture would include economic organization, political processes, intergroup relationships, and technology as integral components of a population's culture, not separate from it" (241). But whether one accepts such a "holistic" definition, or one that privileges the realm of language and thought, representations of culture are necessarily partial.

This book follows Virginia Dominguez's suggestion that rather than quibbling over what does and does not belong in the category of culture, it is important to ask what purposes it serves (239). In the following pages, I examine the "culturalization of difference" and the social construction of value in relation to the patronage of American Indian art in New Mexico from the early twentieth century to the present day. In addition to considering existing institutions such as Santa Fe's annual Indian Market (the focus of chapter 5) and some significant historical antecedents, including the 1931

Exposition of American Indian Tribal Arts, I trace the histories of a network of highly educated middle- and upper-class white women. This network included relatively well-known figures, such as Willa Cather, Mabel Dodge Luhan, and Mary Austin. But I focus particularly on a number of women who are much less well known, especially outside Santa Fe, including four who graduated from Bryn Mawr at the turn of the twentieth century: journalist Elizabeth Shepley Sergeant, suffragist-turned-Indian-policy reformer and art patron Margretta Stewart Dietrich, and two patrons of art and anthropology, Elizabeth and Martha White. In their promotion of American Indian arts, these women saw themselves as championing new ways of thinking about art in general, about culture, and about the continent's Native inhabitants. To members of this network, notions of culture associated with anthropology served as a valuable tool in a number of interrelated struggles—struggles to redefine American national identity; to bridge the separation of public and private, male and female spheres of influence; to gain public influence and authority for themselves; and to construct authoritative standards of value in a society increasingly oriented around the consumption of commodities. Though these women were in many ways more homogeneous as a group than the Native artists they promoted, there were important differences among them. The White sisters had inherited a fortune made in newspapers and railroads; Dietrich moved to Santa Fe as the widow of a man who had been a banker, governor, and United States Senator. In the early 1930s when Elizabeth White launched the Exposition of Indian Tribal Arts and sought to convince Americans that Indian art was "art, not ethnology," she and many of her fellow art patrons were hardly affected by the Depression. Elizabeth Sergeant, in contrast, struggled to support herself as a journalist, and other women discussed here found employment with wealthy women such as White and Dietrich. While some would nostalgically recall what one member called "a city of ladies" as marked by a spirit of freedom (especially from conventions of gender and sexuality), equality, and unity, those with inherited wealth and privilege enjoyed the economic dependence of those without it.

As James Clifford has observed, the concept of culture is an extraordinarily versatile one (1988:337–39), and the cases I examine here demonstrate that in the context of an expanding consumer society, the relatively egalitarian notion of people belonging to distinct "cultures" has coexisted with, rather than supplanted, more hierarchical notions of culture as the "best" and the province of an elite. As the colonial context of earlier Indian arts patronage has given way to one that can usefully be considered "postcolonial" (Phillips 1995), this contradiction survives, indicating continuities between colonial and postcolonial eras.

In addition to being a study of the social construction of the value of objects, this book is a study of the value of the concept of culture itself—including ways in which the culture concept has lent legitimacy to objects and activities with which it might be associated. As I will argue, in the early twentieth century, anthropological notions of culture—at least the notion that there are cultures, rather than just Culture—provided new ways for some particularly privileged women to gain public influence and authority and to win legitimacy for their work, including political and philanthropic activities. Following the lead of women in the late nineteenth century who were involved in social reform and settlement houses, they legitimated their ambition by associating it with benevolence and collective progress.

I will also argue that such women moved into new spaces of influence in part by using the skills developed in the private sphere of the bourgeois household and the more public, and largely feminine, space of the modern department store (Laermans 1993): skills pertaining to commodity consumption and the exercise of taste. In addition to using consumer skills, these art patrons also made use of their experience with pageantry, including the staging of public dramas and ceremonies. As Margaret Finnegan (1999) has observed, the early twentieth-century passion for pageantry fit well with the expansion of consumer capitalism, encouraging a sense that identities could be selected, tried on, and performed to suit the occasion and both individual and collective interests.

While I believe it is important to consider the strategic nature of these women's activities, my intention is not to reduce their patronage of Native art to a struggle to improve their own status; their philanthropic and political concerns were sincere, and taste, I will argue, was not just a tool to gain status and influence, but was an important means by which these women invented and reinvented their identities as well as their relationships with one another. As Leora Auslander has written in her study of style and taste in relation to the history of furniture in modern France, "judgments of aesthetic value emerge from a complex interaction of desires for emulation, distinction and solidarity" (1996:2). The institutions set up by earlier patrons now provide consumers a way to go shopping for new and improved selves. At Indian Market, shoppers steeped in what historian Jackson Lears terms the "therapeutic ethos" (1983) seek to acquire not just objects but also knowledge—of specialized vocabularies, artists, categories of objects, as well as "cultures."

This study has been informed by a number of influential works that have critically examined "Primitivism," markets in "non-Western" art, and a taste for the objects and knowledge of so-called Primitive Societies. Works such as those of James Clifford (1988), Sally Price (1989), and Marianna Torgovnick (1990, 1997) have provocatively and valuably critiqued oppositions between Primitive and Modern, Self and Other, but in a way, I believe, that sometimes tends, however inadvertently, to reproduce the binary structures of thought under critique. To simplify, "How do 'we' relate to 'them'?" is the fundamental question posed—or at least the question that many readers are likely to come away with. In my consideration of attempts to promote American Indian art, I hope to draw attention to how a consideration of distinctions typically falling outside the category of "culture" may complicate the Self-Other dichotomy. Concern with "otherness" and its metonymic objects occurs in specific historical contexts, contexts which may be obscured by analyses of a more global or totalizing nature and by such broad terms—however useful to a certain point—as "Primitivism," "Orientalism," or "antimodernism."

In addition to exploring ways in which ideas about "culture" and "cultures" may be illuminated by a consideration of class and gender, my aim here is also to consider theories of taste, value, and evaluation—as explored by, for example, Pierre Bourdieu (1984), Michael Thompson (1979), and Barbara Herrnstein Smith (1988)—in relation to historical processes of transformation. Bourdieu's justly influential work, *Distinction,* emphasized class differences in the judgment of taste, but paid scant attention to historical change, gender, or racial, ethnic, or geographic diversity. By showing, however, that even the most "avant-garde" of tastes may serve to legitimate and reproduce social inequalities, Bourdieu suggests important complications for ideals of cultural pluralism. His analysis, for example, leaves anthropologists in a rather awkward relationship to markets in art produced by anthropology's historical subjects, where the work of anthropologists and related scholars has often played an important role in constructing the value and authenticity of objects. The role of anthropologists in such art markets becomes even more politically ambiguous as postcolonial Others adopt the often expedient strategy of what Brian Wallis has termed, in an analysis of "national cultural festivals," a "self-Orientalizing mode" (1991:88). As George Marcus and Fred Myers have written, "In the anthropology of art, it is no longer possible for anthropologists to address subjects 'cleanly'—that is, as subjects in relation to whom they, or their discipline of study, do not already have a history of relations" (1995:2). In lieu of any simple answers to the many questions arising from contemporary encounters between art and anthropology, that history of relationships deserves examination.

This book is based on an eclectic research methodology. In part because the network of individuals I was examining included a number of professional writers—for example, Mary Austin, Willa Cather, Elizabeth Sergeant, Oliver La Farge, and Witter Bynner—and people for whom books and other written works were a particularly important part of their lives, I discuss numerous published works, especially some dated from 1910 through the 1930s. For example, in chapter 1, Mary Austin's novel *No. 26 Jayne Street* and the nonfiction bestseller by Stuart Chase, *Mexico: A Study of Two Americas,* are discussed in relation to American cultural nationalism and commodity consumption. In chapter 2, Willa Cather's *The Song of the Lark* (1915) and Elizabeth Sergeant's articles in *Harper's* (1922)—publications that had a direct influence on the network of women whose paths I trace—provide examples of changing constructions of national identity, gender, and cultural difference. Though I believe it is important to analyze such works as strategic and partial representations—of people and places—I am equally concerned with how such works relate to practices of value construction and the formation of value-making institutions.

In addition to examining works of fiction, memoirs, and journalism, I draw on formal and informal interviews with artists, art collectors, dealers, and museum curators, as well as with other people historically connected with networks of art patrons. In my research, such interviews often meshed well with the archival research I was doing at the same time, and I make much use here of letters, minutes of meetings, brochures, reports, scrapbooks, and unpublished manuscripts.

I gained not just information, but insight as well, from involvement in the Indian art world.[2] In addition to attending such events, I worked as a volunteer at Indian Market and its relatives, the Gallup Intertribal Ceremonial and the Eight Northern Indian Pueblos Annual Artist and Craftsman

Show, as well as related events such as fund-raising auctions. At the School of American Research, I volunteered with the visiting artist program and with seminars, including those held in conjunction with Indian Market.

During my two and a half years of living in Northern New Mexico, and on numerous subsequent visits, more chance happenings were sometimes surprisingly instructive about my interests in the art market, both past and present. Not only did I learn from things people said and did, but I learned from my own reactions. There was, for example, the time I decided that I wanted to "participant observe" by purchasing, not just watching others purchase. Several of the collectors I interviewed were fond of insisting that anyone could afford to buy "decent" Indian art if he or she really wanted to—and proceeded to tell me stories of what they had sacrificed to make their first purchases, now, they would sometimes point out, worth ten to fifty times what they paid for them. I, however, was rarely willing to make similar "sacrifices" and felt that on my limited budget, any purchase of Indian art had to be at the absolute bottom rung of the market (below, in fact, what anyone in a position of authority would recognize as "art"). I knew, from my interviews and historical research, that collectors (past and present) would cringe at what I ended up buying—lopsided little pots, made by relatively inexperienced potters from Jemez and Cochiti who did not describe themselves as artists, pots brightly painted after firing with the most thoroughly "non-traditional" of designs. I was intrigued to find myself becoming attached to these marketplace faux pas. Yet when an admired colleague walked into my apartment and laughed at my purchases ("you bought *that???*") I found myself, despite my prior awareness of the positioning of such objects in prevailing hierarchies of value, not immune to self-doubt; consequently I gained new insight into the practice I had been observing of people investing large amounts of money into learning from various experts what to buy and what not to.

During the research and writing of this book, I thought much about careers and works and how they depend upon social networks, relationships, and institutions. The research I did often reminded me that without the generous assistance of many individuals and institutions, my own work would never have been possible. This book draws on research and writing initially supported by the Duke University Department of Cultural Anthropology, a Woodrow Wilson Fellowship in Rural Policy, a Leslie White Memorial

Award from the Central States Anthropological Society, and a Fellowship in Nonprofit Governance from the Indiana University Center on Philanthropy. During my first year in Santa Fe I benefited greatly from living and doing research at the School of American Research, made possible by Douglas Schwartz. Follow-up research and manuscript revision was supported by a Richard Carley Hunt Memorial Fellowship from the Wenner-Gren Foundation for Anthropological Research, Inc. and the Hewlett-Mellon Fund for Faculty Development at Albion College.

This project was in many ways inspired by Richard G. Fox, who encouraged me to think critically about concepts of culture and the social history of American anthropology. My writing and thinking were also aided especially by Rita Barnard, Jerry Brody, Mary Ellen Curtin, Ken Dauber, Cynthia Davis, Virginia Dominguez, Susan Hegeman, Margaret Jacobs, Charlie McGovern, V. Y. Mudimbe, Fred Myers, Joanne Passaro, Dana Phillips, Jan Radway, Kathy Rudy, Carol Smith, and Orin Starn. Michael Brown, in addition to discussing this project with me at length, introduced me to the late Alfonso Ortiz, who was tremendously generous with both information and ideas. At the School of American Research I was assisted by many, including Baylor Chapman, Lynn Brittner, Jane Guillentine, Jane Kepp, Bonnie Mamp, Joan O'Donnell, Peter Palmeiri, Douglas Schwartz, Cecile Stein, and Tony Thibodeau. Willow Powers at the Laboratory of Anthropology shared her knowledge of the archives. Many people spoke to me at length concerning their experiences with Indian art and art patrons; for especially helpful or lengthy discussions, I am especially grateful to Bruce Bernstein, Gail Bird, Jean Buchanan, Maria Chabot, Dick Howard, Yazzie Johnson, Marge Lambert, Julia Lukas, Catherine Rayne, Ramona Sakiestewa, Richard Spivey, Sallie Wagner, Letta Wofford, and Nancy Youngblood-Yugo. Thanks to Santa Fe photographer Corey McGillicuddy for taking the photographs in chapter 5 and allowing them to be reproduced here. My mother, Roberta Wheeler, provided support in many ways and imparted many of the sensibilities and preoccupations that have inspired my work. As was true for many of the people I write about here, my status as a newcomer in Northern New Mexico did not prevent me from feeling that it was a place where I belonged; Jeb Saunders made it easier to feel at home elsewhere, lent his editorial skills to each chapter, and along with our dog, Winnie, provided comic relief.

CHAPTER ONE **CULTURE AND CULTURES**

Let's begin with a piece of property and a cute story about an eclipse, two women, and their hair. Since 1972, the property has been home to the School of American Research (SAR), in the foothills of the Sangre de Cristo mountains, nestled in an exclusive residential neighborhood on the east side of Santa Fe. Despite the name, the SAR is not a school at all, but rather a place where scholars, the majority of them anthropologists, come to participate in seminars and write books in the serenity of the high desert, temporarily relieved from the demands of classrooms and faculty committees. For its sponsors, the SAR often serves, like the Santa Fe Opera or some of the local museums, as an entree to a powerful local elite and a means of establishing a certain kind of regional identity. It is also home to a renowned collection of Native American art, housed in carefully guarded, climate-controlled vaults and visited by art historians, art collectors, and Native artists. The SAR is a place where culture as a marker of class distinction and culture as "peoples of the world" unite.

When visitors arrive at the School for the first time, they usually receive a tour of the buildings and grounds. The tour includes a brief history of the property, as well as an explanation of some of its more unusual features—the administration building, for example, styled after a Spanish mission church, the terraced gardens, and, in a small clearing in a shady grove, the grave of the property's former owners, Amelia Elizabeth White and her sister, Martha Root White.

By the time they reach the grave, visitors are apt to have been told a story about how the Whites came to buy the property. As the story goes, sometime in the early 1920s the White sisters, typically described as "two wealthy women from Manhattan who never married," were on a road trip across the country, aiming to reach California in time to observe a solar eclipse. In Santa Fe they stopped to have their hair done—described, in at least one version of the story, as "the feminine thing to do"—and they were so taken with the area that, on a whim, they purchased the property that Elizabeth White, great friend of anthropology and art, bequeathed a half century later to the School of American Research. Upon hearing this story, the audience is apt to chuckle and smile—at the thought, perhaps, of such a frivolous, personal, and feminine errand having such significant and public consequences.

The story is in some ways misleading. Although the Whites were not above conspicuously indulging their whims in an eccentric fashion afforded by a position of extraordinary privilege, their interest in Santa Fe developed out of Elizabeth White's long-term social, political, and intellectual commitments and was not altogether a spur-of-the moment indulgence. But accuracy aside, the story told about the two women is instructive about common perceptions of relationships between women and history. In an article concerning the history of anthropology in Santa Fe, historian George Stocking described the Whites and some of their acquaintances as "wealthy New England spinsters" (1982:9). Stocking's description, like the story of the Whites' purchase of the property, falls into a pattern of social memory in which what is most often considered worth knowing about women such as Elizabeth and Martha White is that they were wealthy, from the East, and never married—rather than, for example, that they graduated from Bryn Mawr at the turn of the century, participated in the women's suffrage movement, and developed interests in anthropology and American Indians before the First World War. Also often absent from the social memory is the information that the Whites were not just isolated, particularly eccentric "spinsters," but part of a network of highly educated women who, during the 1920s and 1930s, bought property in Northern New Mexico and became important patrons of Native American and Spanish Colonial art.

The story of the Whites' acquisition of the property charms its audiences in part because it seems so incongruous with the property's present purpose as a home for serious scholarship and a hallowed, awe-inspiring art collection. It also strikes people as funny because this is one of the more valuable pieces of real estate in the entire region. Women who never married, a road-trip with no serious purpose, a beauty salon, anthropology, priceless art, and extraordinarily valuable property—who imagines such categories ending up together? If, however, the story about the White sisters is a story about gender, class, a merging of public and private interests, the acquisition of property, and the social construction of value, there are ways in which these categories are not so incongruous after all and their connection to the School of American Research not at all coincidental.

By the time the Whites bought that hillside in Santa Fe in 1923, they had joined a movement among anthropologists, artists, and writers promoting new ways of thinking about culture and cultural difference. Thinking about cultures in the plural, rather than as something singular and European-centered, offered new sources of power and authority and new ways of evaluating commodities, including real estate. At a time when culture, in the singular, had become a valuable commodity sought after by many middle-class Americans, thinking of cultures in the plural offered a new means of distinction, a new identity.

Culture, Cultures, and the Nation

Toward the end of his ironically titled *Europe and the People Without History* (1982), Eric Wolf urged anthropologists to rethink the concept of culture in a way which might take into account continual change and the fragmentation of communities dispersed across time and space, as well as the complicated criss-crossing of global political and economic relationships. In contrast to a view of culture as a concept inevitably developed by scientists motivated purely by a search for truth and understanding, Wolf emphasized the historical connections between anthropological notions of culture and nationalist movements. "The culture concept came to the fore in a specific historical context," he noted, "during a period when some European nations were striving for dominance while others were striving for separate identities and independence. The demonstration that each struggling nation possessed a distinctive society, animated by its special spirit or culture, served to legitimate its aspirations to form a separate state of its own. The notion of separate and integral cultures corresponded to this political project" (387).

The concept of culture, Wolf suggests, is not an inevitable part of contemporary discourse, but has resulted from a history of struggles to redraw maps of identities and differences. Although Wolf wrote in the past tense, the assertion of nations and cultures has continued into the present, often involving more complicated dynamics than a drive for the political independence of nation-states. Moreover, "the notion of separate and integral cultures" did not arise all in one piece, displacing, or existing completely independently of, other notions of culture, such as that which assumes culture to be something of which an individual can have more or less, even something one can acquire for a price. But the concept of culture to which Wolf refers, a concept that assumes that all people belong to "a culture," each worthy in its own way, each internally coherent and unified, has been one that has been useful at various times to individuals, including anthropologists, who have not always entirely abandoned Eurocentric notions of culture as something that makes some people superior to others. Rather, these two different ways of thinking about culture have continued to coexist, however much they might seem to contradict one another, and however much the concept to which Wolf refers may have become predominant.

Wolf's own rethinking of the culture concept has encouraged a consideration of how individuals and groups have used language and ideas to gain and maintain power in social relationships (Wolf 1999). How was the concept of culture used to gain and maintain power in early twentieth-century America? At the turn of the century, American intellectuals did not need the concept of culture to help legitimate the formation of a separate state; their concerns with culture were instead part of an ongoing process of constructing a more positive, confident national identity. The nation's relationship to "culture" was considered by many to be a particularly vexing problem.

In the early twentieth century, struggling to rehabilitate the nation's identity, American cultural nationalists cast about for new ways of thinking about culture as they attempted to reposition themselves on their map of the world and to redraw the boundaries between themselves and others. In this period, the anthropological notion of separate and integral cultures appeared, to many intellectuals at least, to allow for more than one center of the world, including wherever it was that they positioned themselves. To use another metaphor, seeing everyone as belonging to a valid culture allowed people—those who concerned themselves with such things, that is—to rewrite the rules of a game they felt they had been losing. At the same time, they did not entirely forsake the idea that culture was something that could be acquired and encouraged ("cultivated"), and either sense of the term—as a way of identifying groups of people all over the world, or as a matter of elite knowledge and sensibility *within* a group—allowed for important distinctions of authenticity and value.

In the basement of the library of the School of American Research, I browsed one afternoon among books that once belonged to the White sisters' father, Horace White. Among volumes of translated Greek and Roman histories, I happened upon an especially striking illustration of connections between American nationalism and ideas about "culture" and "cultures." The *Anthropology* volume of the *Science-History of the Universe,* published in 1909—just before Elizabeth and Martha White became seriously interested in the Southwest—was part of a compact ten-volume set designed for a popular audience, with other volumes devoted to such topics as chemistry and physics. The volume on anthropology begins with the admission that "no other science deals with a field so ill-defined" and refers to the motto of the Anthropology Department of the 1893 World's Columbian Exposition in Chicago, "Man and His Works," as a reliable indication of the discipline's vagueness. Vagueness notwithstanding, the volume proceeds to provide concise summaries of anthropology's various subdivisions, including somatology, ethnology, ethnography, and culture history ("under the latter we must rank Prehistoric Archaeology, perhaps the most popular subdivision of the field") (Rolt-Wheeler 1909:ix).

After chapters devoted to "Man's Place in Nature" (which includes an illustrated facial comparison of a "Female Hottentot and Female Gorilla"), anthropometry (with its numerous applications to criminology), and prehistoric archaeology, Francis Rolt-Wheeler claims that all these topics come together in the final chapter, "The Development of Culture." This chapter, significantly, makes a stridently nationalist plea for the study of the "culture of the United States"—the importance of which is stressed with the claim that "the New World . . . will, when she reaches a full strength, give to Man a Culture different from any that has gone before" (97).

Rolt-Wheeler concedes, however, that the importance of American Culture unfortunately has yet to be widely recognized and, as explanation, proposes that the lack of recognition is due

> to the fact that the prophets of that spirit have not yet appeared; that the poets, artists, architects, sculptors, dramatists and scholars, are still in the lotus-dream of European ascendency. The engineer, the mechanician, the inventor, the industrial monarch, the railroad king, and the Great Khan of trade, are more in keeping with the growing American spirit, and hence arises the anomaly of those men's names being upon

people's lips who seem to have naught else but wealth to recommend them as the cause of fame. (97)

But, it is argued, "it would be unjust to American culture" to assume that the importance granted to the pursuit of wealth is motivated only by greed. Instead, Rolt-Wheeler proposes in an even more imperialist tone that perhaps "these men" (the engineers, mechanicians, etc.) have only rightly discerned "that the masters of the world in the future will be Americans and that the resources of the world should be under their hands." "America," the volume concludes, "is yet a child, but men are beginning to see that her ideals are not borrowed and that her Culture is her own" (98). I have no knowledge that Elizabeth or Martha White ever read this book, though they did read others that I examine in this study. In many ways, including its pitch to an audience interested in a succinct summary of academic knowledge, it was not typical of the books in their own or their father's libraries. Regardless, the sensibility reflected in this book was one to which the Whites and their associates would appeal, while advocating a shift of emphasis from Culture to cultures.

Even for cultural nationalists without the imperial ambitions expressed in the *Science-History of the Universe*, the relationship between American national identity and culture was fraught with a number of difficulties, including the country's status as a former colony. As the passage quoted above suggests, at the turn of the century the United States was widely perceived as a once poor, now nouveau-riche relative of Europe. In order to imagine the national identity more positively, American intellectuals struggled to assert the possibility of an "American culture." As Russell Lynes noted at mid-century, "through the story of the history of our taste has run a constant theme—if America is to be great, America must have culture" (1954:7). But how, American cultural nationalists wondered, could they articulate an American national identity with cultural forms (art, literature, music) derived from Europe? In a study of nationalism and the arts in twentieth-century America, Charles Alexander argues that "the vision of a genuinely native, nationally representative expression was the single most significant feature of American cultural commentary in the years after 1900 and up to the Second World War" (1980:xii).

In addition to fretting about whether "American culture" was forever condemned to derivative status, many American intellectuals feared that the very concept of culture was being corrupted by its popularity among middle-class consumers. In a society filled with individuals determined to improve their social and economic status, culture was being marketed as something that anyone could acquire—for the price of admission, a book, or a series of lectures. *The Science-History of the Universe* was part of this phenomenon. In 1919, Waldo Frank struggled to retain the validity of the idea of culture and protested against the commercial exploitation of the concept in what he called the "Land of the Pioneers." Frank offered a summary of the history of Americans' relationship to "culture":

> "Culture," which the American had been forced to leave behind in Europe, became a commodity to be won back with wealth: a badge of place and prestige: finally a sort of bait for the catching of less wary fish. The bald truth of this attitude comes out in such institutions as the "Five Foot Book Shelf" first suggested, I believe, by President Emeritus Charles E. Eliot of Harvard, and later exploited by enterprising publishers. Upon this little shelf, in essential and abbreviated form, the busy American finds "culture." Theodore Roosevelt is the author of a similar thesaurus. And today, numerous societies make fortunes advertising in the daily prints how the individual may achieve "culture" at the cost of ten cents a week, by subscribing to a list of "the best of the world's knowledge." (25–26)

Frank joined a number of his contemporaries in putting culture in quotation marks. In Sinclair Lewis's novels of the 1920s, culture is similarly problematized. In his 1929 novel *Dodsworth,* Lewis, echoing Thorstein Veblen's turn-of-the-century analysis of the women of the American nouveaux riches, suggested that the problem of "culture" was connected to the gendered division of labor in the bourgeois household. Bourgeois women, excluded from industrial production and more direct avenues to power, channeled their ambitions into the acquisition and display of "so-called culture." *Dodsworth* tells the story of the midlife crisis and marital failure of a successful automobile manufacturer, Sam Dodsworth. Dodsworth's manipulative wife, Fran, is an ardent social climber who, frustrated and bored after two decades of devotion to provincial domesticity, tasteful consumption, and philanthropic causes, leads him on a frantic tour of the capitals of Western Europe. In one exchange between the couple, Sam asks Fran what it is she expects to find in Europe. " 'A lot of culture?' " he asks, and she replies, " 'No! "Culture!" I loathe the word, I loathe the people who use it! I certainly do not intend to collect the names of a lot of painters—and soups—and come back and air them' " (31). But Lewis depicts Fran Dodsworth's disdain for "culture" as merely a ploy to hide her own affectations, and she ends up too concerned about finding the "right" people and avoiding the standard tourist routines to enjoy even the art galleries and museums of Paris: "Fran had read enough about art; she glanced over the studio magazines monthly, and she knew every gallery on Fifth Avenue. But, to her, painting, like all 'culture,' was interesting only as it adorned her socially" (119). People were eager to buy status in whatever way they could, Lewis suggests, and many were willing to sell it to them under the label of "culture." Those with a little more knowledge of elite tastes knew enough to disavow any interest in such status-seeking, but they still might not convince anyone of their authenticity.

Dodsworth caricatured a notion of culture that was often associated, in the early twentieth century, with the institution known as "Chatauqua." Chatauqua began as a Methodist summer retreat, founded in 1874 in upstate New York. By the early twentieth century, towns and cities throughout the country hosted Chatauqua-style programs, offering a mix of entertainment and education. In the words of two Chatauqua enthusiasts who later wrote a history of the phenomenon, Chatauqua promised "a program of inspiration and culture right at the doorstep" of provincial America (Case and Case 1948:20). In the Chatauqua program, "culture" meant opera, orchestral music, lectures, and poetry—all with "an air of impeccable good breeding" (3). At the peak of the Chatauqua fad in 1924, twelve thousand American towns had Chatauqua tents, into which crowded an estimated thirty million people (3).

In *We Called It Culture*—the title itself revealing—Case and Case contend that Chatauqua's great legacy was "the awakening of rural areas to a consciousness of the part they were both entitled and expected to play in the affairs of the nation and the world . . . No other rural population on the globe forsook its provincial viewpoint so quickly or accepted more thoroughly its responsibilities in a complex but homogeneous social scheme" (239). For its detractors, however, Chatauqua exemplified the provincial rather than transcending it. Accounting for the decline of Chatauqua after 1924, Case and Case cite the imposition of government taxes on entrance tickets, the corporate sponsors' success in turning the profitable events into

"Big Business" (previously one of the traditional enemies of Chatauqua lecturers), as well as the expansion of other sources of commodified leisure:

> People had cars now, highways were building up fast, and bus lines were spangling the countryside, so that Chatauqua's late audiences could run in to the Lyceum attractions in the cities. They had movies along Main Street, which brought them silent dramas like *The Birth of a Nation* and *The Ten Commandments* and comedians like Charlie Chaplin and Fatty Arbuckle. The new radios were coming off the assembly line like peas out of a pod. They would soon be in every home, so the people wouldn't have to stir from their own firesides to hear great orchestras and concerts and lectures. Young people were crowding the colleges, newspapers and magazines were doubling and trebling their circulations, people were travelling abroad, and the strengthening roar of airplane motors was rolling along the horizon. (235)

Perhaps also a factor was that the Chatauqua organizers were so successful in selling "culture" that the term "Chatauqua" had acquired connotations of social climbing, pretentiousness, and provincial insularity, though for many people it retained the notion of an educational and uplifting proram of study and entertainment (Trachtenberg 1982:140–44). As we will see in chapter 4, in the 1920s such different perceptions would clash in Santa Fe, when the White sisters, together with a number of their fellow migrants to the area, would oppose efforts to establish a version of "Chatauqua." At stake would be not just the meaning of "Chatauqua," but also very different notions of culture and competing claims for influence and authority.

In the early twentieth century, anthropologists had begun representing their work as the study of "cultures" and articulating a vision of cultural relativism. Franz Boas, the anthropologist most often credited with establishing anthropology as a distinct academic discipline, decided after spending a year living with the Eskimos in the 1880s that "the idea of a 'cultured' individual is merely relative" (quoted in Langness [1987:530]). Yet neither Boas nor his many influential students often entered the fray of debates about how culture should be defined and about how elitist notions of culture pertained to more relativist ones. A notable exception can be found in the work of Boas's student Edward Sapir, who struggled, like Lewis, Waldo Frank, and many cultural nationalists of the early twentieth century, to retain the validity of the idea of "culture"—in the singular—despite its apparent commodification and association with pretentiousness. As an anthropologist, Sapir sought to reconcile the anthropological notion of the idea of "cultures" with the more popular view of the time that culture was a matter of superior taste. His essay "Culture, Genuine and Spurious" (1924) is particularly striking as an example of how contradictory concepts of culture were colliding, of how culture was a matter of consternation, and how intellectuals were casting about for ways of reconciling the term's contradictions. Sapir—a poet and classical musician as well as a linguist, dedicated scholar of Indian languages, and an ethnographer—was unwilling to dismiss popular questions about culture as merely unscientific or the product of ignorance.

Sapir begins his essay by describing how the term "culture" has become a matter of dispute; he contends tentatively that the term is salvageable, but in need of more accurate definition: "We disagree on the value of things and the relations of things, but often enough we agree on the particular value of the label. It is only when the question arises of just where to put the label, that trouble begins . . . Whatever culture is, we know that it is, or is considered to be, a good thing" (402).

Sapir then goes on to identify three main senses of the term. First, as used by "the ethnologist and culture-historian," "culture" suggests "any socially inherited element in the life of man, material and spiritual." From this point of view, Sapir explains that all human groups are "cultured," regardless of the degree of industrial development or material wealth. Ethnologists, Sapir claims, may distinguish between levels of culture on an evolutionary scale, but ordinarily make no distinctions of value among different societies and their different cultures. Sapir states that, for the purposes of his article, he intends to set aside this ethnological notion of culture, as it is too "technical" to be of much use in clarifying the term for popular usage.

The second usage Sapir identifies is that "rather conventional ideal of individual refinement, built up on a certain modicum of assimilated knowledge and experience but made up chiefly of a set of typical reactions that have the sanction of a class and a tradition of long standing" (403). At its worst, Sapir claims, this notion of culture encourages pretentiousness, "a scornful aloofness from the manners and tastes of the crowd," a sense of superiority rather undeserved since it is a derivative, unoriginal stance, dependent on traditions which may be hard to transplant to other lands.

("In America the cultured ideal, in its quintessential classical form, is a more exotic plant than in the halls of Oxford and Cambridge, whence it was imported to these rugged shores, but fragments and *derivatives* of it meet us frequently enough" [404, emphasis added].)

The third usage Sapir identifies is that used to refer to stereotyped national characteristics, a sort of national spirit, genius, or style, as in the "culture of France" or the "culture of Russia." Here, incidentally, Sapir mentions his profound admiration for "the culture of France"—an admiration shared by the White sisters and many of their associates: "No one who has even superficially concerned himself with French culture can have failed to be impressed by the qualities of clarity, lucid systematization, balance, care in choice of means, and good taste, that permeate so many aspects of the national civilization." Sapir's only dispute with this notion of culture seems to be that it is perhaps overly general and lacking optimism about the possibility of positive change. He thus proposes combining this third notion of culture as national characteristic with the second, more idealistic, notion of culture as individual refinement. This he calls "genuine culture"—neither "high or low; it is merely inherently harmonious, balanced, self-satisfactory." "Genuine culture"—as opposed to "canned culture"—he argues, has no relation to "efficiency" or industrial development. In fact, he contends, industrialism has often been an obstacle to "genuine culture" because of alienated labor, mass consumption, and divisions among socioeconomic classes and rural and urban areas. Focusing on how modern divisions of labor impede "genuine culture," Sapir compares a "telephone girl" to an "American Indian" equipped with salmon-spear and rabbit-snare. "As a solution to the problem of culture," the telephone girl, Sapir claims, "is a failure" since her work, although technically efficient, is routinized and lacking in individual creativity. "The Indian," however, according to Sapir, engages in a "culturally higher type of activity . . . because there is normally no sense of spiritual frustration" (411).

After lamenting a situation in which "[the Indian] has slipped out of *the warm embrace of culture into the cold air of fragmentary existence,*" Sapir goes on to urge support for American cultural nationalism, an American "coming of age," in which there is encouragement of individual creativity and "a feeling of spiritual mastery" (414, emphasis added; 420). Though American Indians of the past illustrated for Sapir that "culture" outside of Europe was humanly possible, unlike many of his contemporaries Sapir was not proposing that Indians, past or present, offered any specific answer to the problems he perceived in contemporary America. Sapir was echoing calls for "a whole restored through culture" (Trachtenberg 1982:142) of the sort that had often been made by American authors beginning in the mid-nineteenth century. With many of these earlier authors and with his fellow anthropologist and poet, Ruth Benedict (Caffrey 1989), Sapir shared a Romanticist idealizing of the individual expression of personal experience; he paid little attention to political and economic aspects of the situation he found so disturbing. Yet Sapir's concerns seem to have involved much more than elitism and a desire for distinction from "the masses": for him, "culture" was a way of capturing all that he thought missing from twentieth-century America, including a sense of common identity and purpose and a concern for the welfare of all members of the national community. In a true "culture," Americans would not be divided by class or occupation and their work would be fulfilling, rather than spiritually draining. His use of "the telephone girl," however, as the epitome of what made twentieth-century America lacking in culture, was indicative of the way in which concerns about culture reflected an elite bias. Over the following decades, many contemporaries of Sapir, including Elizabeth and Martha White, would perpetuate that elite bias as they hailed Indians as an answer to problems of American national identity.

Shopping for Culture on Jayne Street

A few years after the White sisters purchased their hillside abode in Santa Fe, a fairly well-known author bought a property just around the corner. The author was Mary Austin, and although her background—in regard to class, education, and geography—was in many ways quite different from the Whites', she would join forces with them in a number of efforts concerning American Indians, art, and Santa Fe. Though Austin is known for her novels and essays set in the West, largely among the region's Indian and Hispanic inhabitants, her 1920 novel set in New York, *No. 26 Jayne Street,* is in many ways more revealing of the circumstances that would make Santa Fe and its inhabitants so appealing to Austin as well as to the Whites and many other white Americans during the 1920s. Based partly on Austin's experiences during her rather unsuccessful attempt to join the intellectual community of Greenwich Village, and begun while she was still in New York, the novel was completed at her friend Mabel Dodge's new residence in Taos, New Mexico (Rudnick 1984:346). *No. 26 Jayne Street* is in many ways instructive about where Austin and many of her associates were coming from, literally and figuratively, particularly in relation to individual struggles—especially among women—to control space and value and to define national identities in a period where identities were increasingly defined in relation to commodity consumption.

No. 26 Jayne Street only gets as far West as New York but gives a sense of why cultural nationalism found itself more at home in Northern New Mexico than in Manhattan. Set among Greenwich Village antiwar activists, immediately prior to the United States' entry into the First World War, the novel anticipates a theme common in much later American feminist writing: that the "personal is political." The story is that of a young woman of wealth and privilege, Neith Schuyler, who has recently returned to New York after years of travel and residence in Western Europe. While struggling to grasp the nature of her national identity, Schuyler begins a romantic relationship with a socialist activist from "a small town in Iowa," a man who fails to apply his utopian political principles to his personal relationships, particularly romantic relationships with women. Schuyler's love affair ends in disappointment and, at the end of the novel, though she is still committed to her quest for national identity, she is skeptical of political ideology that fails to consider personal relationships between individuals, and (in contemporary terminology) of ideology that considers class at the expense of gender. In addition to being an important and particularly ardent cultural nationalist, Austin could be considered an early "cultural feminist," one who at one point envisioned the creation of a "genuine woman culture" (quoted in *El Palacio* 1921). For Austin as well as for some later feminists, "culture" was a term that could distinguish not just societies and nations, but also men and women.[1]

Neith Schuyler's search for national identity has been inspired by the circumstances of the impending World War, though the war seems only to hasten, rather than bring about, an exploration of identity. Returning to New York after the war has begun in Europe, Schuyler explains to her new acquaintances in Manhattan that she will remain in the country until she has determined "how to reply to some of the things they are saying about us [in Europe]. I really came back to discover America. Now that I am here I am bothered which to believe of the things we say about ourselves" (20).

Schuyler's confusion is not clarified by her awareness of the large numbers of recent immigrants filling the city, and she struggles to resolve how
they figure into the project of national self-definition. The immigrants
remind her that Americans, whatever they are, are not a "race"—and
Schuyler seems to assume that race, nation, and culture are an essential
trinity of identity. While walking "among the alien peoples of lower New
York," Schuyler perceives a "rising sense of race," something which she
thinks makes one of her new activist associates, an English woman, so
personally and politically powerful: "But, of course, the English were a
race. The war would be a good thing if it made them all Americans together" (130). Since Schuyler stops short of advocating a policy of racial
homogeneity, she struggles to think of other ways of constructing a national identity that would have the purity she imagines to reside in race.

Even the sounds of the city confuse Schuyler's quest for identity. After
her contemplative walk among the "alien peoples," Schuyler listens alone
in her Village apartment as the band from the Fourteenth Street Armory
plays "Yankee Doodle!" followed by a cultural cacophony: "A few minutes
later the stringed quartette from a near-by restaurant began to play the
"Star-Spangled Banner" in the street, followed by the "Marseillaise," and
the Italian national air. Far uptown a kiltie band piped along the main
thoroughfare, and a little later the bells of Santa Maria Maddelena began to
ring" (131).

The question of the national identity in the face of so much diversity is
never resolved in the novel—for Austin, any sort of resolution to the question would take place farther West and involve a celebration of indigenous cultural difference rather than of immigrants. Her character, Neith
Schuyler, however, continues to struggle, if rather unsuccessfully, to "discover America." Despite her concerns with public, political issues surrounding the war, labor politics, and immigrants, her search for national
identity is a very personal one, expressed as much through individual taste
in choices of residences, interior decoration, and clothing, as through political activism and public discourse. Since national identity is so closely related to arrangements of and control over space, it is appropriate that the
title of the novel refers to the address of Schuyler's apartment in Greenwich
Village, where she has taken up residence alone, against the wishes of her
relatives.

In the chapters that follow, the connections between consuming places and consuming commodities will be explored in greater detail, using the examples of women who became Austin's colleagues and neighbors in Northern New Mexico. While Austin and her associates celebrated the possibilities for constructing an American identity in the Southwest, Austin represents Schuyler's efforts to construct a national identity in Manhattan as a frustrating endeavor. In furnishing her apartment as well as choosing her clothes, friends, fiancé, and political affiliations, Schuyler deliberately seeks to assert a distinctly American identity—one partly, but not entirely, of her own design. But instead of *discovering* America, Schuyler finds she must continually piece it together out of a limited range of choices. Even things that seemed quite identifiably American are too ephemeral and common to serve as the basis of an authentic identity. While "house furnishing," Schuyler complains, " 'The extraordinary things there are to buy in New York, and the things one can't buy! The miles and miles I have walked trying to find something that isn't in the mode of the moment. I couldn't have imagined such a passion for alikeness' " (96). Ideally, her purchases are meant to reflect both individuality—the "subtle color of her personality" (85)—and a collective American identity, but her shopping expeditions seem to end, inevitably, Austin suggests, in disappointment.

For guidance, Neith Schuyler scrutinizes the decor of her new acquaintances. During a "Peace meeting" of women held in "Mrs. Carteret Keys' handsome drawing room," Schuyler observes critically: "there was nothing native but Mrs. Carteret Keys. There was discreet plunder of every European period, but nothing that could be called American unless one counted the good taste with which it had been assembled. Neith began to understand the significance of [her friend] Fleeta's futuristic furnishings. The future was the only indisputable American period" (123–24).

Schuyler's attempts to clothe herself in Americanness result in similar, somewhat uncomfortable, compromises. In "a made-over apricot satin," a gift designed "after an illustration in *Vogue*," she "looked to be the expensive, hand-grown product that the American man likes to think himself responsible for" (87)—the expensive, again, a typically American disguise of a lack of sophistication and authenticity. Schuyler accepts the dress only after it occurs to her that "looking like an illustration in *Vogue* is one phase of Americanization" (88).

Austin's character never fully revels in this "phase of Americanization," but appears to resign herself to it as a temporary compromise. Mary Austin, however, found much that she thought "could be called American," and with a *past* as well, but found these things more readily in the rural Southwest than in Manhattan. Austin was born in rural Illinois and spent thirty years in California before moving to New York and unlike many of her associates in New York, was not unfamiliar with the Southwest and its inhabitants before the 1920s. Her experiment with Manhattan seems to have been part of an ambition to broaden her intellectual and political influence from its Western, regional origins. In attempting to join the intellectual community of Greenwich Village, Austin aimed to parlay her experience in the periphery—particularly her knowledge of Indians and natural history—into authority and influence in the core.

Austin's experience in New York was disappointing, however, and in the early 1920s she began shifting her base to Santa Fe, where she felt more at home, and where she found support for her views among her neighbors. After she had left New York for good, Austin mentioned in a letter to Mabel Dodge Luhan (who had married Tony Luhan of Taos Pueblo in 1923) that although she was pleased to see evidence of a growing acceptance of "the Indian as a factor in our National life and culture," she felt the acceptance had been too long in coming: "For many years now I have been telling New York new things . . . like the importance of the Indian in our culture." In another letter to Luhan in the mid-1920s, Austin explained her frustration, revealing the extent to which she had hoped that her experience in the West and with Indians would gain her wider influence:

> When I came to New York I was already fairly launched upon my own path . . . though I hoped to find among the so-called radical Intellectuals all that I was looking [for], I also supposed I had something to offer . . .
>
> . . . I sincerely submitted myself [to the Intellectuals] to be taught, I faithfully went to all their gatherings, read what they wrote, and came to realize very slowly that their economics were inadequate— not even they deny that now—their science antiquated. I mean quite literally the things that were offered me for ethnology and biology were far behind what the leading men in those fields were thinking . . . (Mabel Dodge Luhan Collection)

Mary Austin found that constructing a positive American identity was more easily done by turning her attention South and West. Both the south-

western United States and Mexico offered American intellectuals a combination of exoticism and nativism that held especially promising possibilities for remapping the geography and the aesthetics of the national
identity—one far from Europe as well as colonial New England. Three
years after publishing her account of Neith Schuyler's awkward groping for
"things that could be called American," Austin published *The American
Rhythm* (1923), celebrating "Amerindian verse" as an authentic foundation
for an American art form that was simultaneously old and new.[2] In the
Southwest, and particularly in American Indians, Austin found a "rhythm"
apparently more appealing to her than the cacophony of Manhattan's
immigrant-filled streets. Along with many other intellectuals of her day,
Austin became an outspoken advocate of a version of cultural pluralism,
one that appealed to anthropological notions of separate and integral cultures in asserting the validity of difference characterized as "cultural." But
Austin and others like her did not abandon the idea that culture was to be
found in "art" and specially valued commodities—including music, dance,
handicrafts, painting, and architecture—which could serve as a measure of
personal and collective identity.

Not all difference associated with culture or race appealed equally to
Austin. In addition to writing anxiously of the swelling non-European immigrant population in Manhattan, she expressed blatant anti-Semitism in
an attack on her rival author, Waldo Frank (Dilworth 1996:190), and she
appears to have found African Americans a troubling presence. Richard
Drinnon reports that Austin "prided herself on being able *not* to see the
blackness of James Weldon Johnson, W. E. B. Du Bois, and other Afro-
Americans and thus could blissfully 'forget they are black'" (1980:225).
Some of Austin's white contemporaries felt quite differently and were patrons of black folklore and art: Charlotte Mason, better known as Mrs.
Rufus Osgood Mason, was deeply interested in Plains Indians and provided
financial support for Natalie Curtis's *The Indians' Book* (1907) as well as the
work of numerous black artists associated with the Harlem Renaissance
(Hemenway 1977:104). But for Austin, "blackness" was to be overlooked
and "Indianness" something to be sought out and highlighted.

Austin had been a schoolteacher struggling to support herself and a
daughter in California before becoming an author, and her literary success
was neither immediate nor overwhelming. In Santa Fe, not too far from
Mabel Dodge Luhan's home in Taos, Austin found her interests in Indians

and anthropology shared by many of her neighbors, including Elizabeth and Martha White. Such women had long had access to much greater wealth, and it is not surprising that they related their interests in Indians and anthropology even more enthusiastically than Austin to shopping—for household furnishings and objects they would sanctify as "art," as well as real estate, including the property that would become home to the School of American Research. Although it is not clear that Austin's racist concerns about blacks and immigrants were widely shared by her neighbors and fellow art patrons, their cultural pluralism would focus on Indians and was not part of a broader effort to challenge orthodox perceptions of race and culture. Revaluing perceptions of Indian and Hispanic art and "culture" was both a more conservative project and one that served patrons' own interests.

Seeking American Places, Discovering Cultures

Professor A. F. Bandelier, the eminent archaeologist, left this morning for Jemez Pueblo to gather some material and antiquities for the New Mexico exhibit at the World's Fair.
—*The New Mexican*, 20 October 1891

The land! don't you feel it? Doesn't it make you want to go out and lift dead Indians tenderly from their graves, to steal from them—as if it must be clinging even to their corpses—some authenticity, that which—
    Here not there.
—William Carlos Williams, *In the American Grain*

The following two chapters will examine a network of women who bought property in Santa Fe during the same period that Mary Austin did. Their enthusiasm about the Southwest, however, was widely shared among many of the "Manhattan intellectuals" whom Austin had tried so unsuccessfully to influence. Even those who did not develop any lasting commitment to the region perceived it to have important and highly promising possibilities for the project of redefining the nation's identity. Waldo Frank, quoted earlier denouncing the marketing of culture in five-foot book shelves, was one traveler to the Southwest who shared Austin's impression that the region possessed authentic culture. In his 1919 depiction of *Our America*, Frank dismissed the "hegemony of New England" (75) and described how he found a more inspiring, spiritual homeland while traveling by "motor-bus" through the high desert country of Colorado and New Mexico—a region he termed a "Land of Buried Cultures." Frank was particularly impressed with the appearance of the "Mexican" homes he passed, evidence, he felt, that "the Mexican has won *a certain culture* from the arid soil," and he wrote admiringly of "a terrible humility in these squat, straw-grained homes with their bright blue shutters and their crimson flowers" (95, emphasis added).[3]

Cultural nationalists such as Frank and Austin were similarly inspired by visits to Mexico. It might seem odd that they managed to find an authentic national identity for the United States in "Mexicans" in the Southwestern United States, and in Indians in the Southwest and in Mexico—regions and peoples on which an "American" identity so clearly was imposed. Cultural nationalists, however, felt that only by affirming the value of people and things that had long been undervalued would they find an authentic identity, one indigenous to the soil, the land, and the continent. Moreover, they found support for their views among Mexican cultural nationalists at work reinventing a Mexican national identity. Mary Austin claimed in her memoir that developments in postrevolutionary Mexico in the 1920s made her optimistic about "the possibility of the reinstatement of the handcraft culture and of the folk drama" (1932:336). Austin wrote that she was especially inspired by Diego Rivera and his murals—with their celebration of Indians, manual labor, ancient architecture, and abundant agriculture. Rivera was similarly involved in a nationalist project involving a redefinition of "culture." As Rivera wrote in 1924: "When I returned to my native Mexico almost three years ago, after fourteen years in Europe, I found the atmosphere of art fairly stagnant. Many artists of merit, and a true genius or two, were working, but they were so separate in their aims that they were making no headway against the enormous indifference of *the so-called cultured classes,* who support only the kind of art they like . . ." (1924:174, emphasis added).

Rivera thus echoed Sapir's distinction between "genuine" and "spurious" culture and attempted to disassociate genuine culture from class. The many Americans who were influenced by Rivera, in addition to Mary Austin, included the popular American social critic Stuart Chase. After completing his 1929 study *Men and Machines,* Chase traveled to Mexico in search of a restful change of pace and planned to see Rivera's murals as well as to contrast the "machine age" and the "handicraft age," a comparison he detailed in a bestseller illustrated by Rivera, *Mexico: A Study of Two Americas* (1931). The book focuses on a comparison of Tepoztlán and Middletown, the latter being Muncie, Indiana, as depicted by Robert and Helen Lynd. "Tepoztlán," Chase concluded from his comparison, "is far more American than Middletown, when all is said and done, but it is alien to everything we regard as typically 'American' " (15)—an observation that echoed what many cultural nationalists had been saying about the American Southwest.[4]

Chase shared with Mary Austin and Waldo Frank a particular respect for Mexico's Indians. Their authenticity and uniqueness, Chase felt, was evident in their handicrafts and ancient buildings, as well as their bodies. "[I]n race as well as in culture," he declared, "Tepoztlán is almost pure American, while the northern community, in the state called Indiana, is an omelette of English, French, Poles, Italians, Czechs, Russians, Negroes, Germans, Irish" (15). Critiquing popular American notions that a typically American landscape could be found in New England, Chase asked why, "in the face of [a] timeless pyramid, should we arrogate to ourselves the name 'America' at all?" (7).

Chase's books serve not only as an example of attempts to reconfigure American national identity and perceptions of cultural difference; they also exemplify the growing popular influence of anthropology and other social sciences. By drawing, in *Mexico,* on Robert and Helen Lynd's study of Middletown, Chase was legitimating his arguments with the authority of science. In *Men and Machines* Chase made use of Margaret Mead's just-published *Coming of Age in Samoa* in order to compare the lives of a "White Plains Clerk," a "Park Avenue Banker," and "a Samoan." Samoans, Chase contended, lived in a classless society where art remained part of the "organic whole" of daily life, whereas the lives of Americans, he argued, had been diminished by class divisions and the specialization of labor (1929:283–85). Although in his study of Mexico Chase admits that he stayed "but a short time" in Tepoztlán, he justified his brief impressions by citing Robert Redfield's recently published ethnography; Redfield, Chase noted, had spent "nearly a year" in Tepoztlán, and had "studied every phase of the town's life" (1931:14).

In the 1940s, Redfield's ethnography became the focus of lasting controversy in anthropology after Oscar Lewis carried out similar research in

Tepoztlán and produced a drastically different representation of village life. Where Redfield saw harmony and happiness, Lewis found rampant individualism, strife, crime, and distrust, and argued that Redfield's depiction had been completely false. Taking into account the possibility that life in the village had changed in the seventeen years separating Redfield's and Lewis's fieldwork, later anthropologists would see both representations as incomplete and a reflection, in part, of contrasting personalities (Barrett 1996:78–79).

Yet it seems likely that it was not just because of a cheerful disposition that Chase found Redfield's depiction of a happy and harmonious Tepoztlán so convincing and appealing. Such representations of "primitive" or premodern culture appealed to Chase in part because of his situation at a particular historical moment. In the 1920s and 1930s, anthropology and its notion of premodern cultures that could be documented scientifically supported visions of American identity that held much popular appeal: the most "remote" places could be seen as possessing authentic "culture" and might even provide solutions to the problems of modern life.

Culture, Cultures, and Women

As Sinclair Lewis suggested with his tale of Fran Dodsworth dragging her automobile-manufacturing husband around Europe, the concept of culture was tied, not just to race and class, but also to gender. Though usually excluded from the production and authoritative evaluation of "high culture," middle-class women were considered avid consumers of culture through such institutions as Chatauquas and "culture clubs" (Tractenberg 1982:145–47). Culture was associated with forms of consumption favored by the wealthy, and middle- and upper-class women were expected to specialize in consumption, while their husbands preoccupied themselves with supposedly more productive labor. In Thorstein Veblen's analysis, women of "the leisure class" devoted themselves to "conspicuous consumption" in order to display what their husbands could afford. They preoccupied themselves with "household adornment and tidiness" in order to demonstrate that their husbands could afford such "wasted effort" (1899:82). In keeping with the social theory of his day, Veblen was a master of generalization and did not concern himself much with exceptions. Where unmarried women, for example, might fit into this scheme he left unanswered, though presumably it would be the wealth of their fathers that they were expected to display. Nor was Veblen interested in what reasons there might be for women's complicity in such display.[5]

Veblen's contemporary, the German social theorist Georg Simmel, depicted women's relationship to "fashion" differently. More interested than Veblen in understanding pleasure, desire, and individual agency, he did not characterize style and the adornment of houses or bodies, by men or women, as wasteful. Simmel suggested, however, that it was in part because upper-class women were denied other means of achieving recognition, social power, and "individuality" that they were apt to concern themselves so with fashion and adornment (Simmel in Frisby and Featherstone 1997:196–97). "It seems," he surmised, "as though fashion were the valve, as it were, through which women's need for some measure of conspicuousness and individual prominence finds vent, when its satisfaction is more often denied in other spheres" (196). This analysis explains Fran Dodsworth quite well, though Lewis suggested, unlike Simmel, that this was a particularly twisted valve. Fran was never going to be satisfied: as much as she sought to differentiate herself from middle-class Americans, she would never achieve respect from those she emulated and admired.

With Lewis, Veblen, and Simmel in mind, I return to the story of the White sisters and their felicitous purchase of property in 1923. In the year I lived at the School of American Research, whenever I heard anyone explain who the White sisters were, their marital status was always mentioned, and often it was the subject of hushed speculation. Were they lesbians? Or was this just part of their eccentricity?[6] It is true that eccentricity was attributed to the Whites even by their peers. As far as their sexual identity, I came across no evidence that either or both women were lesbians, though some of their close acquaintances were, as the Whites were well aware. Martha White, as an erstwhile math teacher and a devoted athlete and horsewoman, was rarely described in conventionally "feminine" terms. But sexuality aside, the fact that the two women did not marry was not represented as particularly exceptional by the Whites or their associates. In addition to Mary Austin, who was divorced, their network of friends included quite a number of women who were not married. In an age when stereotypical roles for men and women followed the well-known script of "Mr. Breadwinner, Mrs. Consumer" (de Grazia 1996:3, 152), the Whites managed to play "*Miss* Consumer" throughout their lives. In the Southwest, they were able to imbue this role with uncommon prestige and legitimacy: they would go shopping, not just on behalf of themselves and their friends, but also on behalf of American Indians, the region, and the nation.

The Whites shared their interests in the Southwest with a number of their classmates from Bryn Mawr. Amelia Elizabeth White, known to her friends always as "Elizabeth," graduated from Bryn Mawr in 1901, her sister Martha in 1903. The class of 1903 also included Elizabeth Shepley Sergeant (pronounced "Sur-jent"), who became a fairly successful journalist and a respected biographer of Willa Cather and Robert Frost. On one of her first trips to New Mexico, Sergeant would be accompanied by Bryn Mawr classmate Gertrude Ely (who had left the college before graduating to study music in Europe), daughter of the vice-president of the Pennsylvania Railroad. Also a member of the class of 1903 was Margretta Stewart, who would become a significant figure in the campaign for women's suffrage and the reform of child labor laws; after the death of her husband, Charles Dietrich, a banker who served as a U.S. senator and governor of Nebraska, Margretta Stewart Dietrich would become known as one of the Southwest's most influential Indian affairs activists and an important patron of Indian art. By the 1920s all of these women had purchased property in Northern New Mexico and become active, though with varying degrees of commitment, in efforts to influence national and regional policy pertaining to American Indians.

Elizabeth and Martha White were likely the wealthiest of these five former Bryn Mawr students: their father was Horace White, owner and editor-in-chief of the *Chicago Tribune* and the *New York Evening Post,* successful railroad investor, as well as a scholar and translator of classical Latin histories and the author of a popular book, *Money and Banking,* published in 1895. Elizabeth Sergeant was the only one of the group who ever really needed to work for a living. Although Sergeant came from a wealthy, highly educated Boston family with a colonial heritage, her inheritance was not sufficient for her to live on, and there were times, particularly during the 1930s, when she struggled to support herself with her writing, selling "potboilers" to popular magazines and often relying on friends to provide her with inexpensive studios where she could write.[7] For much of her life she received financial assistance from her younger sister, Katharine White, wife of E. B. White and a respected writer and fiction editor at *The New Yorker.* As will be discussed in the next chapter, Sergeant's publications and her correspondence with friends and publishers indicate the calculated nature of her representations of cultural difference and the Southwestern landscape; many of Sergeant's published writings clearly were designed to appeal to middle-class audiences in a way that might provide her with an income at the same time as promoting a desired shift in values and public policies.

Among these women, only Margretta Stewart ever married. Charles Dietrich, much older than Stewart, was the father of one of her Bryn Mawr classmates and he left her a widow in her forties. None of these women had children. Despite the fact that the Whites' unmarried status seems so remarkable in popular memory, it was not so unusual for graduates of women's colleges at the turn of the twentieth century to remain unmarried—a situation that inspired warnings of "race suicide" as a potential hazard of women's education. Such warnings followed nineteenth-century medical opinions that women's education was inadvisable because intellectual activity risked damaging female reproductive organs, where, it was thought, women's energies should be properly directed (Smith-Rosenberg 1985:258–63; Gordon 1976:136). In 1924 two women sociologists at Vassar responded to the warnings of "race suicide" with a study intended to be reassuring, showing that in fact the rate of marriage among Vassar graduates was rising, though like other graduates of women's colleges, Vassar women tended to marry later and have fewer children than did other American women. Among Vassar women graduating around the turn of the century, according to these sociologists, fewer than 60 percent of the graduates had married by the time of the study, about the same rate as the graduates of Bryn Mawr. Among the general population it was reported that only about 10 percent of women did not marry (Newcomer and Gibson 1924; Smith-Rosenberg 1985:253).

Late in her life Elizabeth Sergeant hinted that as a young woman she feared marriage to be incompatible with her ambition for a career, but revealed that she once came close to marrying a French Cubist painter (1963:114–15). Willa Cather, one of Sergeant's closest friends from 1910 through the 1920s, reportedly warned Sergeant that marriage would only compromise Sergeant's desires for a career as a professional writer.[8] Such revelations may have been a way of asserting a heterosexual identity and deflecting speculation about herself, as a never-married woman writing a very personal memoir about Willa Cather, whom many perceived to be a lesbian. Sergeant does seem to have had romantic relationships with men (for example, she carried out a very lengthy and intimate correspondence with the writer Sidney Howard, whom she met in Paris during the First World War; the correspondence ended when he married in 1920 and Sergeant moved to New Mexico). But Sergeant never did marry and, like the other women considered here, centered her life largely around friendships, particularly, though not at all exclusively, with other women.

Some of Cather's recent biographers argue persuasively that it is reasonable to consider Cather a lesbian (e.g., O'Brien 1987)—despite the fact that this was not an identity she claimed for herself. In her published memoir of Cather, Sergeant seems to avoid the question of Cather's sexuality quite deliberately. Younger members of the network that included Sergeant, Cather, and the other women discussed in this chapter told me that their community in Santa Fe included many women who either openly identified themselves as lesbians or were considered lesbians by other members of the community. Sexual orientation, however, may have made little difference in the way these women chose to live their lives or in their perceptions of indigenous art and the Southwest. It is however, significant in understanding their actions as consumers and philanthropists that Cather, Sergeant, and the other women I discuss here tended not to live in nuclear families, but in households with other women—whether lovers, sisters, friends, paid assistants, nurse-companions, or housekeepers. It is also significant that regardless of sexuality, there were ways in which these women felt constrained by prevailing conventions of gender. In a society in which middle- and upper-class women were increasingly encouraged to seek self-realization and fulfillment (Lears 1983, 1994), it was in part a certain freedom from gender that these women sought in their consumption of places and goods.

It is an important fact about the women I describe here that although they did not all have "careers," they shared an ambition to have an influence on the world outside of home and family, an ambition no doubt fueled by their college educations. At the turn of the century, women's colleges tended to encourage a sense of mission among their graduates, and this was perhaps especially true at Bryn Mawr, where college president M. Carey Thomas exerted a powerful influence over her students. Such colleges offered their students, in Thomas's words, "the hope of doing something splendid after all" (Smith-Rosenberg 1985:253)—the hope, that is, of pursu-

ing individual ambition rather than dismissing it as inappropriately un-
feminine, or subsuming it to the needs of the bourgeois family.

Ambition, however, gained respectability when cast as ambition to serve
society rather than self. Middle-class nineteenth-century American women,
making use of notions that women possessed an inherent moral superiority,
often cloaked ambitions for greater public influence in what Lori Ginzburg
calls "benevolent femininity" (1990:35). At Bryn Mawr, Thomas encouraged
her students' interests in the settlement house movement, reformist social
work, and the campaign for women's suffrage, in ways that tended to
maintain the emphasis on social rather than individual ambition. Like Mary
Austin, Thomas held anti-Semitic and overtly racist views and therefore did
not directly encourage appreciation for cultural diversity or racial equality
(Horowitz 1994:448–49), but her students were nonetheless able to represent commitments to such matters as in keeping with an obligation to serve
society. In the same era in which Veblen depicted wealthy women conveying status through idleness, Thomas and her students were determined to
demonstrate their usefulness.

Among the Bryn Mawr women who would develop interests in Indian
affairs and take up residence, at least temporarily, in New Mexico, Elizabeth
Sergeant specifically acknowledged Thomas as having helped shape her
political commitments as a "Bryn Mawrter"—as a woman selflessly and
idealistically devoted to improving the welfare of others. In her memoir of
Cather, Sergeant, describing her own outlook at the time she first met
Cather, recalled the "restless, reforming times" that had engulfed her after
her college graduation and the ideals that inspired her attempt to combine
"social work" and journalism. "A Bryn Mawrter," she explained, "raised by
M. Carey Thomas must try to right these terrible social wrongs which
blistered and festered under the shiny urban surface of Manhattan Island"
(Sergeant 1963:31, 35–36). In 1910 Willa Cather, as managing editor of
McClure's, published Sergeant's first piece of serious journalism, an article titled "Toilers of the Tenements: Where the Beautiful Things of the
Great Shops are Made." In "Toilers of the Tenements," the "terrible social
wrong" Sergeant aimed to expose was the exploitation of Italian and Eastern European immigrants whom she describes producing, in crowded ten-
ement houses, such items as artificial flowers, artificial ostrich plumes,
corset covers, cigarette wrappers, and human hair wigs. By the early 1920s
her interests had shifted from the urban poor to land rights, art, and re-

ligious freedom among Pueblo Indians. In her memoir of Cather, Sergeant represents this shift as compatible with a lifelong interest in correcting social and political inequalities. According to Sergeant, her political concerns were never shared by Cather, whom she describes as surprisingly "respectful of wealth and swagger" (Sergeant 1963:48).

Sergeant's fellow alumnae, the White sisters, Margretta Stewart Dietrich, and Gertrude Ely, were also involved in reform and suffrage politics before their first forays west. After women attained the vote in 1920, Gertrude Ely became active in Democratic party politics; later, in the 1930s, she was an administrator in the New Deal. Although more conservative than Sergeant or Ely, Margretta Stewart Dietrich was perhaps the most politically active of the five Bryn Mawrters discussed here: before taking over the leadership of the New Mexico Association on Indian Affairs, Dietrich served as president of the Nebraska Woman Suffrage Association and its successor, the Nebraska League of Women Voters, and was a director of the National League of Women Voters. Elizabeth White, before committing herself to Indian affairs, also took part in suffrage activities and had contacts among prominent reformers, including Florence Kelley, socialist, feminist, and leader of the National Consumers' League; and activist, social worker, and fellow "Bryn Mawrter" Pauline Goldmark. While Kelley and Goldmark were acquainted with Elizabeth and Martha White, they shared closer friendships with Elizabeth Sergeant.

These Bryn Mawr graduates' intellectual histories suggest some of the ways that particular versions of anthropology became increasingly appealing to Americans struggling to resolve dilemmas of national identity and their relationship to "culture." Although by the 1920s all five of these Bryn Mawr graduates had developed interests in anthropology, especially archaeology, and had begun participating in efforts influenced by American cultural nationalism, their education at Bryn Mawr offered little preparation for their later interests—other than its encouragement of ambition and dedication to art and scientific exploration, to pageantry and dramatic performance, and to travel as an aesthetic experience as well as a way of acquiring and exercising knowledge and taste.[9] As scholars of modern tourism have noted, such an approach to travel and tourism is historically specific and has long been a habit cultivated among the upper middle class (e.g., Urry 1990; Frow 1991).

These were women who had extensive travel experience prior to visiting the Southwest. Elizabeth and Martha White traveled in Europe before and after attending Bryn Mawr. After Elizabeth Sergeant's graduation, she traveled with an aunt in Italy and other parts of Europe. Suffering from undefined psychological and physical troubles, Sergeant was left by her aunt at a sanitarium in Paris and later moved to a similar institution in Zurich, where she is reported to have been analyzed by Carl Jung (Davis 1987:27–28). Decades later, Sergeant dedicated her memoir of Cather to Pauline Goldmark, with whom Sergeant had traveled through Europe in 1908 (it was Goldmark, in 1910, who suggested that Sergeant submit her first article to Cather at *McClure's*, initiating Cather's and Sergeant's long friendship). Sergeant continued to spend time in Italy and France, eventually, in 1914, becoming "the French specialist" for *The New Republic*. When, after the First World War, these women traveled more frequently in the Southwest, in some ways they were both consuming and marketing a commodity of sorts—"the Southwest"—that seemed at once novel and antique.

In the Southwest, such buying and selling could be made to fit the script of respectable social benevolence. In an age when women's activities as consumers were apt to be ridiculed and parodied along with attempts to gain status from "culture," the Southwest offered the possibility of engaging consumer skills in projects of reconstructing personal and national identities, aiding others in the Bryn Mawrter tradition, and participating in the new "science" of anthropology.

CHAPTER TWO **ELIZABETH SERGEANT, BUYING AND SELLING THE SOUTHWEST**

New Mexico is a glorious new universe.

Elizabeth Sergeant, to the editor of Ladies' Home Journal[1]

 In 1923, when Elizabeth and Martha White purchased the property that would eventually become home to the School of American Research, Elizabeth immediately wrote to notify their former Bryn Mawr classmate Elizabeth Shepley Sergeant. Sergeant had purchased property in the area the previous year and had published a four-part series of articles about the purchase in *Harper's* magazine. Such purchases and communications about them are examples of the way this network of women, Northeasterners and Europhiles of long standing, acquired a taste for the Southwest, including regional styles of architecture, desert landscapes, art, and people. They learned how to see the region and where to find value there in part from interactions with one another.

There were important differences among these women. The Whites, especially after their father Horace White's death in 1916, had a steady income from investments and real estate, and though ambitious in that Bryn Mawrter fashion, they had no financial need for gainful employment. But among wealthy New Yorkers, status was not determined by wealth alone; the Whites gained no particular advantage, socially, from Horace White's Midwestern background (although he was born in New Hampshire and prided himself on being a Yankee, he grew up in the Illinois Territory) and the fortune that he had not inherited but made in newspapers and railroads. Elizabeth Sergeant, on the other hand, had the cultural capital of a rather well-known and well-to-do family, with a long history in New England, but she had much less in the way of actual capital. Sergeant struggled to make a living as a professional writer and, at times, as a researcher for the federal government. In the Southwest she attempted to support herself in part by selling representations of the region's landscapes and inhabitants. She went shopping in the Southwest, for land, art, stories, and images, but she also attempted to sell her knowledge of how to do that to readers of magazines such as *Harper's* and *Ladies' Home Journal*.

Sergeant's interest in the Southwest, as well as in anthropology and Indians, came originally from her friend and editor at *McClure's*, Willa Cather. Prior to taking an interest in the Southwest, the two women shared interests in Western Europe, especially France. In a period when many Americans had come to identify France not just with upper-middle-class women, but also status-seeking women of less elite status (Levenstein 1998), the Southwest appealed to both Sergeant and Cather in part because it offered a way of reinventing the geography of national identity and of gender in ways that seemed especially promising. Compared to France or New York, for those of their race and class, the Southwest could be a liberating place, one where they were freed from all sorts of expectations and could wield new power and authority. Both Cather and Sergeant would approach the Southwest in part as consumers—shopping for novelty, authenticity, and new identities—but they would also attempt to sell representations of the Southwest to others.

Cather saw her writing as "pure art," independent of the marketplace. In keeping with the views of many artists and art patrons, she defined art as "something for which there is no market demand" (Bell-Villada 1996:148). In fact, both Cather and Sergeant were selling to markets, but Cather's were consistently more exclusive ones and she sold to them much more successfully. Unlike Cather, Sergeant was not wholly committed to imagining art as separate from the market or from other purposes. In regard to her own career, Sergeant, in contrast to Cather, did not believe that art was necessarily a higher calling than activism and journalism. She attempted to use her writing to finance political activism on behalf of the Southwestern Pueblos and was willing to tailor her work to suit particular audiences. In her perceptions of Indians and Indian art, on the other hand, Sergeant and her fellow Bryn Mawr alumnae would hold more closely to Cather's belief in the incompatibility of art and a mass market.

Cather and Sergeant Discover "Older and Higher Obligations"

As Elizabeth Sergeant described it, Cather "suffered a truly grueling inner pull between East and West" (1963:54). Early in her career, one of Cather's primary models of inspiration was Henry James ("the god of [Cather's] young literary life," according to Sergeant [1963:67]), who wrote of Americans in European settings. In 1902 Cather made a literary pilgrimage to England and France, where she began setting her fiction. When Elizabeth Sergeant submitted her first article, "Toilers of the Tenements," to *McClure's* in 1910 and met Cather there, it was largely their common interests in James and Flaubert that drew the two women together. Sergeant was then twenty-nine, Cather thirty-seven.

Anticipating the importance of elite tastes in Sergeant's later work in the Southwest, it should be noted that the two women shared tastes in all sorts of things, not just in literature. Sergeant's memoir of her friendship with Cather is filled with recollections of how they appreciated one another's clothing, decor, and tastes in food. Sergeant marveled, for example, at Cather's "blythe, made-in-Nebraska look" in "lisle stockings, low-heeled Oxfords, and easy sport coat"; while Cather admired Sergeant's "*outré* sailor" hat and remarked of Sergeant's "Avignon dress with its lace fichu and sprigs of flowers" that she must put it in a story (Sergeant 1963:43, 46, 114). Sergeant even recalls their delight in shopping for vegetables in a Greenwich Village market, where they sought "the perfect leaf lettuce" for "*la salade classique*" (113).

This sharing of tastes went along with sharing one another's ambitions: along with appetites for clothes, food, and books, they shared a commitment to their chosen careers. The year they first met, 1910, the two celebrated Cather's decision to resign from her position at *McClure's* at one of New York's most fashionable restaurants, Delmonico's. Sergeant would later write of Cather dressed that evening in "a very ornate, luxurious, conspicuous red-embroidered frock," and recalled thinking that her friend "was dressing the woman she felt inside"—one bound not to remain obscure. However personal, the two women's preoccupations with appearances would fuel their professional ambitions as well as their friendship.[2]

In much the same way that Sergeant and Cather shared tastes in everyday goods, they also shared one another's aesthetic appreciations of landscapes encountered in traveling and their abilities to represent such landscapes in their writing. Travel, for Cather and Sergeant, was a form of consuming (often for later use in writing) and an important means of expressing and reinventing their identities. Travel was a means for many middle- and even upper-class people to acquire greater cultural capital, a way of gaining greater access to legitimate knowledge, public influence, and authority. Cather and Sergeant, however, took a particularly active approach to their travels, priding themselves on their powers of observation and artful description. The result was a combination of rivalry and camaraderie. Sergeant recalled, for example, traveling by bus with Cather to Central Park, just after one of Sergeant's trips to Europe: "[Willa] esteemed me for having the patina of Europe, as she called it, still clinging to me. I admired her for her vigor, her authenticity, her delight in the landmarks we passed; her frank disclosure of what was pertinent to her in this multifarious universe of New York City. There was so much she did not want to see and saw not. What she did see she had selected instinctively and made so her own that her impulsive sharing of it gave it a halo of brightness" (1963:46).

The way Sergeant later described it, in the early days of their friendship both women saw Europe, especially France, as their ideal destination and the source of "patina." Cather spoke to Sergeant disdainfully of Nebraska's stifling provincialism, saying that if she spent too much time in Nebraska she feared she would "die in a cornfield," where "there is no place to hide" (Sergeant 1963:49). Sergeant represented herself as perceiving Cather's Midwestern ties as exotic, a potential strength rather than a handicap; she claimed to have encouraged a reluctant Cather to write about Nebraska— which Cather did in her first novel to receive wide acclaim, *O Pioneers!* (1913).[3] Of course, in such recollections Sergeant complimented her own perceptions of value and also established her own identity as a Yankee and native urbanite.

Ironically, but not surprisingly, it was Cather's deep ambivalence about her national and regional identity that led to a literary reputation marked by the celebration of rural, provincial America. Cather developed greater confidence in writing about rural American places on an excursion to Arizona. In keeping with the way many Easterners viewed the Southwest as a healthful, restorative place to visit and recuperate from poor health, Cather first visited the region in 1912 following an illness. One of her brothers was working for the Santa Fe Railroad and took her, during her stay with him, to visit cliff-dwelling sites and to observe the Hopi Snake Dance.[4] This trip marked an important turning point in Cather's career, possibly helping her to resolve two significant dilemmas of identity—the conflict between the urban, Eurocentric Eastern literary establishment and a provincial Midwestern background, as well as her attempt to reconcile her gender identity with her aspirations as an artist. Cather later based a section of her 1915 novel *The Song of the Lark* on the 1912 vacation, and her writings about the visit—first in personal letters and later in the novel— inspired Elizabeth Sergeant's first trip to the Southwest several years later. Cather's experiences and the novel based on them were an important influence on Sergeant's perceptions of the Southwest. Sergeant would, in turn, influence her fellow Bryn Mawrters, as well, perhaps, as other readers of her journalism.

Feminist Cather scholars have tended to consider Cather's writing on the Southwestern desert, Anasazi pottery, and the cliff dwellings in psycho- analytic terms, likening her emphasis on "enclosed yet continually open spaces" (O'Brien 1987:410) to the female body. According to Ellen Moers, Cather's Panther Canyon (in *The Song of the Lark*) is "the most thoroughly elaborated female landscape in literature" (quoted in Fryer 1987:33), and to Judith Fryer it is "a textured map of the female body, wild and gentle, rocky and fringed and smooth, seemingly inaccessible, yet sheltering life deep within its hollow center" (1987:33). My interest, however, is in how Cather's concerns with gender intertwined with concerns about national identity and in how the Southwest helped Cather revise her notions of art and culture. While I reject the idea that a landscape can possess an essentially feminine or masculine character—or any particular national essence—it does seem that Cather's writing about the Southwest, like some of Ser- geant's less well known writing, can be considered an attempt to claim the desert and the outdoors as "feminine" space, a way of reconstructing femi- ninity outside of genteel domesticity, and of locating a more authentic American identity in the West, away from Europe and the Northeast.[5]

The Song of the Lark tells the unlikely story of the development of a great opera star, a woman from rural Colorado, Thea Kronborg. Thea leaves the small and seemingly dull town of her birth to study piano and voice in Chicago, but then, unexpectedly, discovers her most profound artistic in- spiration in the "Mexican ghetto" back in her hometown and in an aban- doned cliff dwelling in Arizona. It is these unexpected sources of inspiration that enable her to become successful in opera, not just in the United States, but also in Europe. Like Cather's, Thea's visit to Arizona is intended as a recuperative one, following a period of ill health. Staying on an Arizona ranch, Thea spends her days at an abandoned cliff dwelling in "Panther

Canyon"— based on Walnut Canyon, near Flagstaff, which Cather had visited with her brother in 1912. In addition to regaining her health, Thea unexpectedly, and somewhat mystically, discovers a new power of expression in her voice—or rather, an old power to which she had not earlier had access.

In her biography of Cather, Sharon O'Brien argues persuasively that writing about the development of a woman's voice was, for Cather, a way of reconciling her own ambitions as an artist with her gender identity, by locating artistic identity within a woman's physical body (1987:166–73). Fragments of Indian pottery play an important part in bringing about this reconciliation of woman, art, and body, as we see when Thea, in Panther Canyon, bathes in a pool beneath the cliff dwellings and contemplates the remnants of cliff-dweller art:

> One morning, as she was standing upright in the pool, splashing water between her shoulder-blades with a big sponge, something flashed through her mind that made her draw herself up and stand still until the water had quite dried upon her flushed skin. The stream and the broken pottery: what was any art but an effort to make a sheath, a mould in which to imprison for a moment the shining, elusive element which is life itself—life hurrying past us and running away, too strong to stop, too sweet to lose? The Indian women had held it in their jars. In the sculpture she had seen at the Art Institute, it had been caught in a flash of arrested motion. In singing, one made a vessel of one's throat and nostrils and held it on one's breath, caught the stream in a scale of natural intervals. (1915:240)

In addition to achieving this new understanding of art as a category capable of embracing Pueblo women's pottery, sculpture, and a woman's voice, in the canyon, Thea begins to imagine a different, more empowering, relationship to history, a relationship also inspired largely by the fragments of pottery: "These potsherds were like fetters that bound one to a long chain of human endeavor" (241). Whereas previously Thea had located her past in her provincial, isolated hometown in Colorado, after her days in the Canyon, "[t]he Cliff-Dwellers had lengthened her past. She had older and higher obligations" (243). With this new sense of authenticity and rootedness, Thea resolves to go "to Germany to study without further loss of time" (242).

That Thea's discovery of American authenticity and artistic integrity in the cliff dwellings primarily served to facilitate her European-centered ambitions is perhaps revealing of Cather's priorities. In fact, Cather's interest in Indians never developed much beyond their usefulness as material for her fiction; at least she never took much interest in living Indians and the political struggles to which her friend Sergeant became so committed. But her experiences in the Southwest did encourage Cather to construct an identity focused at least in part on Western America, and her efforts inspired others such as Sergeant and the Whites. Sergeant and her fellow Bryn Mawr alumnae would also embrace Cather's notion, so compatible with consumerism, that value might be found in the most unexpected places, by those with the eye to discern it.

Although Sergeant would become more actively involved in Southwestern politics, there are many important continuities between Cather's perceptions and Sergeant's. By 1912, when Cather first visited her brother in Arizona, the two women had become close friends. During that first trip to Arizona, Cather wrote Sergeant frequent letters, describing her fascination with the landscape and its Hispanic and Indian inhabitants. These letters were, Sergeant suggests, an important first introduction to the Southwest—though not yet ready to hop a train to the desert instead of the steamer to France, she later reported that her interest had been piqued (Sergeant 1963).

In introducing Sergeant to the region, Cather also introduced her to Southwestern Indian pottery and anthropology. In 1914 Cather took Sergeant to visit an exhibition of cliff-dweller pottery at the Museum of Natural History—probably Sergeant's first serious notice of Indian pottery and of anthropology. Recalling the visit nearly forty years later, Sergeant wrote that on their way to the museum, "Willa seemed tense and low-spirited":

> But when we got to those glass cases, where were displayed tan pots with ridged designs in relief, and great black and red pots with complex geometrical patterns, she was rapturously unaware of her physical depletion.
>
> Willa reminded me of the potsherds she had rather shamefacedly shown me after her first visit to the Southwest. It had seemed a sacrilege to take anything for oneself from those cliff dwellings that hung along Walnut Canyon, on "streets" that were hewn from the

chalky rock. Hard-boiled archaeologists, however, had dug up the pots in the glass cases—some were whole, others artfully pieced together. You were able to conjure up the women who, under conditions of incredible difficulty and fear of enemies, had still designed and molded them, "dreamed" the fine geometry of the designs, and made beautiful objects for daily use out of river-bottom clay. (1963:123)

Cather's rapture was contagious, and by the early 1920s Sergeant had become more deeply involved in the Southwest than Cather. She had also developed a number of personal contacts among anthropologists and had become an independent student of anthropology, as well as an influential promoter of Pueblo pottery. The passion with which she devoted herself to Southwestern affairs and Indian art (however more briefly than her Bryn Mawr classmates Margretta Dietrich and Elizabeth White) suggests that her experiences in the Southwest were as important to her as those of Cather's Thea.

At the time of their 1914 visit to the Museum of Natural History, Cather was at work on *The Song of the Lark* and was enjoying the tremendous success of *O Pioneers!* Sergeant, who had returned to New York after a year researching articles in France, had just joined the staff of the *New Republic,* and although her assignment was to write about French literature and culture, she saw herself as taking part in an important development in American cultural nationalism. The influential cultural critic Randolph Bourne was among her fellow writers and would become a close friend; her editors included Herbert Croly and Walter Lippmann. When Cather, who deemed the *New Republic* crowd too political and left-wing, attempted to persuade Sergeant that her talents would be better served writing fiction, Sergeant argued that Cather should sympathize with the publication, because, like *McClure's,* it was edited by people who "regarded our America as an unfinished affair, which needs constant remaking to help its growth" (Sergeant 1963:125).

Despite their political disagreements, Sergeant and Cather continued to influence one another, and Cather often urged Sergeant to visit the Southwest, where Cather returned in 1915 on a visit to the cliff-dwellings at Mesa Verde. After Sergeant completed her first book, *French Perspectives,* in 1916, she made her first trip west. Sergeant traveled to a dude ranch in Wyoming, where she claims to have learned "trail riding from a cowboy" (1963:142), then continued on to California, intending to visit New Mexico on her return east. In California, however, Sergeant received news of the war in Europe, news that caused her to rush her return trip, leaving time only for two stops along the Santa Fe Railroad—at the Grand Canyon and at Walnut Canyon, the "Panther Canyon" of *The Song of the Lark*. Of Walnut Canyon, Sergeant wrote, "In that strange cliff city Thea and her lover were nowhere to be seen. But the ancient voices spoke, and the austere and planetary Southwest gripped my soul in such fashion that I knew I should return. Willa was glad that I'd had even that much of it" (144).

As it happened, Sergeant would not manage to return to the Southwest until after the war. In 1917 she took a position in Paris as the war correspondent for the *New Republic;* in the following year she was severely injured, possibly by a landmine, in a field outside Paris. During her months recovering at the American Hospital in Paris—where Elizabeth White was probably one of her visitors—Sergeant read the page proofs of Cather's new novel, *My Ántonia*. Reading its vivid descriptions of Nebraska made Sergeant homesick for rural, Western America, particularly the Southwest (as a Bostonian laid up in Paris, Sergeant rather blithely blurred West and Southwest into one). Her reaction to Cather's manuscript suggests something of the effect of the war on the geography of elite white identities. It was less easy to romanticize a Europe laid waste by war; accordingly, an identity centered in Western America began to appear brighter, larger, and more liberating: "The luminous light that burns on the Arizona desert, out of long miles of untouched sage and sand. Yes, that's where I want to be, on an observation car traveling swiftly into the Southwest. Losing myself in a shimmer of fine dust, passing the bold, red, ramparts of a land beloved of pioneers, and *large enough to carry Europe in its pocket*" (Sergeant 1920:205, emphasis added).

Bryn Mawrters Go West

For all their shared tastes, Willa Cather did not share Elizabeth Sergeant's commitment to philanthropy and activism—Cather was not a Bryn Mawrter even in sensibility. This difference between the two women intensified when Sergeant returned to the Southwest and became increasingly concerned with matters more obviously political than aesthetic, even though Sergeant's published writing displayed an increasing emphasis on the latter.

Sergeant's work in New Mexico, like that of the other Bryn Mawrters whose paths would lead there, still stressed notions of taste as an important expression of identity. Sergeant also used her aesthetic talents to market a political agenda of cultural pluralism.

While Cather managed to parlay her aesthetic skills in representing Western America into literary fame, in their activities in the Southwest, Sergeant and other Bryn Mawrters found ways of combining such skills with philanthropy and activism. Particularly through their philanthropic patronage of Indian and other indigenous arts, Bryn Mawrters, I will argue, extended the aesthetic skills of the bourgeois household into greater public influence through a form of "politicized consumption." Moreover, by moving to a relatively undeveloped periphery and finding value where others had not, they had a chance of commanding greater public influence and authority than if they had remained in the Northeast.

In 1920 Elizabeth Sergeant realized her dream of returning to the Southwest, continuing to view the region as a place of healing for body and soul. Sergeant traveled to New Mexico, on the advice of her physician, once she had recovered sufficiently from her war injury to be able to walk again. Accompanying her was her old friend from Bryn Mawr, Gertrude Ely. While staying on a Santa Fe ranch, in between horseback trips and "burrowing in Smithsonian reports," Sergeant and Ely purchased a crumbling adobe for $500, six miles outside Santa Fe, in the Hispanic village of Tesuque (Sergeant 1922:414). Ely, like Sergeant and the White sisters, had also spent the war in France, where she worked with the YMCA and was twice decorated with the Croix de Guerre for "distinguished bravery under fire" (*Main Line Times* 1970).

In 1921 Sergeant financed another trip to New Mexico with Ely by writing her four-part article for *Harper's* magazine, "The Journal of a Mud House," in which she recounted her adventures with Ely and other friends while renovating the house in Tesuque.[6] During this period, Sergeant was becoming increasingly involved in Indian-related politics—an involvement she refrained from mentioning in the article. In a letter to another potential publisher, Sergeant explained her concerns quite differently from the way she did for her *Harper's* readers:

> My valley [in Tesuque] has American fruit and dairy ranchers and "Mexicans" who are day laborers for the Americans, and small ranch-

ers on their own account, and a Pueblo Indian tribal group, the Tesuques, that came into sensational prominence last year by tearing
down some American fences that were in fact on Indian land. Practically all of the water in the ancient Indian ditch now goes to the
ranchers higher up the valley so that this year, when there has been
practically no rain, the agent has had to ask for rations for Tesuque,
the first time in anyone's memory; for they are a thoroughly indus-
trious race. (Sergeant to Norman Hapgood, 14 November 1922, John
Collier Papers, microfilm reel 5).

Though Sergeant was able to publish some overtly political pieces successfully (in the *New Republic* and *The Nation,* for example), in the majority
of her articles political context was delivered in a by-the-way, sardonic
fashion. Her *Harper's* article exemplifies her calculated attempts to appeal
to upper-middle-class sensibilities.

In many ways, this article can usefully be considered a Western counterpart to Mary Austin's *No. 26 Jayne Street.* In Austin's novel, a woman returns
to the United States after travels in Europe and struggles to express an
American identity, largely through distinctions of taste—in consuming
both commodities and real estate. Sergeant's article also begins with the
signing of a contract—but to purchase a house on two acres of land in the
country, rather than to lease an urban apartment in the interest of escape
from nearby relatives. Sergeant's work suggests a more positive and independent identity for educated women, but it is an identity similarly centered on purchasing objects and decorating a home. Sergeant depicts consumption and domesticity as liberating rather than constraining, gender as
a flexible sort of identity, and cultural and racial difference as not troubling
or confusing (as in Austin's novel), but worthy of particular celebration.
Like Cather's *Song of the Lark,* Sergeant's article can be seen as an attempt to
claim the Southwest and the outdoors as feminine space, while shifting
constructions of femininity and the geography of national identity. As I
have noted above, it is not that the Southwestern landscape is essentially
feminine, but it did provide an opportunity to give elite women such as
Sergeant and Ely a "home" outdoors.

In "The Journal of a Mud House" Sergeant attempts to answer her
editor's question of "why a woman who might live in France 'should go and
bury herself in the desert' " (Sergeant 1922:410)—the assumption being that

France is the more suitable place for a woman, particularly a woman with Sergeant's education and ambition. Although throughout the article Sergeant celebrates stereotypically feminine traits—attention to style, appearances, domesticity—she also constructs the West as a place where expectations of gender can be transgressed without penalty. Recounting their departure from the East in the summer of 1921, Sergeant establishes Gertrude Ely as the more stereotypically feminine in style, yet also the more politically active and ambitious. "On the Chicago train," Sergeant writes:

> Till the last moment I doubted Gertrude's coming, and at North Philadelphia she gave me, as usual, a scare. Passengers get off, passengers get on, platform empties, conductor signals and then, suddenly, whirl of blue serge, zestful laugh, sparkling eyeglasses, bewildered porter, shower of smart black bags. She always does do it (or almost always), but it keeps her *thin.*
>
> "I'll tell you some news. The Democratic Committee has asked me to run for . . ." No wonder she is still more full of East than West and casts a rather disapproving eye on my war-battered luggage, piled high on the opposite seat. Her own immaculate collection is quite worthy of congressional halls or country house weekends—of a stateroom rather than our crowded section. How will it look in those Mexican rooms in Santa Fe, where we are to live while we rebuild our mud-roofed adobe? (1922:410–11)

In spite of her fear that Ely will seem out of place once they arrive, Sergeant establishes their direction as one toward greater personal freedom. To her Eastern eye, even Chicago is refreshingly "Western," and she writes that what keeps her going across the hot, dull plains en route to the Rockies is "the memory of the Chicago Lake Front on Saturday afternoon. A gorgeous, triumphantly "Western" sight. The swift motor that met us made one leap for that blue-gold shore, and all the miles it devoured on the way to Winnetka seemed lined with shining bathers—bathers who came pouring half naked out of the black city streets . . . imagine a Boston street car full of women in bathing suits! Imagine battalions of bath-toweled males swarming through the Fifties and Sixties to New York's East River! (1922:411).

Thus, the "West," for Sergeant, is a place where one can abandon constraining social conventions the way the Chicago bathers abandon their clothes. Among conventions that one can gladly abandon are those that pertain to gender. In describing one of their new neighbors in Tesuque, Sergeant suggests that she is not alone in forsaking "Paris" for the "desert," in exchange for freedom from gendered expectations. On their way to their new house, Sergeant recalls, she and Ely spied, through "a very inviting rustic gate," "a man in a sombrero, working in a field. But when we hailed him, the "man," leaving his plow, revealed himself as a woman dressed in khaki shirt and breeches. A very vivacious and unmasculine-looking little lady, who affirmed that, after twelve years in Paris, she had come back to her native New Mexico and bought a ranch, which she was working herself" (1922:416).

This "little lady," a Mrs. O'Bryan, in addition to serving as an encouraging role model, provides much-needed advice about life in Tesuque (which "is used enough to American farmers' wives but finds us a remarkable species") and takes many of their troubles on her shoulders—"shoulders," Sergeant writes, "that look very slight and slender, yet lift a hundred pound sack of grain like a strong man's." One day Sergeant and Ely sit on their neighbor's porch with Mrs. O'Bryan and her son, who, Sergeant claims, "only half approves of his mother's reversion to Southwestern type after many years in Paris." " 'She used to be the fussiest little dresser you ever saw,' " he laments, and Sergeant notes that his mother is not offended, but flattered: "Her blue eyes danced. 'Yes, I wouldn't go out till my veil was just so, if it took an hour, like any Parisian. And how many hats and sets of furs did I have when I came home?' . . . All the same the son is proud of his mother's masculine capacity, her fearlessness" (1922:590–91).

In relating this exchange, Sergeant again invokes Paris as that feminine consumer's paradise. Sinclair Lewis did the same in *Dodsworth*, where Paris, in Sam Dodsworth's mind, is "that feminine, flirtatious refuge from reality" (87). Sergeant's New Mexico, however, is also a consumer's utopia, if of a different sort. In their shopping, Sergeant and Ely are untroubled by worries of how to avoid the supposed homogeneity of modern fashions that worried Austin's character in *26 Jayne Street*. Nor need they trouble themselves with knowledge of commodities being the products of sweated immigrant labor, such as had concerned Sergeant during her work on the Lower East Side of Manhattan. Although a decade later Sergeant would express more cynical views of native art and craft production, in "The Journal of a Mud House" she depicts the labor that their Indian and Hispanic neighbors devote to their crafts as unalienated, a fulfilling expression of identity and individuality—for producer as well as consumer.

Hence, Sergeant and Ely delight in adorning their new abode with pots and blankets purchased from Pueblo women and antique furniture "picked up" during jaunts through mountain villages. While Sergeant's friend Katherine Dudley, a painter, visits (and reads to her from Gauguin's journals), they work out where to place Sergeant's great-grandmother's Persian shawl, whether the desk should be black or pink, where to put the "salmon-colored Spanish chest," and whether to place the "big black Santa Clara jar filled with juniper over the hearth, and a round terra-cotta bowl of startling carmine Indian paintbrush combined with purple and yellow blooms on the long table with wrought-iron ends"—and all the while they work, "the green-blue doors stand open deliciously to the riotous brilliance of pink foothills and blue sky" (Sergeant 1922:778). Their delight in aesthetics extends to the outdoors: when not working on the house, Sergeant writes, she and her friends take horse-packing trips through the desert, spend nights camping in cliff dwellings, and attend dances at the Pueblos. As her description of their open door illustrates, Sergeant blurs boundaries between public and private, domesticity and adventure.

In her "Journal of a Mud House," although she did not express it so explicitly, Sergeant, like Cather, was, I would argue, attempting to revalue the periphery of the nation as a homeland of national identity and authenticity. Such reconfiguration was very much to her own advantage as a writer, but it was also as a political strategy to gain national support for Pueblo land rights and civil liberties (as well as being a strategy to fund her own part in this effort). One way of revaluing the region for her readership was to allude to lands more readily associated, among her audience, with spiritual inspiration and elite knowledge. Also like Cather, Sergeant was asserting the authority of her own voice—one not lacking in cultural capital, including the knowledge of foreign lands and the supposed centers of "civilization," despite a newfound taste for what many of their contemporaries would have considered a provincial backwater.

As in so many elite whites' descriptions of the Southwest written during this period, Sergeant invokes the more conventional landscape of the cosmopolitan traveler—particularly the Mediterranean and Middle East. Of the mountains behind their house, for example, Sergeant writes that "the light is Greek, but the gods of the Sangre de Cristo are neither Greek nor

Christian" (1922:422)—despite, it seems, their name and many Catholic inhabitants. The yellow ridge behind them is "classic and austere as Greek marble" (778), and Tesuque village, she claims, "has a sort of ascetic pathos that suggests Palestine" (594). "Ciupodero [a neighboring village] in harvest time will always exist in memory just as we saw it—timeless as the mountain village of the 'Ode on a Grecian Urn' " (58). Although it is possible, and in many ways helpful, to see in such allusions an attempt to make the Southwest "America's Orient" (Babcock 1990; Dilworth 1996:5), the mapping of the one terrain onto the other is, I believe, more complex than an attempt to exoticize and dominate and can be illuminated by a consideration of rhetorical strategy, in an era when "Europe's Orient" had already acquired a certain value as cultural capital among middle-class white Americans. Sergeant depicted her farming, cross-dressing neighbor, Mrs. O'Bryan, as not lacking any familiarity with urban fashion and proper femininity. Similarly, Sergeant demonstrated that her own admiration for Southwestern landscapes did not result from any lack of experience with elite tourism.

Whatever her political agenda, Sergeant was also still struggling to develop a career for herself as a writer, and the Southwest offered the opportunity to market a new sort of commodity to her readers: the Southwestern landscape. As a journalist, and as Cather did as a novelist, Sergeant marketed an adept taste in images akin to her tastes in clothing, food, and household decor. She attempted to use this skill to her advantage, quite explicitly on some occasions, in selling her writing. For both Sergeant and Cather, aesthetically pleasing images were to be consumed and produced. Their writing became a special sort of commodity—a way of consuming a sense of "place" and regional identity. Both Sergeant and Cather planned to write travel books about the Southwest, an ambition that went unrealized; Cather's novels, however, are now sold like travel books and souvenirs to Southwestern tourists in airports, hotel lobbies, and museum gift shops.

In the 1920s the expanding market for American tourism, aided by the proliferation of highways and cars, offered writers like Sergeant an important new readership. Though Sergeant had achieved some success as a journalist before moving to New Mexico in the 1920s, she never achieved any financial stability, and her correspondence reveals that she continued to struggle to sell her abilities and interests to publishers—and frequently did so by downplaying her political concerns and appealing to the interests of potential tourists. Proposing an article on Pueblo "Pottery Women," Sergeant assured the editor of *Ladies' Home Journal* that, despite her political commitments, the article would have "no tang of propaganda" (16 November 1922, John Collier Papers, microfilm reel 5).

One way for Sergeant to avoid the "tang of propaganda" was to concentrate on aesthetically pleasing images, interspersed with "facts." To the *Ladies' Home Journal,* Sergeant proposed in the fall of 1922 a series of articles giving "a bird's eye motor view of the 20 pueblos from Taos to Zuni, done very pictorially, with human interludes, with certain of the new economic and health statistics that are now available" (John Collier Papers, microfilm reel 5). Proposing a similar piece to the editor of *The Century,* Sergeant explained, "New Mexico must be apprehended through the eye, if you don't know how it looks, you know nothing about it" (John Collier Papers, microfilm reel 5). Sergeant similarly wrote to John Collier of her plan to produce a travel guide to the Pueblos. What she envisioned, she explained to Collier, was "a book which every traveler [to the Southwest] will want to read; one that will be at once scientifically based in giving the essentials of what is known of this people on the archaeological and ethnological side; one that . . . will be 'pictorial' in the sense of giving the look and feel and meaning of the country that has produced their civilization. . . . if I have any gift in writing it is in making places and people live" (John Collier Papers, microfilm reel 4).

In her *Harper's* article Sergeant concentrates to such an extent on ethnic and racial difference as an aesthetic matter that one could scarcely guess she had more serious concerns as well—those, for instance, pertaining to the struggle to protect Indian land rights and civil liberties. When writing of one of her horseback trips, Sergeant recalls an Edward Curtis photograph of Indians riding horses through a canyon.[7] In writing of her Indian and Hispanic neighbors, she reproduces Curtis's romantic representations of difference; her neighbors might as well be "Indian dishes stand[ing] against a white background" as in her dining room cupboard (1922:56). An elderly Indian man asleep on the ground alongside the railroad tracks is "a bronze statue of primeval times, akin to rocks and trees and mountains" (412).

Such superficial and romantic celebrations of cultural difference give way to elitism when Sergeant writes of the "inferior Indian pottery" littering the platform of the Albuquerque train station (412), and when she suggests, plaintively, that the tastes of her Hispanic neighbors appear to be

taking a downward slide toward tackiness, away from their more picturesque traditions. Writing of the village church in Tesuque, Sergeant suggests the limits of her cultural pluralism:

> If only the Southwest could be ruled by a Roman Catholic potentate
> with an archaeological and aesthetic tradition! Every year one more
> old church, full of crucifixes and carved beams and strange dark
> saints—the sort of church that Americans cross the ocean to visit in
> Spain and Italy—is transformed into a neat little modern sanctuary
> with polished oak pews and commercial Madonnas all golden hair,
> pink cheeks, and blue robes. The priest tells me that in some places the
> people demand that "the Mexican" shall remain above the altar. Alas!
> not the Tesuque people. But the walls are at least pink and blue, and
> covered with tin candle sconces. (1922:57)

Sergeant's apparent obsession with the picturesque probably stemmed
at least in part from a sense of what might interest her readers and appear
suitably uncontroversial to the editors of the genteel press. In fact, Sergeant
was becoming passionately involved in a campaign for cultural pluralism
and Indian land rights. The campaign mobilized in 1922 in response to
legislation, particularly the Bursum Bill, which supported the claims of
non-Indians to land that had once been claimed by the Pueblos.[8] Sergeant
and other white intellectuals and wealthy elites—including the Whites,
Mary Austin, Mabel Dodge Luhan, Witter Bynner, and Alice Corbin Henderson—used the proposed legislation to draw attention to longstanding
injustices in government policy toward Indians—not just the threat to land
rights, but also the suppression of religious beliefs and other cultural differences, and the government's failure to provide the most basic health care
and to alleviate poverty. In addition to working with her friend Elizabeth
White and other members of the newly formed Eastern Association on
Indian Affairs and its Santa Fe branch, the New Mexico Association on
Indian Affairs (which Sergeant helped found), Sergeant worked closely
with John Collier (the future director of the Bureau of Indian Affairs)
through the Indian Defense Association, discussing political strategy with
Pueblo leaders and writing numerous articles (primarily in *The Nation* and
the *New Republic*) promoting land rights, cultural pluralism, and religious
freedom—particularly in relation to the Pueblos.

In addition to her journalism and work surrounding Indian land rights,

Sergeant was instrumental in organizing efforts to promote Indian art, such as the Pueblo Pottery Fund, which she helped found in 1922 as a way of promoting and preserving the Pueblo pottery Cather had first helped her appreciate. Alarmed by the rapid rate at which old pottery was being sold and taken out of the region, Sergeant explained to John Collier that her aim was to collect "specimens" of pottery from all the Pueblos and house them in Santa Fe, "where the women of the pueblos can always come to study them" (30 November 1922, John Collier Papers, microfilm reel 4).

Such activities kept Sergeant in close contact with those "hard boiled archaeologists" she had once imagined excavating cliff-dweller pottery. In the early 1920s, Sergeant visited F. W. Hodge's excavation of Hawikuh near Zuni; in her political work concerning the Bursum Bill, she frequently relied on Hodge, then affiliated with the Museum of the American Indian, for advice. After one of her first visits to Zuni to discuss political strategies, for example, Sergeant wrote Hodge to inquire about the ethics of publishing the names of the leaders she had interviewed and quoting from their speeches. In the same letter, she mentioned that the warm welcome she received at Zuni was largely due to the fact that she had first visited the pueblo as Hodge's friend and guest (John Collier Papers, microfilm reel 5).

Although many of the articles Sergeant published in the *New Republic* and *The Nation* expressed her political views much more directly than did "The Journal of a Mud House," she continued to revalorize New Mexican landscapes, art, and inhabitants by drawing on her knowledge of places more conventionally associated, among her readers, with elite tastes. Pueblo religious ceremonies, Sergeant wrote in *The Nation*, take place against a "Gauguinesque background" and Pueblo pottery is "as fine as any in Crete" (1923:579).

As well as mustering political support for the Pueblos, Sergeant's articles tended to promote Southwestern tourism enthusiastically, even though this was an industry about which Sergeant, along with many other intellectuals of the day, had serious misgivings. Sergeant was largely dependent upon tourists, actual or potential, as consumers of her writing. She also perceived tourism as a means of alleviating, if not solving, Indian economic difficulties. At the same time, though, that Sergeant wrote articles geared toward enticing tourists, she also warned that tourism could have a corrosive effect on the cultural difference she found so worthy of celebration. The government, Sergeant argued, faced the task of protecting cultural pluralism without reducing "Indian villages and Spanish missions" to "tourist attractions played up by hotelkeepers and chambers of commerce." The government of New Mexico, she wrote, needed to become "progressive without [encouraging] cheapness" (1923:579). Like her fellow Bryn Mawrters and their associates who would express similar ambivalence about tourism, Sergeant was never entirely clear about whether the spectre of tackiness should be of equal concern to all. Pueblo Indians were, as Sergeant was likely aware, much more apt to be concerned about how tourism might encourage violations of religious principles and disrupt their lives and communities (Gordon-McCutchan 1991, Jojola 1998, Teale 1998).

In her work for protection of Pueblo land rights and in her campaign for tasteful tourism, Sergeant drew on the same Bryn Mawrter identity that had inspired, over a decade before, her combination of social work and muckraking journalism among immigrant workers in Manhattan. When researching political strategies and the potential consequences of the Bursum Bill among the Pueblos, at one point Sergeant referred to her unmarried status as a prerequisite for the kind of work she was doing. After a trip to speak with leaders at Zuni in 1922, she wrote on 13 December, in one of her frequent letters to John Collier, of difficulties in achieving acceptance as a woman concerned with politics:

> Lorenzo [Lorenzo Chaves, who had worked as an excavator for F. W. Hodge] told me afterwards that the Sun Priest had been disturbed because I was a woman and occupied in these matters. Why was I not occupied with my children? I said "you should have told him the Zunis were my children." Lorenzo said "that is just what I did tell him. I said 'Isn't it a wonderful thing that women like this woman should take an interest and try to save the Pueblos from this terrible danger that threatens them. If she had children she could not be helping us in this way.' " (John Collier Papers, microfilm reel 4)

Such "maternalist" sentiments suggest the continuity between Sergeant's background among reformers and settlement-house workers and the way she continued to negotiate her gender identity during her experiences in the Southwest. Not unlike the settlement-house workers, Sergeant drew on her ethnic and class background as leverage to gain authority as a single woman working in an area dominated by men. But despite her elitism, romanticism, and "maternalism," Sergeant appears to have struggled earnestly to understand the dynamics and ethics of the patronage of cultural difference, and her attitudes were often more reflective and less dictatorial than those of other whites involved in similar work. Sergeant was, in fact, the author of an exceptionally rare critical study of the effects of the art market on Pueblo society (John Collier Papers, microfilm reel 28), questioning the assumption that arts patronage encouraged the preservation of tradition. Ignoring the fact that in the 1930s farming was hardly a viable source of income among the Northern Pueblos, Sergeant argued that art patronage was radically transforming the economic basis of Pueblo communities, inspiring Pueblo men to give up farming in order to paint. While it was not so unusual for more distant observers to cast stones at white patrons (for a wonderful example, see Gold's 1936 critique of Mabel Dodge Luhan's "slumming" among the Pueblos), among more knowledgeable commentators, Sergeant at times displayed an uncommon willingness to examine basic assumptions critically—her own assumptions as well as those of others.

On the other hand, Sergeant may well have felt spurned by the patrons she critiqued, and her more critical analysis of the art market may have been influenced by resentment. She had experienced a bitter falling out with Elizabeth White in the early 1920s, when Sergeant backed her close friend John Collier in his efforts to defeat the Bursum Bill, departing from the position of the Eastern Association on Indian Affairs, with which White was involved. In an article in the *New Republic* (1923), Sergeant described the Eastern Association as prioritizing the interests of white settlers, at a time when White was representing their position as a necessary compromise. White was outraged by what she saw as a malicious misrepresentation of her group's loyalties.

Though there were probably sincere differences of opinion about political strategies, the disagreement was also about a competition for authority. Although it seems extraordinary that any of these white newcomers from the Northeast would perceive themselves as experts on the Pueblos after such brief experience in the region, White, with others of the "Santa Fe Group" as they came to be known, saw Collier as acting too independently of their advice and expertise. White was also a Republican and may well have been suspicious of Collier's affiliation with socialists and radical reformers. Sergeant, a Democrat and occasional "muckraker," was politically and intellectually less conservative than White, and she and Collier remained friends for the rest of their lives, sharing interests in Jungian psychology as well as Indian affairs. Sergeant hints that her outlook and White's diverged in other ways as well. In *Shadow-Shapes*, the book she published in 1920 about her experiences recovering from her war injury, Sergeant suggests that she and White had very different ideas about the war. In part because White's personal papers reveal that she developed a profound hatred of "the enemy," I suspect that it is White whom Sergeant describes visiting her at the war's end in the American Hospital in Paris: "The psychology of these gentle, passionate, well-bred, brown-haired spinsters who, after two or three years of nursing—nursing gas and wounds, in hospitals sometimes bombed and shelled—yet take pleasure in the street celebration, amazes me. Elizabeth, my second visitor of the species, was glorying besides in the harshness of the Armistice terms. As I think it over, she, who nursed largely in Belgium, is the only hater—not excepting the French pupil nurses—I have seen. The only person thinking about German humiliation as the reverse of our triumph" (1920:74–75).

Not only did she differ from the Whites in their political and intellectual sensibilities; unlike them, Sergeant apparently did not have the means to live in New Mexico without a constant struggle for economic support. Perhaps as a consequence, she seems to have had more ambivalent feelings about New Mexico than did the Whites or Margretta Dietrich, and, for the rest of her life, her writings and travels would continue to shift between East and West. After a failed attempt to mend her friendship with Elizabeth White, in 1923 Sergeant moved back to New York, for the next decade returning to New Mexico only for brief visits. She had, she wrote many years later, experienced an epiphany one day on the road between Santa Fe and Tesuque, realizing suddenly *"This is not my country"* (1963:208; Sergeant's emphasis). In 1929, Sergeant published her only novel, not a successful one, based on the lives of her mother's ancestors in colonial New England—an attempt, perhaps, to recenter her identity in the Northeast.[9] Later that year she moved to Zurich, where she spent two years studying and undergoing psychoanalysis with Carl Jung and Toni Woolf, returning to New York in the midst of the Depression. There she struggled for jobs writing "pot boilers for popular magazines" and found little in common with her old friend Willa Cather, who lived in a luxurious Park Avenue apartment and scorned Sergeant's enthusiasm for the New Deal (Sergeant 1963:250–61).

In 1933, John Collier became head of the Bureau of Indian Affairs and pro-Indian Harold Ickes was appointed Secretary of the Interior. Optimistic that "many of the reforms hitherto impossible would be tried out" (1963:254), Sergeant returned to her house in Tesuque and worked for three years as a consultant and researcher for the Bureau of Indian Affairs and for the Soil Conservation Service. During this period, Sergeant had little contact with the Whites and Margretta Dietrich. It was at that time, however, that she befriended Edward Dozier, from Santa Clara Pueblo, a high school student at the time who took an interest in Sergeant's research among the Pueblos. Dozier went on to become an influential anthropologist and linguist. Long after Sergeant moved back to New York in 1936 they continued a warm and detailed correspondence, frequently discussing Indian political issues and Dozier's research concerning culture and ethnicity in the United States and the Philippines.[10] Sergeant's greatest public recognition came late in life with her well-received 1953 memoir of Cather, followed by a book about Robert Frost (whose identity as "the poet of New England" bore resemblance to Cather's as "the novelist of Nebraska"). Sergeant's efforts to define her own identity continued: at the time of her death in New York City in 1965, she was working on an autobiography.

Sergeant had been only marginally successful in her attempts to market the Southwest as a commodity, but many of her former classmates from Bryn Mawr, including the Whites and Margretta Dietrich, had the advantage of greater capital. Freed from the need to earn an income, they could afford to market the Southwest and its art at a financial loss. Although Sergeant had been unwilling to support their efforts at the cost of her own independence and authority, in New Mexico her former classmates would find many more willing to support them uncritically.

CHAPTER THREE **SHOPPING FOR A BETTER WORLD IN A "CITY OF LADIES"**

Before women won the vote in 1920, philanthropic endeavors—giving, voluntarism, and social reform—provided the primary means through which the majority of middle- and upper-class women fashioned their public roles.

Kathleen McCarthy, Women's Culture: American Philanthropy and Art, 1830–1930

Social capital is above all a matter of personal relations.

Toril Moi, "Appropriating Bourdieu: Feminist Theory and Pierre Bourdieu's Sociology of Culture"

 In a recent study of everyday shopping activities in North London, Daniel Miller (1998) argues that it is a mistake to consider shopping, an activity often associated with women, to be primarily an expression of hedonism and materialism. Shopping, he argues, can be about relationships, a means of conveying care and concern for others. Documenting and analyzing this phenomenon does not require any celebration of consumer capitalism, Miller writes, but can help us better understand it. Particularly in a social formation marked by flexible and impermanent social relationships, people often rely on goods to express and solidify attachments to others. One of Miller's chapter titles, "Making Love in Supermarkets," struck me as farfetched at first, but I found that his analysis fit well with what I had learned from surviving members of a community of art patrons in Santa Fe. In particular, I recalled how frequently people I was interviewing pointed out or recalled gifts they had been given by some of the art patrons I was inquiring about, including gifts of art, but also houses and real estate.

One winter afternoon, for example, I spoke with Jean Buchanan, in the house she had built on property inherited from Margretta Dietrich. Originally from Scotland, in 1949 Buchanan had come to Santa Fe from Denver, where she had been working as a secretary. Intending to move to Arizona, she got off the bus for the night in Santa Fe, and there she stayed. After showing me works of Indian and other art that had been left to her by Dietrich and her artist sister, Dorothy Stewart, Buchanan served me tea. As sunlight poured in on geraniums in a kitchen window framed in blue, she recalled a party held during her early years in the city, a party that she had attended with Dietrich, Dorothy Stewart, and Elizabeth White. In the midst of recounting tales of the various guests, most of them women, Buchanan paused for a moment and laughed, explaining, as if she were letting me in on a secret, "Santa Fe was just a small city in those days—*a city of ladies.*" Buchanan then continued to reminisce but did not appear nostalgic: the city of ladies, I gathered, was, for some of its members, constraining as well as liberating.

Like Daniel Miller, Sharon Zukin has argued for the importance of recognizing the pleasures of shopping. Zukin writes that "people like to consume; they seek their social identity in shopping, comparing goods, and talking about consumption. They find drama, history, and variety in new spheres of consumption" (1991:254–55). But consumer pleasures are not equally shared by all, nor is everyone so inclined to seek his or her identity in commodities. To a certain extent, as Daniel Miller points out, such inclinations—and skills, the exercise of which accounts for a good deal of the pleasure—have been linked historically to divisions of gender and class, even if the lines of division are not tidy or inflexible. As Thorstein Veblen observed in 1899, at the turn of the century consuming was something that middle- and upper-class women were particularly trained for and expected to specialize in: shopping for themselves and their families was the counterpart to their husbands' productive labor (a misleading stereotype, according to historian Mark Swiencicki [1997], who argues that men's consumption has often gone unnoticed). But with no husband or nuclear family to concern themselves with, women such as Elizabeth White and Margretta Dietrich managed to turn shopping into a matter, not just of personal and interpersonal pleasure, but of public consequence. At the same time, shared tastes played a large part in their attempts to refashion domesticity and community, using their class and gender to their advantage in ways that would have been more difficult elsewhere, and enjoying the economic dependence of those without their inherited wealth and privilege.

In the previous chapters, I discussed matters of taste and identity construction in relation to the writings of Mary Austin, Willa Cather, and

Elizabeth Sergeant. For Mary Austin's character, Neith Schuyler, consumption was a means of constructing a new personal and national identity, but within the context of Manhattan, Austin suggested that shopping with such a goal in mind could be a troublesome and unsatisfying affair. For her *Harper's* readers, Elizabeth Sergeant depicted shopping in the high desert country as a matter of pure delight—except, that is, when disturbed by the sight of such "inferior" goods as the tourist ware offered by Pueblo Indians along the Santa Fe Railway. However, from her writings about her relationship with Willa Cather and from their correspondence, it appears that in their own lives Sergeant and Cather were concerned less with shopping for actual objects than they were with shopping for images, experiences, and characters. These were the stock-in-trade of the careers they had established as writers, Cather rather more successfully than Sergeant, and their shared tastes and ambitions formed the basis of their friendship.

In contrast, Sergeant's fellow Bryn Mawr alumnae, Margretta Dietrich and Elizabeth and Martha White, never did establish income-producing careers, having no financial need to do so, although they very much shared Sergeant's Bryn Mawrter ethic of public service. Like many of their fellow activists in the suffrage movement, these women prided themselves on their ability to convey a positive and fashionable impression, thereby gaining legitimacy for their politics. They were also enthusiastic participants in the arts of pageantry. At Bryn Mawr, elaborate May Day and other pageants had been common, and the suffrage movement had demonstrated the successful application of pageantry to politics (Finnegan 1999:78–109). In New Mexico, the Bryn Mawrters applied theatrical skills to the movement to protect Indian land rights, and to promoting a rather colonial version of cultural pluralism, including the development of markets in Native and Spanish Colonial art.

In their "city of ladies," individuals such as Dietrich and the Whites made use of both "cultural" and actual capital in making a new community and a home for themselves as well as in advancing the causes they adopted. Within this community, there was a limited extent to which cultural and actual capital were independent. While Dietrich and the Whites managed to parlay their cultural capital (especially in the form of consumer skills and theater) into greater public influence, other individuals attempted to use cultural capital to establish income-producing careers, including work for philanthropists such as the Bryn Mawrters and for the federal government.

Bryn Mawrters Go Shopping in the Southwest

Elizabeth White's interests in anthropology and the American Southwest developed at the same time as Elizabeth Sergeant's, just prior to the beginning of the First World War. For White, as for Sergeant, such interests represented a departure from the more Eurocentric pursuits fostered by the curriculum at Bryn Mawr. While her sister Martha worked as a high school math teacher at an exclusive private school, Elizabeth White spent the years following her graduation from Bryn Mawr in 1901 by traveling (most often in Western Europe), studying art, including drawing, woodcarving, and sculpture; and working as a teaching assistant in the Bryn Mawr English Department, where she gave occasional lectures on English literature. Elizabeth also did secretarial work for her father and participated in various suffrage activities, including "study clubs" and parades. Judging from the diaries she kept during these years, none of her activities absorbed her to the extent that her later work in the Southwest would. Her most enthusiastic notations concerned social occasions and, not insignificantly, shopping—for just the right dress, interesting art, or the perfect gift (School of American Research, Amelia Elizabeth White Collection; hereafter SAR, AEWC).

During the summer of 1913, White traveled to New Mexico, where she visited friends from New York and Philadelphia, including another Bryn Mawr alumna, Alice Day Jackson. Although this was probably her first trip to New Mexico, White had been west before—having previously made trips to Alaska, the Rocky Mountains, and parts of California. In Santa Fe that summer White met F. W. Hodge and other anthropologists, who immediately inspired her interest in their research in the Southwest and Central America. On White's return trip to the East, she visited the Field Museum in Chicago—a sign of her growing fascination with anthropology (diary, SAR, AEWC). This visit to the Southwest and encounter with anthropologists resulted in White's shifting her interests from Europe and toward the Americas, and from English literature to anthropology.

Upon her return to Bryn Mawr at the end of that summer, White began taking Spanish lessons in preparation for further travels in the Southwest and Latin America. She also began a regular correspondence with F. W. Hodge and Herbert Spinden. Early the following year, White visited Spinden and his archaeological excavations in Central America (and wrote to her sister that she thought Antigua was "the most beautiful place in the world"). Then, in 1915, she returned to New Mexico, where she visited the excavation of the cliff dwellings of the Pajarito Plateau outside Santa Fe. But White's new pursuits were interrupted by the war in Europe in the same way as Elizabeth Sergeant's: in 1916, when Sergeant went to work as a journalist in Paris, Elizabeth White and her sister Martha volunteered as nursing assistants with the Red Cross and would spend most of the war in Belgium and France (postcard album, diary, SAR, AEWC).

Immediately following the war, Elizabeth White became increasingly involved in Indian affairs, joining her anthropologist friends—including Hodge and Spinden—as well as old friends from Bryn Mawr in the newly formed Eastern Association on Indian Affairs (EAIA). White's newfound commitment possibly resulted from greater freedom following her father's death in 1916. Horace White had left his three daughters—Elizabeth, Martha, and Abby—a considerable amount of wealth, enough to purchase three houses on East 55th Street in Manhattan, and, eventually, properties in Florida, Arizona, and New Mexico. Their inheritance also made it possible for them to devote the rest of their lives to philanthropy.[1] Thus, Elizabeth White, with her sister Martha's occasional help, provided major funding and support for the EAIA. The Association initially focused on the protection of Pueblo land rights and the defeat of the Bursum Bill, legislation which was widely perceived by Pueblo leaders and by the region's white artists, writers, and philanthropists as a significant threat to Indian cultural survival in the Southwest. In addition to participating in such collective efforts, White developed her own individual philanthropic projects to promote Indian art and in 1922 began planning to open a shop to sell Indian art on Madison Avenue—not to make a profit, but to encourage the market for Indian art.[2] As she became increasingly involved in buying and selling art, White abandoned her attempts to create it more directly.

During the summer of 1923, Elizabeth and Martha traveled to Santa Fe, where they engaged in a combination of political activism, art patronage, and tourism. Elizabeth made use of contacts provided by Elizabeth Sergeant, and, when not busy purchasing objects to sell in the Madison Avenue shop, she and Martha worked with the EAIA to protect Indian land rights (although Sergeant accused them of giving rights away, rather than protecting them) consulting with Pueblo leaders and writing Washington politicians. Before returning to New York, the two sisters visited F. W. Hodge's

Figure 1 The neighborhood in the foothills of the Sangre de Cristo Mountains, on the outskirts of "the city of ladies," where Elizabeth and Martha White purchased the property dubbed "El Delirio," photographed in the 1920s. Reprinted, by permission, from *El Delirio: The Santa Fe World of Elizabeth White*, by Gregor Stark and E. Catherine Rayne. © 1998 by the School of American Research, Santa Fe.

extensive and much-acclaimed excavation of Hawikuh near Zuni. Nearby, they attended the second annual Gallup Intertribal Indian Ceremonial, a festival and art exhibition organized by local traders and other non-Indian local residents. Just after departing Santa Fe, White wrote to Sergeant. Her letter is suggestive of the way the network of Bryn Mawr graduates combined their political activism with shopping—for art, scenery, and land. Their consumption of the landscape involved not just appreciating it and representing it to others, but also buying it. In her letter to Sergeant, White mentioned her purchase of the Armenta Spanish Land Grant property that would eventually become home to the School of American Research (figure 1). "Dearest Elsie," White began:

> I meant to write you ages ago. Thank you so much for your letter and the names of everybody, everywhere. It has been such a help. I have been dashing from one pueblo to another ever since I arrived which explains (but doesn't excuse) why I haven't written sooner . . . [Martha] and I left this morning. We went to Zuni via Inscription Rock ["El Morro"] which I had never seen. We bought a house and a lot just as

we left, or rather, we telephoned young John Evans [Mabel Dodge Luhan's son] to go ahead and acquire it for us. It is not Tesuque, alas, but out towards Sunmount—the last adobe in that direction—with such a heavenly view! I took Hildegarde Angell to Jemez as my postal informed you, and bought such beautiful pots in the Pueblo. (John Collier Papers, microfilm reel 5)

White's letter goes on to relate concerns over John Collier's political strategies in working to defeat the Bursum Bill, legislation that threatened to give white settlers legal title to Pueblo lands. Within a few months, the dispute would lead White to terminate her friendship with Sergeant, disregarding Sergeant's concerted efforts to appease her, but at this point she emphasized their shared tastes in goods, real estate, and spectacles, ending her letter with reference to a gift, Sergeant's articles in *Harper's* the previous year, and to achieving insider status at Tesuque Pueblo:

The Tesuques gave a little fiesta for Martha and me all for ourselves. But the secret leaked out and there were crowds of trippies [tourists?]. I have never been so touched. We went out there yesterday morning early and they danced the Buffalo Dance and the Eagle Dance for us. It was *too* ravishing in front of the church. I must tell you about it later.

I have just sent you by mail one of the flowered shawls that looks as if it belonged in the mud house. I hope you will like it . . . I shall miss you at Hawikuh, but we'll soon meet [in New York].

White closes the letter "Au revoir dear, Ever thine, Elizabeth" (John Collier Papers, microfilm reel 5). Though her friendship with Sergeant turned out to be short-lived, in Santa Fe White would find other friends and allies. She would establish a role for herself in her new community as a giver of gifts not just to friends, but also to institutions. She would also continue to represent herself as more of an insider than a tourist, though in many ways she and her friends had much in common with tourists, attending spectacles and seeking objects that could serve as emblems of regional identity.

White's dedication to Indian art would peak in the early 1930s, when she organized the Exposition of Indian Tribal Arts, a project that provides much of the focus of the next chapter.[3] In addition to collecting American Indian and Hispanic art, White also made numerous purchases of modernist painting. Although Martha White died in 1937, Elizabeth White continued to be a patron of the arts and anthropology for the rest of her long life, financing archaeological research, serving on the board of the School of American Research, and finally leaving her house and land in Santa Fe to the School. Before she died in 1972 at the age of ninety-four, White made important donations of art to museums all over the country: she gave Pueblo pottery, for example, to the Worcester Museum, slate and ivory carvings to the American Museum of Natural History, and paintings by her good friend John Sloan, a renowned realist painter, to the Whitney Museum and the Boston Museum of Fine Arts (SAR, AEWC, box 15). With her gifts, White also left her philanthropical stamp on Santa Fe. In addition to the School of American Research, White donated the land for the Laboratory of Anthropology, the Wheelwright Museum, and the Women's Club, and established a day-care center (modeled, in some ways, after the settlement houses) and an animal shelter in memory of her sister Martha. Such philanthropy conformed to the ethic of public service that had legitimated Bryn Mawr women's ambition for careers and independent lives.

During the 1948 meetings of the American Anthropological Association in Albuquerque, White hosted a lunch for its members at her home in Santa Fe (Stark and Rayne 1998:132). Playing hostess was by then a most familiar role to White. In fact, during her lifetime, she was perhaps best known in Santa Fe for her elaborate parties, conducted in the spirit of the early twentieth-century passion for pageantry. Her home, dubbed "El Delirio" after a bar she and Martha visited in Spain, was frequently a literal stage, with her friends in costume and herself both actor and director. Some of the rooms at El Delirio had their own themes, and in the "New York Room" hung a full-length portrait of Martha White as an Amazon (Stark and Rayne 1998:3). As Margaret Finnegan (1999) argues was common among early twentieth-century suffragists, Elizabeth and Martha White reveled in performing a range of different identities, chosen to suit the occasion (figure 2).

A similar combination of interests in politics, theater, philanthropy, and the aesthetics of cultural difference can be found in Margretta Stewart Dietrich's path west. In "The Journal of a Mud House" Elizabeth Sergeant wrote that when she attended a Corn Dance at Santo Domingo, she "bumped, the first minute, into friends from New York and Philadelphia and Boston" (Sergeant 1922:780). It is possible that Sergeant's fellow Bryn

Figure 2 The "New York Room" and Martha White's portrait as Queen Penthesilea, an "Amazon queen," in the Santa Fe residence of Elizabeth and Martha White, now the home of the School of American Research. Photographed in the 1960s. Reprinted, by permission, from *El Delirio: The Santa Fe World of Elizabeth White,* by Gregor Stark and E. Catherine Rayne. © 1998 by the School of American Research, Santa Fe.

Mawr alumna, Margretta Stewart Dietrich, was among them. For it was during the summer of 1921, when Sergeant was writing her article for *Harper's,* that Dietrich and her sister, Dorothy Stewart, made their first visit to New Mexico. Since graduating from Bryn Mawr, Dietrich had been deeply involved in the campaign for women's suffrage, particularly in Nebraska, where her husband—the father of a Bryn Mawr classmate and fellow suffragist, Gertrude Dietrich—was governor and later a U.S. Senator. Dietrich spent the better part of the years 1910–1920 canvassing rural Nebraska, making speeches on behalf of suffrage and the reform of child labor laws. Recalling her years as a suffragist, Dietrich revealed that she also prided herself on a certain aesthetic sensibility, important in constructing an identity as a younger, attractive suffragist, in contrast to the media stereotypes of suffragists as masculine and homely women. She recalled taking part in a public debate against an antisuffragist—with the improbable name of "Mrs. Crumpacker," dressed in a "severe, tailored suit and stiff hat—almost the clothes that suffragists were made to wear in the old cartoons." In contrast, Dietrich had made a point of wearing her "prettiest" dress, with "two deep flounces of lace" and "a bodice of flowered silk over a lace tucker." "To this day," she wrote, "I can feel the pleasurable sensation I had when I looked upon Mrs. Crumpacker, for I knew it was I who looked more feminine" (Dietrich n.d.:16). In her study of the relationship between consumer society and the suffrage movement, Finnegan reports that such concerns with appearance and fashion were a trend among Dietrich's generation of suffragists, who attempted "to sell the movement—and thus woman's citizenship—by affiliating it with femininity, good looks, and style" (1999:95).

After passage of the Nineteenth Amendment in 1920, Dietrich joined the more conservative successor to the National Woman Suffrage Association, the League of Women Voters. In the summer of 1921 Dietrich was invited to give a lecture to the Santa Fe chapter of the League and used the occasion to "motor" through the Southwest. Similar to the travels of Elizabeth Sergeant and Elizabeth White, Dietrich's and her sister's travels can be seen as an extended shopping trip—for art, landscapes, knowledge of cultural difference, and new parts to perform. The highlights of their trip included the San Geronimo festivities at Taos Pueblo and the aesthetic charms of Santa Fe. In a memoir written shortly before her death, Dietrich recalled the trip and her first meal in Santa Fe, at a restaurant called the Blue Parrot. Her remarks anticipate the way the wealth she would inherit from her husband would enable her to purchase sizable portions of real estate in a cozy community that included many middle- and upper-middle-class white women, of relatively similar tastes. The restaurant, she wrote, "was run by two delightful women in a lovely old house at the corner of Palace Avenue and Burro Alley . . . The house had many patios, with sheep in one of them, and the windows were of handblown glass. My sister, Dorothy Stewart, begged me to buy the whole block, but at that time we were not ready to invest in Santa Fe real estate" (1961:5).

By 1924, when her husband died, Dietrich was ready to so invest and purchased a house in Santa Fe, where she began spending summers. By 1927, she had purchased an additional house, large enough for apartments, including the one Jean Buchanan would later rent, and she and her sister had moved permanently to Santa Fe's Canyon Road, a dirt lane that had

Figure 3 Margretta Dietrich, 1925, from her memoir *New Mexico Recollections*. Although Dietrich is seen here "playing Indian," her work as an art patron and with government Indian policy can be seen as a way of ensuring that Indians would be given Indian roles. There were ways, however, in which Dietrich put herself in the position of determining which roles might be "Indian." Reprinted with permission from Elizabeth Berry Sebastian.

become home to many artists and writers also recently relocated from other parts of the country. Although Dietrich recalled later that she had assumed when she moved to New Mexico that her "promoting days were over" (Dietrich n.d.:100), she quickly became involved, along with her sister, in the New Mexico Association on Indian Affairs (NMAIA), the Indian Arts Fund (as the Pueblo Pottery Fund had been renamed), and the Spanish Colonial Arts Society. She also soon became one of the area's most influential private patrons of Indian and Spanish Colonial art. Dietrich became president of the NMAIA in 1933, a position she retained for the next two decades, and she was reputed, during the 1930s, to be one of the nation's most formidable activists in Indian Affairs.[4] Included in one of Dietrich's memoirs is a photograph of her, dated 1925, which reflects her newly acquired tastes and commitments, as well as her Bryn Mawr enthusiasm for drama. In the photograph, Dietrich is dressed in the 1920s' fashion of a Navajo woman: long skirt, velvet blouse, blanket, silver concha belt, and layers of necklaces (figure 3). Dietrich was "playing Indian"—a concept that has been used to characterize the appropriation of an Indian identity by white Americans, a sort of cultural cross-dressing in which a white identity is really more affirmed than transgressed (Dilworth 1996; Deloria 1998; Green 1988). In the early twentieth century, it became common for middle-class whites to don "Indian" garb and dabble in "Indian" activities— camping, hiking, making handicrafts—at summer camps and in groups such as the Boy Scouts and the Campfire Girls (Deloria 1998:95–127). Unlike many whites who "played Indian," however, Dietrich and her associates maintained rather serious and long-lasting interests. Moreover, in many ways they were more interested in having Indians "play Indian" than in playing such a role themselves.

Throughout the 1920s and 1930s the Dietrich and the White sisters collaborated on various projects pertaining to Indians, many of them focusing on developing the Indian art market. During her years in Santa Fe, Dietrich not only served as an especially influential patron of Pueblo and Navajo painting, purchasing nearly 250 paintings directly from artists (Bernstein 1993:163–64); she also helped organize several decades of fairs and "Indian Markets," designed to promote the market for Indian art and to influence potential buyers as well as artists.

Despite their sustained involvement in the Southwest from the 1930s on, Dietrich and the Whites continued to travel abroad frequently. In the 1930s, for example, Dietrich and her sister made frequent trips to Mexico, and in 1936 Dietrich spent a year traveling in China with an old friend and living companion, Alice Brock. Elizabeth and Martha White made frequent trips to Europe and in the 1930s traveled to Morocco, where Elizabeth studied attempts by the French government to promote indigenous arts. In her late eighties, ever the tourist despite her need to distinguish herself from the tourists in New Mexico, Elizabeth White visited India and the Middle East, accompanied by Catherine Rayne.

Politicizing Consumption and the "City of Ladies"

I have been discussing just a few examples of a network of women who made their way to Northern New Mexico during the 1920s and 1930s. Santa Fe, though, was filled with such women, and the perception, among middle- and upper-class whites, of New Mexico as a place of freedom from the conventions of gender and class seems to have been fairly common. "The Southwest" has typically been constructed by white Americans as a masculine space—in "the Western" novel and film as a space where men might escape feminine influence, consumerism, and domesticity (Tompkins 1992). But in writings by the Bryn Mawrters—Margretta Dietrich, Elizabeth White, and Elizabeth Sergeant—as well as those of their associates, Willa Cather and Mary Austin—the Southwestern landscape, outdoors and in, is depicted as a space where women are at home, a space where they can bridge conventional boundaries between public and private, a space where they reinvent their identities in relation to gender, class, nation, and ethnicity.[5]

Reflecting on the powerful community of white women she encountered in Santa Fe during the 1930s, when she rented an apartment from Dorothy Stewart and began working for the Bureau of Indian Affairs, in May 1991, Julia Lukas told me, "The landscape was very masculine. It attracted strong women—and weak men. The landscape was powerful and masculine and it attracted women who weren't really one thing or another. You know, maybe their genes were mixed up. Women who were powerful without men, powerful together as a group." Lukas suggested that the Southwest attracted women from other parts of the country who, for whatever reason, fit uneasily into the category of their gender. Lukas's description of the landscape as "masculine" is no more accurate than

Cather scholars' description of the landscape as "feminine"; such attempts to connect the landscape with any particular gender only reveal the way that genders and landscapes have continually contested meanings. But regardless of such contests over definition, it is clear that many elite white women perceived the Southwest as a place where gendered and class-structured conventions, including those involving sexuality, could more safely be violated (as Mary Cabot Wheelwright put it, it was a place where one could "be a sport and also drink tea" [Wheelwright n.d.:8]). Santa Fe's cultural diversity encouraged a certain tolerance of individual "eccentricity," a tolerance extended to those, especially among the wealthy, who departed from gendered expectations.

As noted earlier, many of the women connected with this particular network of women were lesbians, although those who were not also led lives centered, in many respects, around other women. Santa Fe, from the 1920s on, was perceived as a haven for all sorts of white Americans who would not have found such easy acceptance elsewhere, including many gay men and lesbians. In a newspaper article on the history of gay people in Santa Fe, an elderly resident recalled, "There were people back then known as 'remittance persons.' They were men, or ladies, from wealthy families on the East Coast and the Midwest who were seen to be an embarrassment because of their lifestyles: alcoholics, deformed people, gays and lesbians, retarded people, kleptomaniacs. Their families would send them here, maybe put them up with a room in the La Fonda hotel to live, give them money to live. They lived and died here as perfectly acceptable members of the Santa Fe community" (Evans 1992:17).

The same article suggested that the popularity of Santa Fe among lesbians was related to a more general freedom from conventions of gender; the author quoted one "longtime lesbian resident" who recalled, "There was a casualness here, a laissez-faire attitude—it was a little freewheeling . . . Since there were early ranch-type ladies living here, wearing ranch-type clothes, you could get away with that without drawing attention. I liked that I could dress the way I wanted to" (18).

Truman Capote's *Answered Prayers* includes a corroborating spoof of Santa Fe lesbian life in gossip told about a Sarah Lawrence graduate who abandoned bourgeois heterosexual family life in New York for " 'the dyke capital of the United States' ": "What San Francisco is to Les Garçons, Santa Fe is to the Daughters of Bilitis. I suppose it's because the butchier ones like dragging up in boots and denim . . . [The Sarah Lawrence graduate and her lover] live in a rambling adobe in the foothills . . . Oh, it's a bit corny— the piñon fires, the Indian fetish dolls, Indian rugs, and the two ladies fussing in the kitchen over homemade tacos and the 'perfect' Margarita. But say what you will, it's one of the pleasantest homes I've ever been in" (Capote 1987:180). (Yet from my discussions with elderly heterosexual women, I gathered that they too reveled in "boots and denim," or at least the freedom to wear such outfits if they chose.)

One reason that wealthy white women such as the Bryn Mawrters found the Southwest such a liberating space was that the constraints of gender were offset by the power and control afforded by their class and race. While Hispanic and Indian inhabitants of the region struggled to cope with a newly imposed foreign language and political and economic system, land and labor were cheaper than in the East, and it was easier for wealthy white women to wield authority over others, men as well as women. In "The Journal of a Mud House" Elizabeth Sergeant emphasizes the fact that she and Gertrude Ely spent much of their summer in Tesuque directing the labor of their Hispanic carpenters and masons (when not employing sage old Indian men to guide them on horseback through mountains and canyons). For example, Sergeant describes her rush, with Ely, to make progress on their house: "It is a very cyclone of activity that now hurls us—with a train of brown men following after—from kitchen to corral" (1922:598). To women of greater wealth, Elizabeth and Martha White for example, such casual labor was perhaps less remarkable; when spending summers in New Mexico (before Elizabeth made it her permanent home), they brought a household of servants along with them.

The patronage, among such women, of Southwestern indigenous arts can be similarly considered in light of political and economic inequalities and the struggle among middle- and upper-class women for greater public influence. American Indian and Spanish Colonial arts were, in some ways, fields open to new sources of authority, museums, and exhibitions, and unusually privileged white women stepped into that opening more easily than they could have in art fields with a more established institutional and masculine structure.

When the Bryn Mawrters began promoting the indigenous arts of the Southwest, there were only fledgling markets for "American" art of any sort. Women have often been important early forces in new, still marginal, art movements, as demonstrated by Kathleen McCarthy's study of gender and patronage in the history of some of the country's major art institutions. In the early twentieth century, prices of modernist and American folk art were considerably lower than those in more established markets, and furthermore, the newer fields were not already dominated by an evaluative structure of male collectors, curators, and critics. According to McCarthy, "Folk art, laces, textiles, ceramics, and modernist paintings were all relatively inexpensive compared to the prices that men like [J. P.] Morgan were willing—and able—to pay for the masterpieces that they so avidly pursued" (1991:180).[6]

McCarthy argues that among the new consumers and patrons of modern American art, women tended to take the lead. In 1926, she reports, only seven commercial galleries in New York showed contemporary American art. Edith Halpert, one of the period's most influential gallery owners showing modern American art, recalls only one other New York gallery owner who was a woman and claims that " 'practically all the adventurous collectors of modern art and the majority of gallery visitors were women' " (198). As McCarthy argues, "women were able to take the lead [in avant-garde arts patronage] because this type of art was undervalued among traditional collectors, and still held at arm's length by the major museums" (209). Women were largely responsible for the founding of the Museum of Modern Art and the Whitney Museum, but typically had been excluded, McCarthy argues, from museums with longer histories.

McCarthy points out that many middle- and upper-class women attempted to extend their influence into the public sphere by exercising talents previously developed in the private sphere of domesticity and consumption. In nineteenth- and early twentieth-century America, the shift to an economy increasingly oriented around consumption opened up entirely new professions—including that of "consumer experts" who offered to alleviate anxieties about taste among the upwardly mobile. These new authorities proffered their advice as interior decorators through the new venue of "how-to" books and magazines like *Ladies' Home Journal*, *House Beautiful*, and *House and Garden*, publications marketed primarily to women (just as the new "cookbooks" made accessible skills that presumably had once been absorbed through years of gradual personal exposure, usually within the family). Women were commonly perceived as especially suited to these new professions. For example, they were said to be "natural" inte-

rior decorators because of "their instinctive knowledge of textiles and intimate knowledge of the conveniences of domestic life" (Candace Wheeler,
quoted in Lynes 1954:182). In 1913 Elsie de Wolfe, who made her fortune
decorating for wealthy clients, published *The House in Good Taste,* in which
she claimed that "good taste" was within reach of any woman willing to
learn. Although some might be gifted with "natural good taste," de Wolfe
reassured all women that good taste could also be acquired for the price of a
book (Lynes 1954:184–85). The Bryn Mawrters similarly marketed knowledge of Indian and Spanish Colonial art and also employed contradictory
notions—that taste couldn't be taught, and that it should be taught.

At the same time that women around the country were beginning to
market their talents professionally as specialists in domestic consumption,
they also made taste an area of philanthropic concern. Philanthropic attempts to improve popular taste were intermeshed with appeals to cultural
nationalism and bourgeois morality, reinforcing notions of women as ma-
ternal guardians of the good society (Ginzburg 1990). In the 1890s, for
example, when the Central Art Association of Chicago sponsored traveling
exhibitions of paintings, Hamlin Garland wrote in praise of the endeavor,
"with all this crudeness and bad taste [in the world], there is a pathetic
desire [among Americans] to do better. People, *especially women,* long to
share all that is brightest and best in art" (quoted in Lynes 1954:153, emphasis added). Graduates of women's colleges working in turn-of-the-
century settlement houses promoted art as a means of "upliftment" for the
poor, offering lectures in "art appreciation" and sponsoring exhibitions and
loaning paintings (see Lynes 1954:158–59).[7]

Historians of the settlement-house movement have found it useful to
consider settlement-house projects a form of "politicized domesticity"
(Evans 1989:162) or, in the title of a Smithsonian exhibition, "Housekeeping
on a Grand Scale" (see Boris 1991:191)—a way for women to break down
boundaries between "private" domesticity and "public" political activity.
Similarly, it is possible to consider the patronage of indigenous arts in the
Southwest a form of politicized consumption. Upper-middle-class white
women such as Elizabeth Sergeant, Margretta Dietrich, and Elizabeth
White had prided themselves on their skills in shopping—that is, in select-
ing and excluding, in making judgments of value, and in constructing and
reconstructing relationships among objects. They had also developed extraordinary confidence in their own tastes. Promoting the indigenous arts

of the Southwest gave shopping a new importance, making it a matter of political, not just personal, consequence. In this way, the Bryn Mawrters' patronage of indigenous arts anticipated the 1990s' idea of "Shopping for a Better World" (Council on Economic Priorities 1990): the belief that more informed consumers can affect positive social change through individual acts of commodity consumption. In New Mexico, Bryn Mawrters were no longer just shopping for themselves and one another, as when White sent Sergeant the "shawl that looks as if it belonged in the mud house." In shopping for museums and as part of a project to develop the art market, they could see themselves as shopping for the benefit of indigenous artists—often women—and their communities, the region, and—since they perceived Indian and Hispanic arts as "national treasures"—on behalf of the nation.[8]

Although Elizabeth Sergeant, the Whites, and Margretta Dietrich promoted the art of male artists as well as that of women and did not make frequent connections between their patronage and their feminism, there is some indication that, as Willa Cather demonstrated in her description of Pueblo pottery fragments, they appreciated the fact that many indigenous artists were women, particularly among Pueblo potters and Navajo weavers. When Elizabeth Sergeant helped to establish the Indian Arts Fund, she emphasized that she hoped it would allow Pueblo women to use the collection as a source of study and inspiration (whereas the Fund's archaeologists were inclined to stress its value as a resource for scientists) (Dauber 1993:143–47). Margretta Dietrich, in her memoir, recalled that "New Mexico in the 1920s and '30s was a good place for a feminist to live," and one of the reasons she offered was that there were so many Indian women establishing successful careers as artists (Dietrich n.d.: 100–01). Dietrich established close friendships with Pueblo women painters and potters and made a point of fostering their careers by purchasing their work. One painter, Pop Chalee, told me in May, 1991 that when she started her career in the 1930s there were so few other women painting that she hardly imagined painting for a living until she sold her first painting to Margretta Dietrich, who told her she would buy anything she painted.[9]

One of the artists Dietrich mentioned in her memoir was Tonita Peña, who had received particular encouragement in the early 1920s from anthropologist Edgar Hewett and became one of the first Pueblo women to establish a successful career as a painter. Though J. J. Brody notes that in

EXHIBITION

of

WATER COLOR PAINTINGS

By TONITA PEÑA

From the collection of
MISS AMELIA ELIZABETH WHITE

Water colors by Tonita Peña may be purchased from the
Exposition of Indian Tribal Arts, Inc. through the Gallery
of American Indian Art, Inc. 850 Lexington Ave., N. Y. C.

Figure 4 Tonita Peña exhibition brochure. Reprinted with permission of
the Catherine McElvaine Library, School of American Research.

patrons' correspondence from the early years of Peña's career there is no indication that her gender was considered at all notable (1997:115), it was highlighted by Margretta Dietrich and Elizabeth White. In the early 1930s Dietrich helped White sponsor a special "one-woman" traveling exhibition in the Northeast to promote Peña's work (figure 4). In the accompanying brochure, Peña was described as not so well known as "the men painters" of the Pueblos, but as producing work that "takes rank with the best that has been produced," work that "should be viewed, not from the point of view of Indian art alone, but as art, pure and simple" (SAR, AEWC, miscellaneous clippings, box 3d).[10] In displaying such work in fine art galleries and arguing for its importance as art, White and Dietrich were establishing themselves in a new authoritative role, one based more on aesthetic appreciation than was the role of the "hard-boiled archaeologists" whose display of Pueblo pottery had so intrigued Sergeant and her friend Cather. Their patronage of Peña was typical, however, in that her work had already gained approval from an anthropologist, one who encouraged painters such as Peña to produce paintings that would suit a combination of his interests: ethnographic illustration of ceremonial dances and crafts and the development of marketable emblems of cultural and regional identity (Bernstein 1993, Brody 1997). White and Dietrich, as patrons who were not anthropologists, were more inclined than Hewett to celebrate Peña and other Native artists as "artists" and to treat them and their work accordingly, but in some ways they were building on Hewett's authority rather than breaking with it. As discussed in chapter 4, their friend Mary Cabot Wheelwright seems to have acted more independently of anthropologists in her study and patronage of Navajo art.

As well as promoting indigenous arts, the Bryn Mawrters were concerned with protecting religious freedom; along with more commercially motivated patrons such as Hewett, they actively worked to foster appreciation for religious difference, fighting, for example, against government suppression of ceremonial dancing. Such pluralism was a fairly new development among white activists and philanthropists. Prior to the 1920s, philanthropic and charitable projects, especially among women, were primarily confined to church-sponsored activities that were more intolerant of cultural or religious differences. The shift toward pluralism in religious matters, like that in art, can partly be explained by the transition to a more consumer-oriented economy. Although the Bryn Mawrters came from families with affiliations with various Protestant faiths, they embraced an individualistic approach to religion, considering it a matter more of spiritual fulfillment, self-actualization, and romantic mystery than of obedience, something that could be, in a way, "shopped for" and consumed through spectacle and sacred objects. Thus, for these women, enjoyment of others' religious ceremonies and objects could express their own taste, and a community that encouraged cultural and religious pluralism was one where cosmopolitan patrons like themselves were free to enjoy the pageantry of one ceremony, the intimacy of another. Although in general the wealthy white women moving to Santa Fe in the 1920s and 1930s were more concerned with the spirituality and ceremony they associated with Indians rather than with Hispanic Catholicism, many appreciated ceremonial dances at the Pueblos as well as masses at the Cathedral in Santa Fe.[11]

The network of women described here applied their aesthetic sensibilities not just to objects they defined as "art" and to religious spectacles, but also to the Southwestern landscape. Women seeking greater influence and authority were able to approach the Southwest as a sort of undervalued commodity, a new market where they had greater chance of establishing a significantly marketable authority. At the same time, for example, that Elizabeth Sergeant collected Indian art and Hispanic furniture, she collected images with which to construct a sense of Northern New Mexico as a unique place in her writing for popular magazines. In marketing herself as an authority on the Southwest and encouraging others to acquire a taste for its charms, Sergeant, as we have seen, was at least temporarily following the steps of her friend Willa Cather, who, Sergeant observed, only achieved great popular success as a writer when she turned away from her Jamesian transatlantic settings and established her identity as "a true novelist of Nebraska" (Sergeant 1963:131), marketing a relatively new sort of commodity: rural, western America as a visually appealing tableau.

Similarly, Sergeant's associate Mary Austin, who struggled unsuccessfully during the years prior to 1920 to make her way into the community of Greenwich Village intellectuals, returned in the 1920s to the West, where she devoted the rest of her career to "our Amerindian life," the Southwestern landscape, and Indian and Spanish Colonial art. During the same period, Austin's good friend Mabel Dodge Luhan, after becoming well known as a patron of modernist art, traveled to Taos seeking "Change" and apparently found what she was looking for, becoming an important patron of indigenous arts as well as a writer celebrating Indians and the Southwest. Yet in 1912, just several years before her Southwestern conversion, Luhan had returned to Manhattan from Italy, warning her son that they had "left everything worth while behind." "America," Luhan later claimed she instructed her son, "is all machinery and money-making and factories . . . ugly, ugly, ugly" (Luhan 1935:447). She went on, however, to introduce so many Eastern intellectuals to the Southwest that Maria Chabot, for many years the companion of Luhan's most famous recruit, Georgia O'Keeffe, described her to me as "a one-person immigration bureau."[12] Although such transformations reflected a deep ambivalence about their national identity, in their conversion to the Southwest these women resembled apostles of some newly emerging religion, a religion that allowed them greater authority and influence than was available to them in more established institutions. Like Willa Cather's Thea Kronborg, they had discovered "older and higher obligations"—obligations that were also opportunities for the exercise of power, a power cloaked in the familiar rhetoric of social benevolence.

Making the Tea for Others to Drink

Last day on the desert. We need a Navajo dictionary, compass, water bag, accurate reservation map. Dust, sand, and rain.
—Maria Chabot, Indian Arts and Crafts Board field notes, 1936

I have focused here on women of unusual wealth and privilege, but there was a younger generation of white women associated with the "city of ladies" who were not wealthy but dependent, in many ways, on those who were. There was, for example, Jean Buchanan, with whom I began this chapter. Buchanan had worked briefly as a secretary for Elizabeth White, and later served as a live-in companion and caretaker for Margretta Dietrich. Buchanan introduced me to her neighbor, Sylvia Glidden Loomis, who had served as Dietrich's secretary and also as a secretary for the Old Santa Fe Foundation, an organization devoted to the preservation of historic buildings, and for the Spanish Colonial Arts Society. For over thirty years Loomis lived in an apartment that once belonged to Dorothy Stewart and Margretta Dietrich (and, reportedly, in the nineteenth century, to the anthropologist Adolph Bandelier). In the 1950s Loomis arranged for the apartment to serve as an office for both organizations, and for many years the organizations paid part of her rent. I spoke with Loomis at length on several occasions in early 1991, when she was in her mid-eighties. Very soft-spoken and frail-looking, she lived alone with a cat, surrounded by paint-ings—many of which were her own work; others included a painting given to her by the New York artist Ben Shahn (well known for his socially engaged, populist artwork) and a painting by Awa Tsireh (Alfonso Roybal), given to her by Margretta Dietrich—books about art, and heavy, dark pieces of Spanish Colonial antique furniture. The first time we spoke she had just finished reading a biography of Frida Kahlo. Outside her windows one could see and hear a steady stream of pedestrians making the rounds of some of the city's most chic and expensive art galleries and boutiques.

Loomis informed me she was originally from a small town in Chatau-qua County, New York, where, she mentioned proudly, her father had been active in coordinating the original Chatauqua summer programs. In the 1930s she had attended art school in Manhattan, where she studied modern-ist painting and eventually found work with the Work Projects Administra-tion and at the Pratt Institute. It was a divorce, she said, that motivated her to move to New Mexico, but later she spoke hesitantly of other reasons. At the beginning of the McCarthy era, she had had friends who were commu-nists, but she had never been one herself, she insisted. She stated this as if deeply embarrassed at an idea especially preposterous to her, as, she pointed out, "an eleventh-generation American." It was true, she acknowl-edged, that she had belonged to a union—"because you had to back then, if you were going to survive." But because of her friends and her union membership, she was accused of being a communist and was pressured to provide information about people she knew. "I was so disgusted," she said. "I wanted to leave it all behind me." Santa Fe, where she had a list of contacts obtained from fellow artists, had seemed as good a place as any.

A Quaker, Loomis joined a lively community of Quakers in Santa Fe and rented a room from Dorothy Stewart, with whom she became close friends. While Loomis was describing the Quaker community of the 1950s, which included a number of other painters, she mentioned a wealthy les-bian couple from Philadelphia who were particularly influential members, and a story about them led to mention of a sizable community of "Anglo" women in Santa Fe who were openly lesbian. I asked if Dorothy Stewart had been a lesbian, having heard that she was. "Yes," she replied immediately, but then either embarrassment or fear seemed to take over and she added "whatever that means . . . but yes." It was a part of Dorothy's life, she said, about which she didn't really know very much. "She always dressed mannishly, of course." I knew this, having come across photographs of Stewart, with a beaming smile, in cowboy hats and ties. "But, oh," she exclaimed, "Dorothy was such a wonderful person!"

Later, Loomis noted that "for all her unconventional ways" Dorothy was really much like her sister, Margretta Dietrich, "very Main Line Philadelphia." The two sisters had belonged to one group of "somebodies" in Santa Fe, a group that included Elizabeth White; they were very "cultured" people, she said, some of them quite "Victorian," particularly White. I had often heard this word "Victorian" used to describe White and Dietrich. But there was another group of "somebodies," Loomis said, "more bohemian," including artists, writers, and people drawn to Santa Fe for its tolerant social climate. The two groups overlapped and mingled, she recalled, but were different in their degree of wealth, as well as in their sensibilities. I wasn't sure, but I had the sense that Loomis did not see herself as belonging fully to either of these groups, but on the margins of both. She was more dependent upon the wealthy philanthropists than the more "bohemian" crowd, but was distanced from her benefactors by her class background and her connections to trade unionists.

However, as a younger woman with a very limited income, she found, it seems, welcome benefits in her association with the "Victorians." Pulling a moonstone necklace from "Ceylon" out of a drawer, Loomis recalled how Margretta Dietrich and her companion Alice Brock had brought it back from their trip to China in 1936; Dietrich used to offer it to Loomis to wear when she served as Dietrich's "escort" to various social and "cultural" events (including Elizabeth White's elaborate parties). A lot of the ladies needed escorts, she explained, and she'd been happy to oblige, as this allowed her to attend events she would not have been able to attend otherwise. I heard similar stories from other women in Santa Fe, stories of the social and economic advantages of association with women of greater wealth and prestige.

I heard more about Dorothy Stewart from Maria Chabot, whose name I had first come across in archival documents dating from the mid-1930s. Even in the impersonal minutes of meetings, where her name appeared, something about her seemed different from the women whose names surrounded hers. Perhaps it was that her name appeared rather suddenly and then often, during a particularly active period. When the anthropologist Alfonso Ortiz mentioned that he thought Chabot lived in Albuquerque, I found her name in a phonebook. We met twice at her home and several times at museums in Santa Fe, where I also heard her speak at a forum on Pueblo pottery.

In November 1990, Chabot explained that she had moved to Mexico from San Antonio at the age of fifteen, having received "not much of an education" in public school. But she had grown up fascinated by Indians and wanted to know more. After living for some months in Tepoztlán, Chabot moved on to Mexico City, where she enrolled in university and took courses in anthropology and Nahuatl with the prominent Mexican anthropologist Alfonso Caso. It was in Mexico City in the early 1930s that Chabot met Dorothy Stewart, Margretta Dietrich, and a number of other Santa Feans who regularly traveled there during the winter months. They invited her to return with them to Santa Fe. They convinced her, she recalled, that "they were doing something about Indians." By 1936 Chabot was living in Santa Fe and was employed by the New Mexico Association on Indian Affairs (NMAIA), her salary paid for by Elizabeth White, her task to coordinate the Association's efforts to promote Indian art. She edited a series of articles for *New Mexico Magazine* designed to educate potential consumers about standards of quality and authenticity. More significantly, in terms of the long-term impact on the Indian art market in New Mexico, Chabot initiated a program of events she called "Indian markets" at which Indian artists might sell their work in Santa Fe's central plaza.

However influential, Chabot's work for the Association was short-lived; in 1936 she was hired by a representative of the newly formed federal Indian Arts and Crafts Board (IACB) to investigate the possibility of implementing similar programs to promote Indian art on a larger scale. Chabot's fellow researcher and traveling companion was Julia Lukas, a textile designer from Manhattan, who had been sojourning in Santa Fe, recovering from what she described as physical, mental, and spiritual exhaustion, while renting a room in Dorothy Stewart's apartment house, known as "El Zaguan." Both Chabot and Lukas were quick to tell me that Lukas knew nothing about Indians or Indian art. Lukas, in fact, whom I located in New York in May 1991, was quite adamant about her ignorance of Indian art, and readily confessed that arrogance had been a youthful flaw. "I was very arrogant about my judgment and taste in anything that had to do with the visual," she told me, laughing, it seemed, at her younger self. "I just assumed that I knew. I was ridiculous."

But Chabot, describing Lukas the way she had met her at El Zaguan, as "elegant looking, beautiful in her dress and in her demeanor," told me that she could tell immediately that Lukas "had a good eye, she had taste . . . I could tell that her appreciation of the Indian was for his culture." For Chabot, taste, culture in the singular, and an appreciation for culture in the plural were all part of the same package—but she was insistent that this package did not always include money. Discussing how it was that women such as Margretta Dietrich and Elizabeth and Martha White had come to promote Indian and Hispanic art, she explained that they were "people of culture" and "cultivated minds" who would "naturally" have taken an interest in such things, especially once they realized how little appreciation there was for Indian and Hispanic culture among other white residents. "But then," Chabot added, "there were also people who had great taste who had no money." It was these people, Chabot suggested, who performed the work that "philanthropically interested people" such as the Whites were willing to fund. When asked which particular individuals she had in mind, Chabot named Dorothy Stewart, the archaeologist Marjorie Lambert, art curator Kenneth Chapman, and Dorothy Dunn, an art teacher at the Santa Fe Indian School who fostered the careers of many Pueblo painters. But Chabot and Lukas would seem also to fit the category. In October 1990, at a public discussion of her work with the NMAIA, Chabot hinted at a critique of the economic inequalities that made her dependent upon the wealthier members of the association: "I made the tea. And they drank it. That's just the way it was."

Yet in their work for the IACB Chabot and Lukas displayed a sensibility quite similar to that of the Bryn Mawrters, despite backgrounds that had been much less privileged. Like the philanthropists, they espoused a goal of developing an art market that would be more profitable for Indians; yet their goals of developing economic opportunity continually merged with more aesthetically and personally motivated concerns for cultural recovery and revitalization. In other words, it was not always clear whether the changes they desired were for Indians, or for themselves—though they assumed a neat convergence of interests.

The two younger women were unlike White and Dietrich, however, in that they saw themselves as professionals, rather than as philanthropists. Traveling through the Southwest and the Plains states, Chabot and Lukas took notes on what sorts of things Indians were selling, who might be interested in buying them, how displays and goods might be improved to attract more well-paying customers, how it might be possible to change popular tastes, as well as artists' ideas about how their work should be marketed. Though many of their concerns were practical, others reflected an assumption that the aesthetic qualities of everyday life were inextricably linked to the well-being of individuals and communities. The way they saw it, through policies of coercive assimilation, the federal government had impoverished Indians not only economically and spiritually, but also aesthetically. Some of their harshest words were for the drab, institutional appearance of federal Indian schools, such as the one at Fort Wingate, where they noted, "Decorations atrocious, rugs hideous, pictures worse, colors unspeakable. What kind of taste can be developed in such a background?" (field notes, RIACB).[13] After a visit to a school on the Pine Ridge Reservation, Lukas wrote that she was beginning to "hate the word *art*," a sentiment, she explained, "inspired by portfolios with decorated covers all labeled fancily with 'ART'—inside were drawings [mark meaning "no good"] . . . paper canoes . . . 'sacred Sioux' designs . . . We've impoverished ourselves by separating 'art' from our daily lives—and now we're thrusting the same poverty on the Indians. The 'art' of the Indians used to be a part of their food, clothing and shelter, their religion, their play and their wars. Now we find it in the classroom in a portfolio labeled 'ART' " (field notes, RIACB).

In their notes, both women revealed a hope that improving the aesthetics of Indian lives might have a therapeutic effect, one that might help serve as an antidote to the ravages of colonialism. Traveling among the Sioux in South Dakota, Chabot admitted that "we can never go back to the past"; instead, she claimed, "it is the elements of the past—the essence which must be recaptured: symbolism and decoration of living" (field notes, RIACB).

Both Chabot and Lukas appeared, in some ways, to see their work for the IACB as an experience that had aesthetic value in itself, similar to the way that Elizabeth Sergeant and Willa Cather had approached the Southwestern landscape as something to be appreciated aesthetically. Lukas spoke of regretting that she had not carried a camera with her but took pleasure in having had stories to tell ever since, about, for example, the time in South Dakota when she and Maria Chabot and a Lakota man named Billy Thunder were trapped in a snowstorm for three days. "Don't let another day go by," she advised me, "without becoming a good photographer." Unlike Lukas, Chabot never established a conventional career; she was, however, interested in writing, an interest that comes through at times in her field notes and memos, some of which read as drafts of articles or short stories about her encounters with artists. For example, in a document titled "Memorandum to Mr. Lewis West," she describes a trip to Santo Domingo to discuss the possibility of setting official government standards for silver and turquoise: "'Do you have to go,' they asked, aware of the night, the approaching storm, the bad road"—and she describes staying with them and running her hands over pieces of turquoise, silver, and coral, the "real" and the "good" as well as what they saw as cheap imitations, and laughing with the men about the difference, in a way in which she appears as much to be attempting to capture an experience and tell a captivating story as to report information. Her more hastily written field notes often reveal a focused attention to the aesthetic qualities of the landscape: "Nothing more beautiful than natural clay colors of this country, varying so in shades of pink browns—fluted like the mountains—depending entirely on form and color . . ."

In their work for the IACB Chabot and Lukas expressed a vision even more ambitious than anything articulated by the Bryn Mawrters, but their enthusiasm was more short-lived. After several months traveling and sending back field notes to the IACB office in Washington, the two women turned in their resignations and moved on to other endeavors. Both cited disillusionment as the primary reason. Chabot stressed that her disappointment centered on government bureaucracy and petty politics. Lukas remembered hers as more about realizing that she had very utopian ideas about Indian art, a utopianism that appeared to conflict with the logistics and politics involved in developing a market and an industry in a way that would have surely involved difficult dealings with the numerous traders making substantial profits from sales of Indian art. In New York, she said, she was used to thinking of art and design as a "cutthroat" business; but she had expected that Indian art would be different in that respect—in fact, she said, she realized that, unrealistically, she had very much *wanted* it to be different. After returning to Manhattan in 1937, Lukas lost touch with Maria Chabot, but remembered her affectionately.

Chabot's immediate path led to Europe, where she spent two years traveling and living with Dorothy Stewart. Eventually she returned to New Mexico and in 1940 was briefly employed by the NMAIA once again, where she completed an investigation on economic conditions on the Navajo reservation.[14] Chabot then spent many years as, in her words, "ranch foreman," for Mary Cabot Wheelwright, before becoming Georgia O'Keeffe's live-in assistant and companion. When Dorothy Stewart was dying of cancer in 1955, Chabot accompanied her to the town in Mexico where she desired to spend her last days ("A Book About D.N.S.," SRCA, 1955). At the time I spoke with Chabot about her work with the NMAIA and the IACB, she was living in a house in Albuquerque that she had purchased from the travel writer and tour guide Erna Fergusson, working on an autobiography and studying Japanese painting.

Gender, Taste, Capital, and Culture

By focusing on this network of women patron-philanthropists and their employees, I have attempted to explore historical connections between the exercise of taste and gender. Bourdieu's *Distinction* (1984) foregrounds the importance of taste in relation to class structure—but without much consideration of its relationship to gender (or ethnicity, race, or geographic inequalities between core and periphery). Bourdieu also offers an unnecessarily static picture of the workings of taste and power. Not only is there much more resistance to dominant judgments of taste than Bourdieu suggests, but as Toril Moi points out, "the position of women—and of men—in relation to social power is far more complex and contradictory than Bourdieu would seem fully to acknowledge" (1991:1033). Moi urges us to consider that "gender is always a socially *variable* entity, one which carries different amounts of symbolic capital in different contexts" (1036; emphasis in original). I hope to have shown this complexity and variability in this analysis of the Bryn Mawrters and the younger and less privileged women who worked with and for them.[15] While middle- and upper-class women have been positioned as specialists in areas of taste and consumption, they have nonetheless had difficulty gaining access to positions of substantial authority in art fields with a more established institutional structure. Disadvantaged by their gender status on their home turf, these women managed to increase their cultural capital by entering and commandeering an area both literally and figuratively at the periphery of the political and economic system.

I have also attempted to historicize relationships between the categories "women" and "culture." The network of women discussed here operated at the forefront of a social and intellectual movement that advocated new conceptions of "culture," not entirely severed from more hierarchical conceptions, but linked with the discipline of anthropology, affirming particular varieties of cultural difference as something not only to be tolerated, but even celebrated, protected, and nurtured. In recent years, feminist scholarship has tended increasingly to consider "women" a category to be deconstructed and to be understood as varying historically and in relation to other categories, such as "race" or "nation" (see, e.g., Riley 1988). The category of culture is no more stable, yet is less often subject to question.

In 1974 Sherry Ortner proposed to answer the question—at that time *the* question for many feminist scholars—of the reasons behind the "universal devaluation of women" (1974:68) by examining the relationship between "women" and "culture." Ortner argued that throughout history, "nature" and "culture" have worked as oppositional categories, with "culture" the more highly valued of the pair. Women, Ortner contended, consistently have been aligned with "nature" rather than "culture," with only occasional exceptions. Among the exceptions, she noted "Nazi Germany, in which women were said to be the guardians of culture and morals" and "European courtly love, in which man considered himself the beast and woman the pristine exalted object" as well as "some aspects of our own culture's view of women" (86). As an example of the latter, Ortner might also have pointed to the "Western"—in which, as Jane Tompkins argues, women have been associated with culture and men with nature (Tompkins 1992).

Rather than attempting to impose categories like "nature" and "culture" on such a diversity of thought and experience, I have considered efforts to contest and transform these terms and their definitions, such as the ones ongoing when the Bryn Mawrters went West. According to Kathleen McCarthy (1991), this period in late nineteenth- and early twentieth-century America was one in which middle-class women were typically thought to be, as Ortner claims women were in Nazi Germany, the "guardians of culture and morals," yet even the most wealthy of women had to struggle to gain influence in institutions such as art museums, which were considered the embodiment of culture. In reaction to this situation, women in the network described in this chapter began to advocate new notions of culture, supported by the emerging discipline of anthropology; such transformed concepts of culture allowed them new sources of authority, new "territories," as well as a way of transcending the ideologies of bourgeois domesticity that made them guardians of a culture they found constraining. When Willa Cather, for example, was writing about cliff dwellings and finding authenticity in the "Mexican ghetto," she celebrated a notion of culture defined partly in opposition to that associated with the women's "culture clubs" and Chatauqua summer programs, touted by their enthusiasts as offering courses in culture, found in small towns and cities throughout the United States. Cather, the Bryn Mawrters, and some of the other women discussed here resisted the notions of "culture" associated with "women" in such institutions, partly because of their own ambitions, but also because they resisted the accompanying restrictions of their gender— restrictions which otherwise would have made them guardians of culture and morality in a private, personal, domestic sphere, but which excluded them from more public influence and authority. In these women's perceptions of the Southwest, those restrictions and exclusions were conspicuously absent.

For white women without the financial resources of Dietrich and the Whites, it was more apparent that the city of ladies offered constraints as well as opportunities. Elizabeth Sergeant, with similar ambitions of public influence, had been unwilling to sacrifice her political independence in exchange for employment or friendship. Others found compromises more acceptable. "It was rather a confining sort of life," one woman told me, wistfully. But like Buchanan, Loomis, and Chabot, she had inherited part of her former employer's estate, and was much more apt to express gratitude and affection in her recollections than she was to regret.

CHAPTER FOUR THE PATRONAGE OF DIFFERENCE: MAKING INDIAN ART "ART, NOT ETHNOLOGY"

The art of the Indians, so eloquent of this land, is American art and of the most important kind. A hundred years ago, men could not have realized this. Art was then a thing to be seen in the Vatican or in the Louvre.

Walter Pach, "The Indian Tribal Arts"

 When the Exposition of Indian Tribal Arts (EITA) opened at Grand Central Art Galleries in Manhattan in 1931, critics announced the "first truly American art exposition." The Exposition brochure described the event as the first exhibition of "Indian Art as art, not ethnology" and quoted one critic's statement that "the cry for 'American' art has been answered." According to John Sloan, the New York–based painter and one of the key organizers of the Exposition, "spreading the consciousness of Indian art in America affords [a] means by which American artists and patrons of art can contribute to the culture of their own continent, to enrich the product and keep it American."[1] Such statements suggest connections between a popular acceptance of relativist notions of culture associated with anthropology, and attempts to use art—an honorific category intimately related to class-structured distinctions[2]—and taste as a way of reimagining American national and regional identities. These newly imagined identities celebrated a rather narrowly defined version of cultural pluralism, particularly as expressed through commodities validated as art.

This chapter concentrates more specifically on how this utopian affirmation of cultural difference—an early predecessor, in some ways, of multiculturalism—reflected elite responses to the rise of consumer capitalism. As discussed in the preceding chapters, the 1920s and 1930s were a period of heightened concern with representations of the national identity as well as with the implications of mass consumption (e.g., Alexander 1980,

Susman 1973, 1984). For patrons of Indian art, including those who sponsored the 1931 Exposition, in matters of identity, commodity consumption represented both problem and solution; part of the solution involved recasting carefully selected commodities, produced by ethnic and racial Others, as "art."[3] At the same time, appeals to culture and national identity served as a useful strategy to gain value and legitimacy for attempts to broaden the category of art and change popular perceptions of the continent's Native inhabitants.

Although the "art, not ethnology" description suggested an antagonistic relationship between "art" and "ethnology"—the one approach revolving more around aesthetic appreciation and the other emphasizing the pursuit of scientific knowledge—in fact the Exposition grew out of a rather congenial coalition, fairly typical of the period, of artists, art patrons, and anthropologists who saw themselves united in their tastes as well as in their politics against forces of assimilation and intolerance. The Exposition's accompanying booklet, "Introduction to American Indian Art," was jointly written by John Sloan and Oliver La Farge—a collaboration of painter and anthropologist-turned-novelist (La Farge, in fact, had just won the Pulitzer prize for his 1929 novel of Navajo romance, *Laughing Boy*). Book orders were taken at the Exposition, and the catalog of available literature included works by poets, novelists, and folklorists, along with those of anthropologists and archaeologists. The "art, not ethnology" slogan did indicate a slight shift of emphasis in the discourse of evaluation—from "authenticity" to "quality." The Exposition and its slogan also reflected an attempt to broaden the authorities of taste and value with respect to Indian art, helping to establish it firmly as the concern not just of those "hard-boiled archaeologists" whom Elizabeth Sergeant had once imagined digging up Pueblo pottery, but also of non-anthropologist patrons and collectors. Still, the Exposition represented no radical challenge to anthropological authority, just as anthropological notions of "culture," especially in their popular applications, were not so very incompatible with the more Arnoldian notion of culture as a marker of superiority.

The first half of the twentieth century was a formative period for anthropology as a discipline, a period when anthropologists were securing their place in the academy while constructing their most marketable conceptual tools—notions of culture and cultures which could be described authoritatively by the professional ethnographer. But, as we have seen, interest in "cultures" was by no means confined to anthropologists, who both influenced, and were influenced by, widespread social and intellectual trends. Discussing the 1930s in America, historian Warren Susman has argued that the period was one marked by the widespread "discovery" of the concept of culture (1973:2–8, 1984:153–54)—a concept already of central importance to anthropologists and many other intellectuals. Not only were works by anthropologists Margaret Mead and Ruth Benedict reaching wide audiences, but other prominent intellectuals and popular authors, including Stuart Chase, Ernest Thompson Seton, John Collier, and Charles F. Lummis were using ideas and research derived explicitly from the work of anthropologists. The examples I discuss here further explore some of the ways the idea of "cultures" resonated outside the academy and how this new division of peoples accommodated a search for national consensus and drew attention away from class divisions and political and economic inequalities.

Places and Objects

For many American intellectuals, objects made by Indians were especially attractive because they were thought to represent nonalienated labor, a merging of the utilitarian and the creative, art and community, community undivided by class and the distinctions of taste ensuing from mass consumption. Indian art—in New Mexico, "Old Mexico," and elsewhere—was also important because it could so easily be seen as embodying regional character (though there was, as we shall see, the constant matter of whose Indian art? whose definition of regional character?). Indian art was perceived as truly distinctive—each piece "one of a kind"—and as inseparable from the natural landscape (or "our soil," according to art critic Walter Pach [1931]). Perhaps more important for cultural nationalists, it seemed to possess an integrity resulting from obliviousness about what might be the fashion in other places. Indian art expressed, for its enthusiasts, an utter self-confidence in isolation. It appeared an island of self-sufficiency in opposition to the trend toward global political and economic integration and the hegemony of center over periphery.

Indian art was also able to satisfy demands, increasingly popular during the 1920s and 1930s, for connection to an American past—something cultural forms associated with Europe and the "genteel tradition" were seen as lacking. American intellectuals had long struggled to resolve the question of how the nation could develop an independent national artistic tradition (Alexander 1980), and Indian art promised connection to a distinctly "American" time (as well as an American race). This connection had been made quite clearly in Willa Cather's description, in *Song of the Lark,* of "Panther Canyon," where her heroine "lengthened her past" and discovered "older and higher obligations" largely through fragments of cliff-dweller pottery (1915:243).

Eventually this attachment to national and regional history, place, and race would impede the extent to which Indian art could be admitted to fine art circles—particularly after the Second World War when, as Alexander argues (1980), American cultural nationalism in the arts gave way to a more universalistic high modernism—but it especially facilitated the efforts of philanthropists who, during the 1920s and 1930s, sought to develop new, more prestigious, and profitable markets on behalf of Indian artists. As the nation emerged from the First World War with greater political and economic power, Americans were prepared to embrace a more confident national identity, represented by art. But although such cultural nationalism would seem to stress the unity of the nation, cultural nationalism also hinged on regionalism and an acute awareness of the uniqueness of particular places.

The demand for regionalism was driven by an insecurity about the nation's identity, but also by a perception that regional "character" might soon disappear, replaced by a generic modern uniformity. As David Harvey has explicated so clearly in *The Condition of Postmodernity* (1989), the greater the mobility of capital and abstraction of space, the stronger the nostalgia for place-specific identity (though such nostalgia tends not to be equally distributed and may be more often the concern of elites). As Americans began to perform more "indigenous" identities, they demanded new sets and props. From the early twentieth century in Santa Fe, migrating art enthusiasts from the East thus shunned bungalows in favor of adobes (Wilson 1997; Weigle and Fiore 1982). And while the Eastern transplants were decorating their adobe dwellings with Indian and Spanish Colonial art, across the continent in Appalachia, patrons of similar (mostly Northeastern, upper-class) backgrounds were promoting the "revival" of mountain folk arts (Whisnant 1983, Becker 1993). In 1931, the year the Exposition of Indian Tribal Arts opened in Manhattan, Abby Aldrich Rockefeller, a supporter of the Exposition, was beginning to purchase "folk arts" collected throughout the country—the collection which in 1939 would be her gift to Colonial Williamsburg, showpiece of the national identity and veritable masterpiece of white revisionism (Handler 1997).[4] Such new fields of knowledge and consumption paved the way for new arbiters of taste and value.

The struggle to capture national and regional character was not due entirely to fears of creeping uniformity. It was imbued also with more class-specific visions of the nation being engulfed by cheaper, "commercial," and "inauthentic" tastes. Tourism was becoming a national pastime, the development of highways and the mass production of automobiles giving new meaning to the slogan "See America First" (which Charles Lummis claimed to have coined before the turn of the century [1925]). At the same time, celebrities were emerging with the rise of mass media and the commodification of leisure, contributing to a sense that identities could be entirely self-made, requiring only ambition and personal success, independent of any inherited status or of more bourgeois forms of cultural capital. As Warren Susman has argued, the national economy was shifting from an emphasis on production to one centered on increasing consumption; along with that shift, working-class and middle-class consumers were perceived as having increased cultural influence, an influence disturbing to intellectuals of diverse political allegiances (Susman 1973, 1984).

In 1922 Natalie Curtis, a classical musician and a dedicated collector of Southwestern Indian music, wrote of an emerging Indian-focused Southwestern literature and revealed some important connections between anxieties about the proliferation of commodities and the loss of regional character, while offering a vision of the redemptive possibilities of art:

> Although New Mexico is so foreign to the character of much of our country that visitors have been known to talk of going back to New York as "returning to America," it is nevertheless, a very real part of these United States, with a distinct utterance of its own. A land lives through its artists, even after the people themselves have perished. That type of Americanization which is largely a matter of mail order house clothes and crockery, of chewing gum and "movies" will soon wipe its erasing hand across the Southwest like a well-meaning but ignorant servant, who zealously "setting to rights" an artist's studio, dusts off his pastels. One can not sufficiently praise this growing litera-

ture of the Southwest which reminds us of the worth and beauty of a section of America that is still free from machinery and—marvelous to relate—free from bill boards as well. (1922:99)

The anxieties Curtis expressed about "Americanization" were not only expressed as passive laments (nor was her servant metaphor insignificant). The ideology and institutions of "art" provided a means by which patrons could actively attempt to influence "the public taste," expressions of cultural and regional difference, and ultimately, the national identity.[5] The EITA, which toured major cities of the East and Midwest for two years, with a side trip to Venice, is but one example of attempts to draw on newly popular notions of separate and diverse cultures, while also—even if unintentionally—supporting the notion of culture as the province of an elite.[6]

Although John Sloan served as president of the EITA, his title was mostly an honorary one and intended to draw public attention; the driving force behind the show was actually Sloan's Santa Fe neighbor, patron, and good friend, Elizabeth White. Since purchasing her Santa Fe property in 1923, White had become an increasingly influential patron of Indian art and an activist in Indian affairs. As discussed in the preceding chapter, White and her sister, Martha, had joined the Eastern Association on Indian Affairs (EAIA) in Manhattan in 1922, and during the following year became active in its Southwestern affiliate, the New Mexico Association on Indian Affairs (NMAIA). In the EAIA, the White sisters worked with a number of anthropologists, including F. W. Hodge and Herbert Spinden. The NMAIA had been founded by Elizabeth Sergeant and Santa Fe resident Margaret McKittrick (recalled by Santa Feans as "a St. Louis debutante"), who enlisted local Anglo-American elites including anthropologist Edgar Hewett, poets Witter Bynner and Alice Corbin Henderson, Dolly Sloan (former business manager of the influential leftist magazine, *The Masses*), the painter Gerald Cassidy and his wife, Ina Sizer Cassidy, an artist who had been active in the campaign for women's suffrage.

The NMAIA and EAIA, along with their chief rival, John Collier's Indian Defense Association (with connections to the General Federation of Women's Clubs), marked an important break in public perceptions of Indians and cultural difference. Organizations of non-Indians focused on the rights and conditions of Indians had been operating since the late nineteenth century. Such organizations also had enjoyed the support of some prominent anthropologists, even though they tended to take assimilationist positions, advocating increased legal and political rights for Indians, but at the price of conversion to bourgeois values and Christianity. The NMAIA, its Eastern affiliate, and the Indian Defense Association were formed in the early 1920s, initially in reaction to the Bursum Bill, which threatened Pueblo Indian land claims; in addition to protecting land rights, these organizations sought to improve physical health at a time when Indian populations were being devastated by malnutrition, tuberculosis, and influenza. Additional aims were to improve access to political and legal power and to promote economic self-sufficiency as well as respect and tolerance for Indian cultural difference—particularly those differences visible in religious ceremonies, dress, and art.

The shift in emphasis, on the part of white activists in Indian affairs, away from coercive assimilationism and towards a paternalistic version of multiculturalism was prompted by a number of factors, including the influence of early twentieth-century reform movements, the rise of American cultural nationalism, the increasingly popular influence of anthropology, and the expansion of tourism. As we have seen, there were also connections to the campaign for women's suffrage and a more general struggle among upper-class women for greater public influence through philanthropy and political activism.

The alliance of artists, experienced political activists, and anthropologists in the new Indian rights organizations reflected more widespread sentiments that anthropology held increasing intellectual, aesthetic, and political importance. Among intellectuals who were not professional anthropologists, there was a sense of discovering anthropology as a profoundly significant new area of knowledge, a discovery which accompanied their new attention to more peripheral regions of the United States, the attractions of "the primitive," and cultural difference. When Elizabeth Sergeant "discovered" the Southwest through her friend Willa Cather, she felt obliged to study "new fields of scholarship." "American archaeology alone," she remarked to Cather, "what a 'literature' there is . . . " (1963:165). Sergeant's sentiments were common among new arrivals in Santa Fe. The artists who migrated to the region from Europe and the East Coast in search of the "picturesque"—and somewhat later, during the 1920s and 1930s, seeking a landscape perceived as distinctly "modernist" in its bare simplicity—found kinship among local anthropologists who had already established themselves, in the region, as authorities on cultural difference, history, and authenticity.[7] In the years after 1910, anthropologists Edgar Hewett and Sylvanus Morley, with the cooperation of local white artists, had begun promoting the preservation and restoration of "authentic" pueblo architecture in the city. Their concerns tended to be simultaneously economic, political, and sentimental.

In an interview with Ruth Barker conducted in 1926, Charles Lummis, a good friend of Edgar Hewett, summarized this particular combination of concerns. Speaking of the importance of architectural renovation and restoration in Santa Fe, Lummis claimed, "You can't do business on sentiment, but you can't do it without sentiment. . . . You've got a monopoly on sentiment here—the rarest and most prized thing in the United States. There are only two or three places in the country that have it and they prize it above everything else. It's what people go to Europe to see— sentiment. . . . You seem to have come to a realization of keeping Santa Fe not 'Different,' but itself. I believe you've come to realize the value of sentiment and of preserving that above everything else [. . .]. Santa Fe must be kept as nearly historically true to itself as possible [. . .] streets should be stamped with the individuality that has made this place important for three centuries." When his interviewer suggested the portales should be restored around the plaza, Lummis countered: " 'No—restore the original wall around the town. "The Only Walled City in America"—that phrase in itself would be worth a million dollars a year' " (Barker 1926). Although Lummis may have expressed his economic motivations more blatantly than Hewett, his remarks are suggestive of the conflict that would ensue between those trying to make the "difference" of Santa Fe profitable and those who wanted to keep it for their own exclusive consumption.[8]

Culture Conflicts in Santa Fe

Patrons of Indian art drew moral force from the collision of two different, but not mutually exclusive, notions of "culture." From anthropologists, they borrowed the idea of culture as the unique essence of a society— culture as a worldview, a system of value, an expression of essential identity through language, religion, labor, and dress. With a crusading spirit of social reform carried over from early twentieth-century reform movements and the campaign for women's suffrage, they proposed "saving" and "protecting" those marked as culturally different and the objects perceived as embodying such difference. But patrons also drew moral force from the elitist notion of culture as a mark of superiority in relation to others of the "same" society—a superiority expressed through the exercise of taste in commodities, creative expression through the production and consumption of art, and knowledge acquired through travel and formal education (an education increasingly likely to include anthropology and archaeology). As Maria Chabot explained in November 1990 to my colleague Ken Dauber and me, when asked why it was, during the 1920s, that Indian art acquired such importance for the community of "Anglo" art patrons and artists in Santa Fe: "they were people of culture, and they were interested in the Indian. They would naturally . . . [T]he Anglo had the money and the interest and some of them the cultivated mind to appreciate [Indian art] and to try to save it."

Although many activists had more ambivalent feelings about tourism than Lummis did, in Santa Fe, the artists, anthropologists, and pseudo-anthropologists like Lummis often felt united in their interest in "authenticity," "uniqueness," and cultural difference, particularly that ascribed to Indians. When Waldo Frank passed through Santa Fe in 1918, he scoffed at the artists whose interest in Indians, he claimed, was only as "seekers of the picturesque" (1919:116). But he felt that Edgar Hewett, because of his seemingly more serious devotion to scientific knowledge, was "a true friend of the Indian" (ironically, among anthropologists Hewett's reputation was more dubious). Hewett, who for several decades sought to make Santa Fe a regional center for both art and ethnology, actively recruited artists to the area, among them the painters Robert Henri and John Sloan. Many observers saw more coherence than Waldo Frank did between anthropological and artistic interests in the community of recently transplanted whites, a community Witter Bynner described as a "mumble jumble of chumminess" (Museum of New Mexico 1989:191). Artist Gustave Baumann recalled "times when the artists forgot their business and went completely archaeological. We learned all the familiar terms and became quite expert in identifying potsherds as belonging to this or that period" (1989:125–26). Elizabeth Sergeant wrote in the *Saturday Review* that "in this unindustrialized New Mexico, even science is largely the science of archaeologist, ethnologist, anthropologist—the sort of science that unconsciously feeds the novelist, the poet" (1934:352).

There were occasional tensions between professional anthropological interests in cultural difference and those of local artists and activists. Witter Bynner, a successful poet and translator of the *Tao Te Ching*, saw his taste in Indian art as happily divorced from any ethnographic knowledge. Bynner's Santa Fe neighbor and friend Margretta Dietrich, after becoming one of the country's most respected Indian affairs activists, recalled her first encounter with an anthropologist, one she declined to name, with a sense of superiority. Dietrich met him while attending the San Geronimo festivities at Taos Pueblo in 1921, and she claimed that while she observed the ceremonies, the anthropologist remained at his hotel reading ethnographic reports. Dietrich went on to remark proudly that despite her enthusiasm for attending such events, unlike anthropologists, she made a point of never inquiring into Indian religious beliefs (1959:5). When I was conducting interviews for this project, Indian art collectors (many of whom had undergraduate or master's-level training in anthropology) occasionally made similar comparisons between themselves and anthropologists, and at times it seemed as if they resented anthropologists' institutional authority and legitimacy as "experts," while at the same time recognizing a close and legitimate affinity between anthropology and collecting Indian art.

In the early twentieth century there was a less clear separation between amateur and professional ethnographers. Occasional conflicts erupted in Santa Fe over the relative authority of professionals and that of knowledgeable, dedicated amateurs, endowed with private wealth rather than institutional funding. A case in point is the controversy that developed in the early 1930s over a proposal by amateur ethnographer Mary Cabot Wheelwright. Wheelwright proposed building a center for the study of Navajo "religion, art, and culture" (quoted in Parezo and Hoerig 1999:220) on the grounds of the newly established, John D. Rockefeller-funded Laboratory of Anthropology, not far from the White sisters' home in the hills above the town. Wheelwright first had proposed the museum be built at the University of New Mexico in Albuquerque, but administrators objected that the hogan-shaped building she envisioned was incompatible with the campus's pueblo- style architecture. Board members of the Laboratory of Anthropology offered the same objections, but there are indications that architectural style was not their only concern.

Wheelwright had studied Navajo sandpainting, weaving, and religion extensively with the celebrated Navajo singer, Hosteen Klah, and consulted with nearly fifty other singers and sandpainters (Parezo and Hoerig 219–20). But Wheelwright, whose background was otherwise quite similar to the White sisters', lacked any formal education. In an era when the Lab's archaeologists were especially concerned with distinguishing themselves from amateurs and establishing their discipline as a science (Dauber 1993:137–46), Wheelwright's independence must have been particularly threatening, especially since she made it clear that her plan was for a museum that would break down the standard distinctions between art and artifact, science and religion—distinctions that had guided the development of existing natural history and anthropology museums. The Lab's Harvard-trained chairman, Alfred Vincent Kidder, was inclined to steer the Lab away from museums, contemporary art, and public education altogether, maintaining the Lab's emphasis on summer field schools for archaeologists and the development of a collection of ceramics being used to reconstruct the prehistory of the Southwest (Dauber 1993:140–42). Although Kidder supported ethnographic research conducted in the region by professional anthropologists such as Elsie Clews Parsons (Givens 1992: 62–63), it seems unlikely that he would have supported Wheelwright's work, regardless of whether her focus was Pueblo or Navajo. Elizabeth White, as Wheelwright's good friend, made a concerted effort to negotiate an agreement between Wheelwright and the Laboratory. When those efforts failed, White donated land for the museum adjacent to the Laboratory, but managed to remain on good terms with the Lab's archaeologists, including Kidder.[9]

Edgar Hewett, largely excluded from the Lab, had his own, very different, conflicts with Santa Fe's artists and art patrons. One of the most bitter conflicts occurred in 1926 over a plan of the Federated Women's Clubs of nine states of the South and Midwest to establish a Chatauqua-inspired summer colony in Santa Fe. The Federated Club women, with the encouragement of the Chamber of Commerce, Edgar Hewett (who delivered a lecture to the women titled "A Thousand Mile Archaeological Trip in the Southwest"), and the Railway proposed a "cultural [colony] of permanent summer homes in a vacation and educational atmosphere" (Doll 1926:176). Deciding against the name "Chatauqua," because of the undesirable connotations it had acquired, the Club women settled on "The Cultural Center of the Southwest" (Doll 1926:173). The local opposition to the center—which included Elizabeth White, Margretta Dietrich, Mary Austin, and Alice Corbin Henderson, among others—ignored the "Cultural Center" designation and continued to refer to it as a "Chatauqua" with all the connotations the name had acquired of status-seeking, pretentiousness, and provinciality.

In an article published in the *New Republic*, Mary Austin passionately wrote of "The Town That Doesn't Want a Chatauqua"—an article infused with the same sort of urgency with which she and her friends had written against the Bursum Bill several years before. The fight against the Chatauqua, Austin contended, amounted to a "fight for the freedom of the creative spirit." This battle was taking place, she argued, in a town with a large population of Spanish-speaking residents ("[Santa Fe's] hours ring to soft cathedral chimes[;] religious processions still wind along its kindly streets, and guitars make musical its summer dusk") as well as "the largest and most important group of creative workers, painters, poets, novelists, etchers, sculptors, architects, between Mississippi and the Pacific Coast." In addition to mentioning the city's many talented residents, Austin noted that "workers in many fields of research, *such as the country naturally calls for,* archaeology, ethnology, geology and aboriginal literature, make it from time to time the headquarters of their work" (emphasis added). Santa Fe's residents and studious visitors, Austin suggested, were developing an "authentic culture," a culture threatened by "Chatauqua-minded" invaders who, not having any real culture of their own, sought to acquire that of others. "There can be no doubt," Austin wrote, "that a vast majority of Americans, particularly American women, sincerely suppose that 'culture' is generated in 'courses,' and proceeds as if by nature from the lecture platform" (1926:195). For Austin, Santa Fe, by virtue of its artists and its "otherness" in Indian and Hispanic residents, had "true" culture.

Elizabeth White expressed similar sentiments, with even less subtlety, in a letter written in May 1926 to her friend, the anthropologist Alfred Kidder (by that time the leading figure in Southwest archaeology, with an authority that far surpassed Hewett's):

> I do not know whether you have heard the awful news but Dr. Hewett and the Federated Women's Clubs are cooking up a scheme to hold a Chattauqua [*sic*] in Santa Fe every summer. Do write to Dr. Hewett if you feel as we do that old Santa Fe would vanish before this swarm of locusts.

You can imagine what a Chattauqua of Texas and Oklahoma club women would be. Of course, Martha and I would move away and it would mean that people of our kind would avoid Santa Fe like the plague. In the interests of the School of American Research [Hewett] ought to stop it. As a matter of fact he is one of the main backers.

The Hendersons and all our other friends in Santa Fe naturally are in despair. In fact Santa Fe is raging in factions, as you can imagine. (SAR, AEWC)

During the Fiesta parade that year—the parade itself partly a protest against Hewett's orchestration of Fiesta activities—local activists had various ways of spoofing the Chatauqua plan, while at the same time establishing the activists' own authenticity and their status as "locals" (despite the fact that many of them had only very recently become residents). For their part in the parade, Margretta Dietrich and her sister, Dorothy Stewart, drove a horse-drawn vendor's cart sporting signs announcing "Dr. Quack's Remedies for the Uncultured," "Culture Absorbine: Recommended When Quick Results are Desired," "Magic Chatauqua Balm," and "Culchew Gum" (figure 5). Years later, Dietrich reported that her sister and a friend, Kate Jackson, had also worked to foil the plans for a "Cultural Center" by buying up the pieces of land on which it was to be built (Dietrich 1961:14).

In the end, the Federated Club women abandoned their plans, leaving their opponents with a sense of having "saved" their city from "the locusts." Although Hewett's alliance with business and tourism continued to alienate him from many local patrons of art and anthropology and from other anthropologists, there remained considerable support for his notion that, especially in Santa Fe, the interests of art and anthropology were combined in an appreciation for antiquity, authenticity, otherness, and the picturesque. There also remained a sense that these were qualities that had to be carefully controlled by the elite. Especially because many of the local art-and-anthropology enthusiasts lacked professional credentials or even much experience in the region, their own "culture-seeking" was at risk of a loss of prestige if it became overly popular, especially among women such as the "Texas and Oklahoma club women" who, presumably, had enough actual capital to make them threatening to their opponents so rich in cultural capital. Women such as the Bryn Mawrters had the clout of their ties to the Northeast and to artists, authors, and scientists; Austin had a hard-won

Figure 5 Margretta Stewart Dietrich campaigns against "the Uncultured" at the Santa Fe Fiesta in 1926, connecting the marketing of culture with more mundane commerce. Courtesy of the Museum of New Mexico, negative number 10932.

literary reputation. Thus, drawing on both class and regional prejudices, the Chatauqua opponents projected their insecurities onto others and established themselves—in their own minds at least—as local authorities on "cultures," art, and good taste.

"On Art They Could Agree"

Despite the occasional disagreements, the network of artists, activists, anthropologists, and other intellectuals affiliated with the Bryn Mawrters continued to work throughout the 1920s and 1930s to promote Indian welfare and art. As Maria Chabot said to me in 1990, despite Santa Fe patrons' political disagreements, "on art they could agree . . . [T]here was never any question of taste [when it came to art]." Particularly during the earlier years, the philanthropic patronage of Indian arts went hand-in-hand with projects devoted to cultural preservation, legal rights, health, and economic conditions. Elizabeth Sergeant wrote to John Collier in 1922, "Miss

White has sent $400 to the NMAIA—one-half for food, the other for handicraft work" (John Collier Papers, microfilm reel 4). Until the improvement of government-sponsored health care on Indian reservations during Collier's Indian New Deal, the EAIA and NMAIA also employed "field nurses" to provide basic health care among Pueblos and Navajos. Increasingly, however, the leaders of both organizations concentrated on promoting Indian arts as a form of cultural preservation and a means of improving economic conditions.

Throughout the 1920s members of both the NMAIA and EAIA sponsored small public exhibitions of Indian art, mostly of Pueblo paintings (which could most easily fit into the category of "art"), in Boston, New York, and Chicago, as well as Santa Fe. Even before the involvement of the NMAIA and EAIA, Edgar Hewett had begun exhibiting Pueblo paintings, with the help of John Sloan, for example, at the 1922 show of the Society of Independent Artists at the Waldorf-Astoria in New York City. Although it was not until the Exposition of Indian Tribal Arts that the slogan "Indian art as art, not ethnology" was used, a similar combination of aesthetics and anthropology was implicit in many of the early exhibitions.[10] More local institutions and events in Northern New Mexico probably had a much greater and longer-lasting impact on the Indian art market than the 1931 Exposition in terms of influencing public opinion and Indian artists, but in many ways the Exposition exemplifies the processes through which Indian art as a valid category gained credence.

Michael Thompson has written of the important role that naming and categorizing plays in producing the value of objects. Thompson uses the example of how it may be to a dealer's advantage to identify objects in an advertisement as "antique" rather than "second-hand" (1979:6). Categories can, of course, be contested and their accepted use transformed, though as Thompson explains, the ability to use labels with any degree of legitimacy is dependent upon political and economic power and control over time and space (52). A cartoon from the *New York World* in 1929 (figure 6) suggests the ambiguous status of Indian-related objects in popular opinion in this period (as well as the prevalent association of women and shopping): unsure of how to categorize or evaluate a Hopi kachina carving and, perhaps most important, what to do with it, the woman proposes it as a gift, thereby leaving such decisions to the recipient. Events such as the EITA and the

"Isn't it cute—for a present, I mean"

Figure 6 Cartoon from the *New York World,* 1929.Reprinted with permission of Denys Wortman IV.

accompanying publicity were calculated to instruct consumers in how to think about such objects and what one might do with them, apart from giving them away.

By naming the 1931 show an "exposition," the show's sponsors were appropriating a term from what they saw as opposing forces. Since the late nineteenth century, American Indians and their wares had been put on display at World's Fairs, often called "Expositions"—one of the most influential being the 1893 World's Columbian Exposition in Chicago—events which Curtis Hinsley has aptly termed "carnivals of the industrial age" (1991:344). The Indians on display at such events served as a foil for industrial progress and were treated as exotic objects of curiosity. The sponsors of the Exposition of Indian Tribal Arts sought to ally Indians with the romantic discourse of art rather than commerce, with the museum rather than the carnival, the elite rather than the crowd. Such distinctions were in fact far more important to patrons than any they might make between "art" and "ethnology" (though, as argued in the previous chapter, "art" opened up spaces for authoritative tastemaking for individuals, particularly wealthy women, more easily than "ethnology").

In addition to Indian displays at the World's Fairs, the Exposition had other, increasingly influential representations of Indians with which to compete. In an article on the importance of Indians to Southwestern tourism during the 1920s and 1930s, Marta Weigle (1989) describes a process of "Disneylandization" whereby Indians were used as main attractions.[11] Also, in the 1920s the film industry was expanding rapidly and, particularly because of cheaper production costs in Hollywood compared to the East, films were increasingly made as "Westerns" with stereotypical Indian characters, a fashion perhaps adding to the popular appeal of the Southwestern desert. Although the rise of mass media was in itself of concern to elites, promoters of Indian art were concerned about counteracting commercial influence on popular perceptions of Indians and their art.

The cultural nationalism emphasized in the Exposition literature, though not insincere, was surely also a rhetorical strategy for gaining public attention and support—during years when it must have been difficult, especially in New York, to draw concern away from breadlines, Hoovervilles, and massive unemployment. While their motivations were clearly complex, Indian art patrons such as Elizabeth White and Margretta Dietrich perceived their actions as pure philanthropy; by placing Indian handicrafts in the category of fine art, they aimed to make art production a more economically profitable, pleasant, and respectable activity for Southwestern Indians, a means of livelihood which would enable Indians to remain in their rural homelands and to continue to follow the rhythms of tribal calendars, observing important occasions with ceremonial dances (dances at which arts patrons were frequent, and appreciative, observers). Encouraging arts production was also a way of avoiding sharp divisions between the domestic and public economy; many of the artists promoted were women, often elderly, with strong ties to home and family, who created their art in backyards and kitchens with the help of husbands and relatives. Establishing Indian art as art would not be a simple task since its forms were associated with the domestic and utilitarian, not to mention "primitive." The patron-philanthropists perceived their task to be twofold: to encourage Indians to make pieces in accord with elite tastes and to educate potential buyers.[12]

Such patron-philanthropists did not see themselves as imposing alien influence on Indian artists; rather, they considered themselves to be counteracting the tastes that had already been imposed by others. That they did not see their actions as paradoxical or hypocritical is partly explained by their view that it was in fact the masses of consumers and middlemen who were imposing the most "alien influence" in their demand for Indian-made objects that reflected popular stereotypes. Moreover, the tastes the patron-philanthropists wished to impose on Indian artists were influenced by other Indians (especially older ones, assumed to be more in touch with "traditional" Indian standards of value than younger people) as well as anthropologists, and they took older Indian artwork (or "artifacts") as their standard of excellence.[13]

Of course, one of the most direct and elementary means for patrons to exercise authority in the Indian art market was to purchase what they liked—for themselves and for others—and at higher prices than most tourists and traders were willing to pay. As discussed in the preceding chapter, one of Elizabeth White's initial steps to promote Indian art was to open an Indian art shop, "Ishauu," on Madison Avenue in Manhattan, one of the first of its kind. Eventually renamed the "Gallery of American Indian Art" and moved to Lexington Avenue, the shop was operated by White at a loss for over a decade (SAR, AEWC, Ishauu files).

In 1922, shortly after White returned from working with the Red Cross in Belgium and Paris during the war, she wrote in September of her intentions to Mabel Dodge Luhan, who had recently moved to Taos. "My idea," White explained, "is to show people here in the East the very best things the Indians make and to pay the Indians a fair price for the *best*. I hope in time the Indians will stop making the trashy stuff that is sold as 'Indian art' along the Santa Fe road" (MDLC).

Although White would become one of the most dedicated promoters of "Indian art as *art*," the very transitional state of the market in this period is revealed by White's calling "Ishauu" a "shop" rather than a "gallery." Moreover, White encouraged consumers to use many of the objects she sold for practical, rather than purely aesthetic, purposes. Today many of those objects would be considered too valuable for such everyday use: large hand-coiled Pueblo pots made into lamps, Apache baskets to be used as "waste baskets and clothes hampers," and "Indian tanned buckskin shirts for use during the hunting season in the Adirondacks and Canada" (SAR, AEWC, Ishauu files). Though the shop was not a financial success, its business occupied much of White's time for a decade: she purchased the pieces she sold on her travels in the Southwest and she often placed large orders with dealers; she also carried on a busy correspondence with customers who saw her shop mentioned in national magazines.

In 1932 White had a telling exchange of letters with Dorothy Deane, who was trying, she explained to White, to use handicrafts as an economic development strategy among Chippewa women. Deane sent White examples of the work the women were making in the hope that White would sell them in her shop. White responded, "I am sorry but the things you sent on to my shop were not in the class of material that is sold there. Have you anything of their own design and workmanship? It is the truly Indian work that appeals to the class of people here. I am sorry that I am not very familiar with the Chippewa work so cannot tell just what you might have. I am very much interested in what you are doing as it seems to me the real way to help the economic difficulties of the Indians" (SAR, AEWC, Ishauu files). Note that White was able to state confidently that the pieces Deane sent were not "truly Indian," yet she admitted that she did not know what would count as "truly Indian" among Chippewa work.

Deane wrote back asserting that the work was in fact "authentic," since it was handmade by Chippewa women. But, she explained, "they have in some cases copied southwest designs because those who are not familiar with Chippewa workmanship often find them more attractive. I am trying, however, to keep them to their own traditional designs as much as possible" (SAR, AEWC, Ishauu files).

Although through her shop White sought to influence popular taste, and more indirectly the work of artists, the Exposition was a project designed more specifically to influence the tastes of potential buyers. To ensure this influence, White, Sloan, and their colleagues used all their contacts and authority: in addition to obtaining additional financial backing (including $5000 from the Carnegie Corporation, a substantial amount at the time for an art exhibition), the official endorsement of the College

Art Association, and nominal sponsorship by the Secretary of the Interior and the Commissioner of Indian Affairs, they enlisted the support of newspapers, prominent art critics like Walter Pach, archaeologists like Frederick Webb Hodge, and well-known collectors of Indian art including White's friend, Abby Rockefeller, and Lou Henry Hoover (annual report 1932, SAR, AEWC, EITA files). Press releases listed the elite sources of the artwork on exhibit, including conspicuous mention of the collections of Elizabeth White, Abby Rockefeller, Lou Henry Hoover, and Mary Cabot Wheelwright. For its part, the Junior League of New York City staged a fashion show featuring Indian silver jewelry (the Associated Press reported that "Miss Challis Walker, a prominent debutante, wore a gown of sheer black velvet with a jet and turquoise necklace, and a silver belt . . . all made by Navajo Indians"). White, meanwhile, distributed photographs of Indian art used as decor for her Manhattan apartment and of Pueblo pottery displayed in her garden in Santa Fe, photographs which were used to illustrate articles in newspapers and in magazines including *House and Garden* and *House Beautiful* (one of the accompanying slogans was "If You Would Decorate Your Home *Earliest* American"). As Dolly Sloan wrote in 1933 to White concerning the importance of such publicity, "we must let people know that some people are collecting Indian art" (SAR, AEWC, EITA files).

The success of the Exposition, at least in gaining public attention, may be indicated by the fact that the show began to be accompanied, not entirely to the sponsors' satisfaction, by Indian displays in department stores, including Macy's and Bloomingdale's. (In 1932, Dolly Sloan wrote to Elizabeth White, "After seeing our show in New York and Springfield, I never thought Indian art could look as rotten as it does at Bloomingdale's" [SAR, AEWC, EITA files].)

In making celebrities of some of the Indian artists whose work was included in the Exposition, newspapers played up a connection—or an opposition—between the artists' apparently geographically limited backgrounds and their aesthetic genius. When a group of Pueblo artists and two Navajo sandpainters was brought to Manhattan to promote the Exposition, syndicated newspaper articles repeatedly quoted Pueblo painter Alfonso Roybal's (Awa Tsireh's) response to the question of how he liked New York: "Have you ever seen Santa Fe?" (SAR, AEWC, EITA press clippings).[14] Describing the opening of the Exposition, one journalist remarked on "designs so dashingly modern that one can scarcely believe they were woven into a blanket by an Indian woman who never heard of Paris" (Seinfel 1931). Similarly, an article titled "She Learned from the Corn, the Rain and the Buffalo" about Tonita Peña (the painter whose work was purchased by Margretta Dietrich, Elizabeth White, Abby Rockefeller, and the Whitney Museum) made this observation: "Tonita Peña's paintings have traveled far more than she, for this Indian woman, mother of six children, seldom journeys from the Cochiti Pueblo in New Mexico" (*Providence Sunday Journal* 1933). Such comments suggest the sensationalism—and appeal—of the idea that there might be systems of aesthetic values existing independently of the core of the modern world-system and the historic centers of fashion. Those with the ability to "discover" and appreciate such "primitive geniuses" were implicitly endowed with cosmopolitanism and sophistication.

Institutionalizing Evaluations of Difference

Miss White said the big question now was: how to combat the tourist trade. The Indians can sell much more of the junky type of pottery than the good. Some means must be found to improve the pottery . . .
—Meeting Minutes of the NMAIA, SWAIAC, SRCA, 1935

The Exposition claimed to present works "chosen entirely with consideration of aesthetic value," but in fact the break with more ethnological approaches to such objects was not at all complete. For example, even the artists promoted were those who had first received the backing and support of anthropologists. However, in many ways the Exposition organizers sincerely sought to break down distinctions between objects valued as "ethnology" and the "fine arts." Certainly they did not consider Indian art the exclusive province of museums of natural history, and they felt strongly that it should be represented in the Whitney (which opened in 1931), the Metropolitan Museum of Art, and the many museums, at that time springing up throughout the country, devoted to "Modern Art" and "Fine Art." Indeed, an explicit purpose of the Exposition was to challenge the ethnocentricity of notions that only objects linked to a European or Euro-American tradition were worthy of the category of "art." And in an attempt to counteract the anonymity of artists in "ethnological" exhibitions, the Exposition was also intended as a way to obtain public recognition for individual Indian artists.[15]

The assumption informing the Exposition—that aesthetic value could be adequately judged by those possessing sufficient knowledge and "good taste"—aided patrons of Indian art in their attempts to influence white and Indian tastes and identities and to exercise a form of cultural authority which could attempt to compete with that of tourists seeking trinkets and, at least on occasion, with anthropologists. In the Exposition's booklet, "Introduction to American Indian Art," John Sloan and Oliver La Farge end their discussion of beadwork by noting that the cultural authenticity of designs is increasingly difficult to determine; they offer as example the fact that Indian beadworkers "began depicting horses and American flags long ago," making it difficult, therefore, to "draw the line between what is, and what is not, truly Indian." Their solution to the dilemma is revealing in its vagueness: "The criterion has to be largely one of taste, and of the Indian feeling. They turn out many silly things, such as ornamented rabbits' feet or poorly conceived designs slapped onto factory made moccasins, but there are many of them today who prefer the old, rich masses of decoration, containing still the vigour and brilliance of their ancient warriors" (La Farge and Sloan 1931:25).

In a similar display of open-mindedness, La Farge and Sloan praise the new bright colors of Hopi and Jicarilla basketry (which they claim ethnologists frown upon), asserting that certainly Indian art cannot be expected to remain unchanged; but then they admit that many "white buyers" have led basket makers astray in encouraging the use of "fancy pseudo symbols" (1931:11). Of course the assumption behind their swift flips between "authenticity" and "good taste" is that these are actually two sides of the same coin. Their fellow patron, the poet Witter Bynner, who lent his collection of silver jewelry to the Exposition, was even more willing than they to dispense with ethnologists as the primary authorities of evaluation and to rely on his own, supposedly innate, "good taste." Discussing his collection of Indian silver, Bynner stated frankly that he knew "nothing of the history of silver-work among Indians, nothing of the origin or significance of the designs they use. For me that is not the point. I can only wheeze with other amateurs that I know what I like. But at the same time I can instinctively and instantly reject the false design, the design which means nothing to its maker except foreign instruction or intended sale" (1936:337).

Thus such patrons established both their own taste and artistic creativity as something that could not be learned or taught or shaped to suit the demands of the market. For patrons such as White and her fellow Bryn Mawrters, however, there was much to be gained from the idea that taste could be taught, for they could do the teaching.

While projects such as White's Manhattan gallery and the 1931 Exposition were meant to influence Easterners' perceptions of Indians and their arts, more local activities in Northern New Mexico allowed Indian arts patrons to have a more direct influence on the artists themselves (among whom, patrons felt, there had been too much "foreign instruction" and catering to the vulgar, uneducated tastes of tourists). In 1922 the School of American Research had begun to sponsor annual "Indian Fairs" in Santa Fe, including exhibitions of Indian art at which cash prizes and ribbons were awarded for the "best" pieces. The exhibitions were organized by anthropologist (and, one might argue, professional cultural nationalist) Edgar Lee Hewett, whose academic credentials were rather dubious, but who, nonetheless, had managed to position himself as one of the more influential anthropologists in the region (Stocking 1982). Typical of the division of funding and expertise in local Indian arts patronage (where women were most often patrons and men official authorities), prizes for the Fairs were funded by a "Miss Rose Dougan, of Richmond, Indiana . . . who has become deeply interested in the life of the Pueblo Indians and has given unsparingly . . . in an effort to raise the standard of their native arts and handicrafts" (El Palacio 1922a). The early exhibitions were held in conjunction with Santa Fe's annual Fiesta, a pageant and three-day event billed as celebrating "the culture of a thousand years and more," inviting audiences "to live over a cycle of American culture history that has been rescued from oblivion" in a setting filled with "picturesque landmarks" and "stupendous mountain scenery," with remains nearby of cliff dwellings "which housed a great culture in the days when Europe was still in the shadow of the Dark Ages" (El Palacio 1922b).

But Hewett, who coordinated the early Fiestas much like a circus ringmaster, was rather too accommodating of tourists (and probably too lax in his standards of authenticity) to suit the tastes of the artists, art patrons, and more sophisticated anthropologists who gradually gained more control over the events.[16] In 1927 the Indian Fair aspect of the Fiesta was taken over from Hewett and the School of American Research by a committee of volunteers, among them Margretta Dietrich and Elizabeth White;[17] in addition to continuing to award prizes at the big annual spectacle in Santa Fe, the committee also began to hold Fairs at the northern Pueblos where "experts"—including anthropologists, modernist artists, and collectors— would award ribbons and cash prizes to Indian artists. Some of the items displayed and sold at the Exposition of Indian Tribal Arts were, in fact, acquired through Indian Fairs held during the summer of 1931 (KCC, LA, file KCO.026). After a fair held at Cochiti Pueblo in 1935, judge Kenneth Chapman reported sadly to the committee that the quality of art was so "disgracefully poor" that reprimands were given instead of prizes, but more often the artists were at least deemed worthy of encouragement (LA, KCC, file KCO.030).

My focus here is on patrons rather than on artists or their communities. The effects of the sort of patronage described here on Native artists and communities and their individual and collective responses, past and present, deserve much more extensive study than they have heretofore received.[18] Archival records and discussions with elderly artists and their descendents, however, give the impression that despite the blatant paternalism expressed by Chapman and others, the relationships between artists and their patrons were typically congenial, with artists and the Pueblo political leadership usually in support of an arrangement which promised to bring at least some of their members economic rewards. By the 1930s, farming in the Pueblos had become an unreliable mode of livelihood and other income earning possibilities were few. Indian artists welcomed the opportunities patrons provided for them to sell their work directly to the public, bypassing traders. Pablita Velarde and Tonita Peña had been discouraged from painting by Santa Clara elders who felt that painting was best reserved for men, and consequently they particularly appreciated patrons' lack of concern for conventional gender roles. Moreover, many of the artists approved of the evaluative distinctions made by patrons, especially when they concurred with their own preferences. Although individually expressed resentments were common (when, for example, an artist was offended by an award going to another artist), there were only occasional efforts to resist the overall patterns of patronage (for examples of individualized resistance, see Jacobs 1999:172–73). The merging of interests among Native artists and elite white patrons is apt to be contrary to contemporary expectations, especially among those who imagine Native communities as homogeneous entities,[19] a subject that is discussed in chapter 5.

In the 1930s the pueblo of Tesuque offered an exception to the more general trend toward embracing the opportunities patronage offered. When Maria Chabot, working for the NMAIA, tried to bring Tesuque potters to an Indian Fair in Santa Fe, she was advised that the potters might be reluctant to participate because they did not want to compete with one another for prizes. Chabot reported that the potters feared Tesuque would become divided into "good" potters and "those who make the poorer painted type" and suffer the sort of factionalism which had occurred nearby at San Ildefonso (NMAIA meeting minutes, SRCA, SWAIAC, folder 38),[20] where potter Maria Martinez was becoming something of a national celebrity and where several other potters and painters had begun to establish significant reputations and to command much higher prices for their work. Though Association members, with their eyes more closely focused on objects, seem to have been remarkably unconcerned about the potters' anxieties, Elizabeth Sergeant, no longer associated with the NMAIA, did write, that same year, a harshly critical analysis of the social consequences of patronage at San Ildefonso; Sergeant argued that patronage, inevitably selective and arbitrary, encouraged rivalry, political and economic inequality, and divisiveness among the Pueblos (1935).[21] Such consequences, she argued, were not being taken into account by patrons in Santa Fe, including Elizabeth White, whom she mentioned specifically as wielding important influence over the Pueblo through her purchases.

Though patrons encountered little direct resistance to their plans overall, it is clear that there were tensions among individual artists and collectors, particularly when collectors served as judges of the Fairs. The judges placed ribbons on the various pieces as the producers sat beside them. Because many of the judges and artists had become friends over the years, such awards at times inspired resentment as well as gratitude. Marjorie Lambert, an archaeologist who judged pottery at the Indian Fairs during the 1930s and 1940s, told me that one of the most well-known potters, Rose Gonzales, who was also her friend, refused to speak to her after she awarded a ribbon to another potter. Hard feelings about the prizes were not merely a matter of personal pride, but a consequence of the direct economic impact of the awards. By the early 1940s, judges at Santa Fe Indian Fairs were trailed by collectors, who sought to buy the prize-winning pieces and were willing to pay considerably more for them.[22]

The standards of evaluation instituted by patrons did, of course, vary over the years, in response to artists' initiatives as well as changing tastes of patrons, but there was little in the way of serious disagreement among judges of the Indian Fairs, some of whom were archaeologists or curators, others serious collectors, some artists as well as collectors, but none of them Indian. According to the regulations of the Fairs, distributed months in advance every year, "All articles in order to compete for prizes must be strictly Indian in material, handicrafts, and decoration. For instance, pottery should not be made in the shape of non-Indian dishes or other utensils; and blankets, textiles, beadwork, and other articles should not contain flags, lodge emblems or other non-Indian designs" (El Palacio 1926:205–06).

Additionally, artists were rewarded for keeping the designs of each pueblo as distinct as possible, and the borrowing of designs was considered a departure from authenticity: Zuni pieces, for example, needed to be recognizably Zuni, and made by a Zuni. In addition to following guidelines derived from anthropology, the emphasis on clear-cut tribal styles reflected the demand for an intimate relationship between place and object. While these standards revealed the preferences of patrons, it is possible that they also grew out of the aim to develop a more exclusive market for Indian art, the patrons recognizing that a wealthier, more educated clientele would be willing to pay more for objects approved by museums and universities and which demanded the exercise of institutionally sanctioned knowledge and taste in the labor of consumption (of course, links to museums and universities also help to reproduce the value of objects, allowing buyers to justify their expenditures as an "investment," though that is certainly more a concern in the contemporary market than it was in the 1930s).

Although anthropologists and other professionals, including the curator and scholar Kenneth Chapman, did serve as judges at the Indian Fairs, whatever their occupation, most judges tended to blend ethnological and aesthetic notions of "quality." (Chapman, however, according to surviving members of the judging teams, was more inclined than others to urge exact replication of highly valued work.) Following the Indian Fair in 1930, Margretta Dietrich, chairman of the Southwest Indian Fair Committee, expressed satisfaction with the exhibition's high standards—standards influenced by anthropologists, but not completely dependent upon them: "Nothing," she claimed, "was accepted for the Fair which did not show good workmanship, correct materials and fine design" (Dietrich 1930).

Though "fine design" was generally considered synonymous with "traditional," later on Dietrich recalled that exceptions were made for "particularly fine innovations" ("History of the Indian Market," SRCA, SWAIAC, folder 106).

Along with holding the Fairs in Santa Fe, members of the Committee volunteered to judge exhibits at events held throughout Northern New Mexico, including the Gallup Intertribal Ceremonial and the Shiprock Fair, competitions similar to those held in Santa Fe but organized largely by traders and federal Indian agents, who were considered by Santa Fe patrons to lack the taste and expertise to award prizes appropriately (apparently a matter of much concern). As Oliver La Farge wrote to "Pueblo Revival" architect John Gaw Meem in 1933, "It has been painfully brought out at the Shiprock Fair and other such events that no prize list is good without good judges . . . At Gallup, . . . through our Committee on Judges, judges of what we may call 'our group' have been secured . . . What we want is to have the entire judging of Arts and Crafts at such Fairs turned over to us" (SAR, AEWC, NMAIA files).

Although La Farge and friends were not entirely successful in their attempt at total control, by 1936 Margretta Dietrich reported that she, La Farge, and their colleagues had been particularly successful in influencing the exhibits at Gallup, where, to her horror, a prize had once been given to "a reproduction of an oriental rug" woven by a Navajo, and by 1938 she was pleased to report the "increasingly Indian character" of the work on display (SRCA, SWAIAC, folder 38).

The Santa Fe patrons designed numerous other projects to influence Indian artists. In the early 1930s, for example, a committee of the EAIA, including Mary Cabot Wheelwright, her cousin Lucy Cabot, and Elizabeth White, campaigned to revive older styles of Navajo weaving. Disapproving of the loud colors produced with chemical dyes and new designs which they felt showed the influence of white traders, the committee encouraged a return to the more subtle hues of vegetable dyes and the weaving of designs without borders. In addition to working with chemical companies to develop inexpensive, packaged vegetable dyes (including one mixture called "Old Navajo"—innovative technologies were apparently considered quite acceptable when in the service of tradition), Association members traveled the Navajo Reservation, distributing photographs of old Navajo blankets among their own collections and encouraging weavers to use them as examples (SAR, AEWC). Similarly, it became a common practice (one that has continued ever since) to encourage Indian artists to study the collections in museums in Santa Fe. These collections were used as a standard by which exhibition judges, curators, and artists could evaluate new work. Artists were encouraged to use museum collections as models of authenticity and institutionally sanctioned taste, a route which many of the more ambitious artists were quick to pursue on their own (in many cases, of course, departing from, as much as reproducing, the older designs, but with the validating connection to authoritative institutions).

Other local activities during the 1930s were aimed at educating tourists, encouraging them to purchase "articles of real worth, not Indian curios" (Dietrich 1936). As head of the NMAIA, Dietrich reported in 1935 that as well as continuing the Indian Fairs, members of the Association would also sponsor a series of lectures in hopes of educating "the public to an appreciation of Indian Art, for Art's sake and for the sake of creating markets for Indian goods" (Annual Report, SRCA, SWAIAC, folder 38). In 1936 the Association published a series of articles, officially "approved" by the Laboratory of Anthropology, which attempted to educate potential buyers. Maria Chabot, editor of the series, wrote to Elizabeth White, who provided funds for Chabot's salary, "we all feel that anything we can do to make the thunderbird and other such imported designs 'bad taste' in tourist articles will be to the good" (SAR, AEWC).

During the same period, Association members decided to return to holding the Indian Fairs in Santa Fe's central plaza, rather than at the more remote pueblos as they had been for several years, since, as they saw it, "naturally the number of strangers attending and being educated unconsciously is limited" (annual report, SRCA, SWAIAC, folder 38). During these events, educational tactics took a more direct turn, and placards were placed around the exhibition area explaining to potential buyers how to identify the "best" pieces. Objects which were considered acceptable were marked with stickers: "Approved by the NMAIA" ("History of the Indian Market," p. 6, SRCA, SWAIAC, folder 106). The same patrons worked to establish permanent collections of Indian art in Santa Fe, which could serve as a standard by which other works could be judged (in addition to serving as a source of study for artists).[23]

Later in the 1930s, some of the Indian arts professionals and patrons in Santa Fe, including Kenneth Chapman, worked with the Roosevelt Administration's Indian Arts and Crafts Board, which, among its other activities, developed official government standards for Indian silver work and placed official stamps on approved pieces (stamps designed to reward artists and to educate buyers). Pieces were rejected if, for example, they used stereotypical but "inauthentic" designs, such as arrows, thunderbirds, or horses, or if the workmanship was considered careless.[24]

Making "Strange Dark Saints" Spanish Colonial Art

In her 1922 articles in *Harper's,* Elizabeth Sergeant expressed concern not only about threats to Indian cultural differences, but also about what she perceived to be a declining level of taste among her Hispanic neighbors in Tesuque. Sergeant pointed to the example of the demise of the "old church[es], full of crucifixes and carved beams and strange dark saints—the sort of church that Americans cross the ocean to visit in Spain and Italy" (1922:57). Sergeant had acquired from Willa Cather high expectations of both Indian and Hispanic aesthetics. Cather's Thea Kronborg had, after all, found her greatest artistic inspiration in two places—the abandoned cliff dwelling and the "Mexican ghetto" of her town in Colorado. Although Sergeant made Indian art and Indian politics her primary commitment in New Mexico, many of her friends and colleagues were also devoted to encouraging what they defined as authentic Hispanic artistic traditions, expressed in furniture, weavings, woodcarving, tinwork, and architecture.[25]

The patrons who sponsored the Indian Fairs and the EITA devised similar projects to move Hispanic "crafts" into the more honorary category of "Spanish Colonial Art," a term Mary Austin claimed to have authored (Weigle 1983:183). In the late 1920s Austin and a number of other Santa Feans, including Margretta Dietrich, Martha White, Alice Corbin Henderson, Ina Sizer Cassidy, and modernist painter Andrew Dasburg, started the Spanish Colonial Arts Society, an organization similar to the NMAIA, though more narrowly focused on art. The patrons, who developed extensive private collections, also sponsored exhibitions and awarded prizes during Santa Fe's Fiesta (awarding prizes for " 'new work that conformed most exactly to the old models' " [Weigle 1983:183]) and opened a shop in the center of Santa Fe. Their stated goals were essentially the same as for their patronage of Indian art—to improve artists' economic opportunities while preserving traditions (Weigle 1983:184). Though Spanish Colonial art has never achieved the same sort of national success as Indian art, the institutions that were set up during the 1920s—namely the art exhibitions during Santa Fe's Fiesta, Fiesta itself, and the Spanish Colonial Arts Society—would exert a lasting impact on ways of organizing ethnic and racial difference in the regional art world.[26]

In developing markets for Indian art, however, patrons were more easily able to draw on the legitimating authority of anthropologists and archaeologists. Spanish Colonial art belonged less clearly to any such field of respected scholarship (Weigle 1983:196). As far as the development of a national market, Indian art's closer association with ethnology, I suspect, was not so much a hindrance as an advantage. Spanish Colonial art shared with Indian art the notion of intimate relationship between place and object; it was able to evoke a sense of a unique local character that could be contrasted with the impersonal character of factory-made goods. Yet Spanish Colonial objects were less likely to appeal directly to American cultural nationalism: while Indians have long been perceived as quintessentially American, the "first Americans," the status of New Mexico's Hispano settlers was more ambiguous, especially to people living outside the Southwest. It is also possible that Spanish Colonial aesthetics were too familiar—the white middle class was also largely Christian, if not Catholic, and it may have been more difficult, outside New Mexico, to exoticize objects created in a tradition of Spanish folk Catholicism and to disassociate them from class-structured boundaries of taste.

Many of the individuals I interviewed for this project were influential patrons of both Indian and Spanish Colonial art. They expressed an interest in supporting contemporary artists who produced "traditional" Spanish Colonial art, and most were also interested in work by "nontraditional" Hispanic artists. However, their interest in Hispanic and Spanish Colonial art was often more recent than their interest in Indian art, and several patrons admitted that it was only after years of exposure that they began to find Spanish Colonial art aesthetically pleasing, rather than disconcerting in its "obsession" with Christian saints. One very dedicated patron had been, since the 1930s, active in major institutions devoted to Indian and Spanish Colonial art. She mentioned that although she had been enthralled by Indian art for as long as she could remember, long before she had moved to the Southwest, Spanish Colonial art had been an "acquired taste."

The Specter of the "Garish and Restless"

Throughout their efforts to serve as tastemakers, a role they sought to play quite deliberately and with an extraordinary measure of confidence, patrons lamented that their influence—over artists, but especially over tourists—was limited. As Witter Bynner protested in 1936:

> . . . the fact is that many Americans, with their creative minds destroyed by the effect of factory products, can come even into this mountain country whose clear air should clear their taste, and prefer Indian jewelry made wholesale in factories at Denver or Albuquerque or in the petty factories set up by white traders . . . An unimaginative and tinny jewelry is being imposed upon credulous and tasteless buyers in the name of Indians who, left alone, let me repeat and repeat, can create for themselves and through themselves for us, decorative belongings as distinguished and personal and aesthetically important as the decorative belongings which for centuries have graced the Orient. (1979:338)

Bynner's moral fervor concerning the slippery slope of standards of quality was common. After one of the first Indian Fairs, Kenneth Chapman wrote optimistically of the effect they would have on "the tourist," who, Chapman complained, instead of seeking "honest quality," chose "the trivial, the gaudy, and the cheap" and was "heedless of the part he was playing in the demoralization of Indian crafts" (1924:215–16). But despite Chapman's optimism, eighteen years later Margretta Dietrich complained similarly of the obstinacy of popular tastes. By that time the Indian Fairs had been renamed "Indian Markets" after one of the organizers, Maria Chabot, sought to replicate characteristics of village markets in "Old Mexico." Dietrich explained that the events were designed to help Indians sell their work as well as to "educate the buying public." But she reported in 1938 that she had to doubt their educational effectiveness when faced with "the enthusiasm of the tourist over the poorest articles" (annual report, SRCA, SWAIAC, folder 38).

Indian artists, Dietrich observed, found it easy enough to sell pieces that had been rejected by the Indian Market authorities outside the official boundaries in the central Plaza—in nearby hotels, restaurants, and side streets (a practice continuing to plague authorities throughout the 1980s and 1990s). Despite the placards on display at the Fairs which alerted buyers to the qualities of "good" Indian art, Dietrich reported that "tourists, even if they had read the placards, bought pottery which had designs painted on with show-card colors, after firing, which perhaps fortunately wash off" ("History of the Indian Market," SRCA, SWAIAC, folder 106). And in a *New Mexico Magazine* article which was part of the series of articles reprinted and sold to tourists in the hope of educating them, Dietrich summed up her attitude toward authenticity and Indian arts, an attitude shared by many of her associates. "It is impossible to give a recipe for good taste," she admitted (despite the fact that so many of her and her colleagues' efforts centered on trying to do just that), "but the Indian, uninfluenced by the white man, had taste of such universal appeal that his work is treasured by people of all lands . . . It is only when ideas of an alien race, our own, are imposed on the Indian that the patterns and colors become garish and restless" (1936:27). Committed to upholding an abstract notion of "culture" and "tradition"—not altogether separate from "race"—Dietrich and her colleagues did not see their own efforts as imposing "alien" influence, but rather as encouraging the "authenticity" which others had undervalued.

Although it is easy to dismiss such evaluative judgments as old-fashioned racist paternalism (or, perhaps more appropriately, "maternalism"), it is more difficult to dismiss the fact that the efforts of patrons such as Dietrich did play a part in developing a more lucrative market for Indian artists—the "approved" ones benefiting more, of course, than the "garish and restless"—but one could argue that most Indian artists in the long run benefited, economically at least, however indirectly. The officially "approved" market in Indian "art" still fueled the market in less expensive "junk"—just as the popular acceptance of the practice of hanging original paintings on walls encourages sales of less expensive posters. In the contemporary market for Indian art, tourists and newcomers are often shocked by the prices (just as many are shocked to hear of prices paid for other sorts of art or other commodities with limited markets, such as rare baseball cards or "collector's items"). To many people, prices they at first consider high become legitimate once they have become familiar with Indian art exhibitions, scholarship, and museums—including a web of public and private, professionally staffed institutions vastly expanded since the 1930s. These institutions provide terminology, frameworks, and classificatory schemes for making distinctions among objects and artists, "art" and "trash" (at least as much, nowadays, using indices of "quality" as of "authenticity") and stress the labor-intensiveness of the art's production and its connections with "culture," "tradition," and regional history. Many buyers of Indian art, as with any art, would simply not buy—unless, of course, items were quite cheap—if they did not have curators, writers, and exhibition judges to help legitimate their purchases.[27]

On the other hand, it is also worth noting that although patrons such as White and Dietrich did work hard to establish opportunities for artists to sell their work directly to consumers, bypassing traders and dealers, their patronage in the form of public exhibitions and publicity certainly would have been to the benefit of non-Indian traders and dealers (whose markups, in the case of Navajo textiles, could be 100 to 1000 percent in the early twentieth century and 300 to 400 percent in the 1990s [M'Closkey 1994: 210]). It is possible that the romantic attitudes and self-interest of patron-philanthropists kept them from making more serious attempts to address the huge profits being made by middlemen.[28]

Patron-philanthropists also made little attempt to develop economic opportunities for members of Native communities who might not be especially suited to careers as artists. Supporting more diverse economic development strategies would have been somewhat difficult for most of the patrons discussed here, who really were most skilled in matters of art and tastemaking, but the priority they placed on art production seems to have reflected their own self-interest and their ideological assumptions. As an example of the latter, patrons generally accepted the popular stereotype that Native people were all endowed with artistic talent; they presumed that if given the appropriate support and encouragement and possessed with a suitable amount of determination, most Indians were capable of becoming great artists.

If patrons' priorities reflected their own interests and their acceptance of stereotypes, they also reflected an upper-class bias against other whites, and the anthropology they drew on, predominantly focused on archaeology, offered little to dissuade such bias. Until fairly recently, anthropologists, including archaeologists, often tended to assume tacitly, like Dietrich, that there are objective standards of quality and aesthetic value. They have also tended to draw the line of "authentic culture" at the border of consumer capitalism, whether more explicitly, as in Sapir's 1924 essay "Culture, Genuine and Spurious," or implicitly, by excluding mass media and commodity consumption from ethnographies and assuming such topics irrelevant to the student of "culture" (Miller, 1995). In the contradictory popular merging of Arnoldian notions of culture with anthropological ones, there are still some people left without culture. Those "with culture" are presumed at risk of losing it.

On the surface it is apparent that the organizers of the EITA, the Indian Fairs, and the Indian Markets were concerned with differences between "cultures." But the art patrons' concepts of cultural difference were shaped by concerns pertaining to class. Consider Margretta Dietrich's terms for the antithesis of what she and her colleagues sought to promote: *garish* and *restless, gaudy,* and *cheap;* these are heavily class-laden terms. In her article for *New Mexico Magazine,* Dietrich explained that she and her colleagues felt that Indians made "better artists than mechanics or houseworkers"— *mechanics* being a period euphemism for proletarians (1936:27). While it is easy to sympathize with the patrons' belief that producing art is more fulfilling than wage labor, in their patronage of specific visions of "cultural" difference, Indian art patrons implicitly crusaded against other forms of difference, differences which to them were more threatening than any they would attribute to "culture." In the equation of oppositions, Indians ("authentic" ones, that is), and others thought of as "primitive," were authentic particularly in opposition to the largely white working and middle class (not in relation to the soft-spoken descendants of New England settlers, as Elizabeth White was described in newspaper accounts of the 1931 Exposition [e.g., Seinfel 1931]).

Similarly, "art" was constructed in opposition to the "masses" or to the mass-produced commodity. Such constructions helped to legitimate the creation of new public roles. Whereas in the world of mass-produced goods, art patrons were only consumers with relatively more money to spend, in the world of "art" they could be authorities and institution-builders. In her autobiography Mabel Dodge Luhan recalled that when she sailed home to America after her pre–World War I years living in an Italian villa, she wept at the thought of returning to "a world of dull, grubby men and women, street cars, cigar stores, electric signs and baseball games" (1935:447)—a world, perceived as quite masculine and unlike that of art, one where she could have little influence. Of course, she found a place for herself in the midst of all this American ugliness as a patron of modern art, and then later in Taos, as a patron of Indian and Spanish Colonial arts.

Recounting her arrival in Taos, in a telling passage, Luhan admired the haggard faces of "Mexicans"; though their faces showed the effects of hard labor in a harsh climate, she felt that "they were not deprived of their essence, as seemed the few lower-class Americans I had seen [in New Mexico]. The faces of *these* were often depraved and dead; it did not seem to agree with them to live in this wide state" (1987:34).

To her credit, Luhan, along with others of her network, was sincerely trying to combat more blatant expressions of racism and to promote respect for differences that many deemed marks of inferiority. In a 1949 article in *The New Yorker*, Edmund Wilson revealed a similar combination of anti-racism, elitism, and a belief in the lost Eden of the "primitive" in describing a visit to Zuni. At first, Wilson writes, he was bemused to hear that Zunis "continue to believe that their village was exactly at the center of the world" (1949:81). But after admiring the pageantry of the Shalako ceremony, Wilson came away with greater respect for the Zuni and expressed horror at the sight of his fellow travelers on the returning train, depicting them as representatives of all that might be wrong with the nation's historical trajectory: "From the moment that the whites of the American West have not had to be hard and alert under pressure of rugged conditions, they have been turning soft, fat, and blank to a degree that is disgusting and dismaying. What do these puffy-faced dough bags do? . . . If the Zuñis are human beings, these must be something else" (80).

The tendency to leap from racism and ethnocentrism to romanticism has been well documented (e.g., Said 1978). What has been less well documented is the way that romanticism of one kind of "otherness"—such as we see in Wilson's reverence for Shalako—can serve to legitimate other prejudices and reflect anxieties about other kinds of difference. The "ugliness" of commodity-dependent "masses" is the implicit threat looming on the horizon in the discourse of Indian arts patrons in the 1920s and 1930s, as well as much other discourse of the period concerning "culture." In the Indian art market the threat came primarily from tourists, who were seen as degrading Indian art because of their low standards, acceptance of misleading stereotypes of Indians, and desire for cheap souvenirs. Tourism, however, was just part of a larger transformation. There were also concerns, though less powerful among art patrons, that Indians themselves might be drawn into ranks of "the masses," particularly as they increasingly produced handmade wares for sale and purchased mass-produced goods for their own use. When Elizabeth Sergeant wrote in the *New Republic* in support of Indian religious freedom, she employed the threat of "mass culture" to inspire Americans to appreciate Indian religious differences; when the government-suppressed Indian dances were finally eradicated, she warned, "Then will every Indian purely prefer . . . the movies to the Deer Dance," resulting in "Death to [America's] Golden Age" (1923:357).

Misgivings about consumer capitalism were not, of course, limited to those concerned with preserving some sort of unchanged "primitive" authenticity and were expressed by many of remarkably diverse political persuasions. In 1935 a writer for the communist *New Masses* argued the importance of encouraging "a healthy and progressive culture to take root in the masses of people" and railed against "the manufacturer" who "is interested primarily in profits, not in elevating the level of public taste and standards of design" (Alexander 1935:21). It was also at this time that scholars of the Frankfurt School and other critics were beginning to debate the ideological and aesthetic implications of "mass culture," debates which continue into the present.[29] In a classic essay, typical of the contradictions embraced by popular concerns with "culture," Clement Greenberg, the modernist art critic, pondered how "a painting by Braque and a *Saturday Evening Post* cover" could be "part of the same culture" (Greenberg 1957:98) and warned that kitsch ("ersatz culture") was taking over everywhere: "It has gone on a triumphal tour of the world, crowding out and defacing native cultures in one colonial country after another" (103). Similarly, Stuart Chase, who admitted frankly that, comparing them with Indians, he did "not like white Mexicans so well, not the cities they live in, nor their taste in interior decoration" (1931:304), concluded his comparison of Mexico and the United States by stating that his "gravest misgivings" in regard to the Mexican future concerned the appeal of commodities mass-produced in the United States. "Will the machine roll Latin America flat, trampling down the last vestige of authentic American culture?" Chase asked (306). Concluding his chapter of "Advice from a Parvenu Cousin," Chase outlined what he felt was Mexico's "chief menace from the machine age" and, more specifically, from "the Yankee invasion." His primary concern, he explained—in the typically 1930s fashion of manically listing proliferating things—was that of "cultural penetration in the form of American sports, radios, jazz, words, habits, subdivisions, billboards, Rotary clubs, plus-fours, Arrow collars . . ." (315).[30]

Such misgivings are partly an example of cosmopolitans wanting to preserve the differences which make cosmopolitanism possible (as Hannerz notes, "there can be no cosmopolitans without locals" [1990:250]). But what is perhaps stronger in this discourse than the desire to preserve difference is an apocalyptic sense that difference is getting *out of control*— particularly out from under the control of elites (including anthropologists). Critics like Stuart Chase confronted the rapidly expanding range of goods available for purchase—such as the "100,000 items, and 36,000 different kinds of things" offered by the Sears Roebuck mail-order catalog (1929:276)—and questioned whether the problem of modernity was really one of "standardization." Similarly, those who sought to express distinctive national and regional character were hindered by their less geographically concerned neighbors who were apt to erect, as Mary Austin put it, "any imaginable style of architecture except one native to the soil" (1933:122). Travelers to remote parts, once exceptional, were being joined by tourists— as in Chase's warning that Mexico would soon be visited by "clouds of Buicks, swarms of Dodges, shoals of Chevrolets" (1931:187)—hordes uninformed about, even uninterested in, standards of authenticity and tastefulness as constructed either by anthropologists or art patrons. But even if consumers could not, or would not, abide by elite standards of value, many would increasingly honor both "art" and "ethnology" as respectable fields of knowledge—and as not necessarily oppositional, but as compatible categories of distinction.

CHAPTER FIVE **CULTURE AND VALUE**
AT INDIAN MARKET

Consumption is . . . a stage in the process of communication, that is, an act of deciphering, decoding, which presupposes practical or explicit mastery of a code. In a sense, one can say that the capacity to see (*voir*) is a function of the knowledge (*savoir*), or concepts, that is, the words, that are available to name visible things, and which are, as it were, programmes for perception. A work of art has meaning and interest only for someone who possesses the cultural competence, that is, the code, into which it is encoded.

Pierre Bourdieu, Distinction: A Social Critique of the Judgement of Taste

 Neva Goodwin writes that "a salient characteristic of a consumer society is that it is one in which a principal focus of leisure or nonwork time is the spending of money" (1997:xxx). Shopping in the United States has been reported to rank second only to watching television as a leisure pursuit (Lury 1996:29). Though shopping can involve as much labor as leisure, increasingly it is seen as a pleasurable activity, considered in contrast to "work." The popularity of shopping helps to account for the enormous expansion, in recent years, of Santa Fe Indian Market.

In the past decade the two-day event has swelled to include more than a thousand artists per year, occupying more than six hundred booths around the city's central plaza. For many artists, whose work and Indian identities are approved by the Southwestern Association on Indian Arts (SWAIA), Indian Market has served as the foundation of their careers. Many artists claim to save their very best pieces for "Market," the term used by long-standing participants, many of whom remember attending the event as children, year after year. Many earn a substantial portion of their annual income there and speak of Indian Market weekend as the culmination of a year's work. A few particularly favored artists are reported to sell out and pack up by early afternoon; but although many report not having slept much in the days or even weeks before, by far the majority plan on two long days of sitting beside their work, greeting customers, both new and familiar, handing out business cards, processing credit cards, wrapping purchases, and visiting with dealers, gallery owners, museum curators, and fellow artists. Local business owners, including dealers of Indian art as well as hotel and restaurant owners, commonly credit this one weekend in August with keeping them in business the rest of the year. Given the occasion's financial significance, it is not surprising to hear Santa Feans gauge the size of crowds relative to previous years the way financial analysts might review the stock market.

Among the tens of thousands of potential buyers, some line up at artists' booths before dawn, if not the middle of the night, in the hope of acquiring the most sought-after pieces, often those that have won awards. Many attempt to select purchases the evening before, when awards are announced and SWAIA members are permitted an exclusive preview of the fifteen hundred or so pieces submitted for judging. Other buyers have eyed pieces while working as volunteers, receiving and returning work to artists, and recording the decisions of judges. Though some are local residents, many more come from distant parts: California, the Midwest, Texas; in some cases, other countries. I have met buyers who have flown in from Germany and Australia. Some have arrived with carefully planned lists of purchases (listed by tribe or pueblo, style, or individual artist) either on paper or in their heads. If buyers are successful in getting what they want, they may leave by mid-morning and celebrate over brunch. But many area residents come not necessarily planning to purchase anything at all; they come to people-watch, perhaps catch a glimpse of the occasional movie star, look at the exhibited works, spot trends, talk to the artists.

It is true that many Santa Feans wouldn't even think of attending what some like to call "Indian Markup"—out of a general lack of interest or disapproval of what it represents to them, most notably "out-of-control" commercialism, conspicuous consumption, exclusivity, and hype.[1] But for those seriously interested in contemporary Southwestern Indian art, it's an important occasion. As Santo Domingo potter and Indian Market award winner Robert Tenorio informed me on more than one occasion, there are a lot of Indian art fairs, but Indian Market is "the Cadillac" of them all. The atmosphere is especially festive early on Saturday morning (figures 7, 8), an

Figures 7, 8 Indian Market patrons in 1995, photographed by Corey McGillicuddy. Reprinted with permission of the photographer.

atmosphere aided by the sight of customers decked out in purchases from previous years (lots of silver, jingling concha belts, necklaces of coral, turquoise, and shell) or just the sort of things wealthy people in Santa Fe might wear to summer parties or the opera. It is an event long anticipated and it arrives with a bustle of activity and excitement; especially in a "good year," it feels like a celebration of abundance—an abundance of money, goods, people.

Not all visitors are equally impressed. For example, the last time I attended Indian Market, in 1998, I spoke to a man who had just moved to Santa Fe from Los Angeles (the crime and the traffic, he said, had become unbearable) and was attending the event for the first time. "A lot of this just looks like junk," he remarked, with a wave down the Plaza. "Stuff you could see in Cleveland." I had the impression that he assumed that most of the surrounding crowd would not agree with him, but in fact, many of the event's most enthusiastic supporters and many of the artists would concur. The pleasures of Indian Market shopping are to some extent an acquired taste.

I learned something important about the way in which some people acquire an appreciation for Indian Market in 1990, the second year I attended, when I shared a house with two visitors who went to the event for the first time and also came away disappointed. An English architect and a Lithuanian mural restorationist, both in their twenties, they had been eager to attend. But when I saw them later in the day, they expressed frustration. They had expected more opportunities, they explained, for the artists to "share their culture." They were dismayed to witness instead what appeared to them to be a mass shopping spree and they were shocked by the amount of money changing hands, the emphasis on objects for sale. Most of all, they found the vast array of items bewildering: "We had no idea what we were looking at," the restorationist explained; "Everything looked the same to us." Of course, there is a very long history of non-Indians presuming that Indians, of all people, should be above or beyond matters of money and materialism. There is also a long history of imagining that art, of any kind, is sullied by any close association with commerce. I presumed that such expectations and desires accounted for my friends' reaction.

By that evening, however, my acquaintances had undergone a remarkable change of perspective, one that impressed upon me the complexity of consumers' perceptions of value and their relationships to particular markets. Returning from an exhibition of contemporary and ancient Pueblo pottery, titled "From This Earth," at the Museum of Indian Art and Culture, they said how eager they were to return to Indian Market, where they felt sure they would have so much better a sense of "what [they] were seeing." At the museum, the architect said, they had acquired an appreciation for how Pueblo pottery was made; they could attempt to distinguish the styles associated with the various pueblos; they could tell the difference between seed pots and storage jars; they would enjoy looking for "fire clouds" and the resemblance to pots they had seen in the museum that were two thousand years old. Perhaps they were even willing to assume that in time silverwork, textiles, or basketry might offer the same sorts of pleasures. While it is true that there were ways in which the exhibition they saw attempted to counteract popular stereotypes about Indians and Indian art, it did not seem to me that such efforts were responsible for my housemates' change of heart. What seemed more important was that the exhibition allowed them to acquire knowledge, vocabulary, and skills of discrimination, legitimated by the museum, that they could then continue to exercise in a way that provided pleasure, pleasure that stood in marked contrast to the bewilderment inspired by not "knowing" what you are looking at.

The museum exhibition also allowed these visitors to perceive a new legitimacy in shopping, an activity which their initial impressions of Indian Market as a "mass shopping spree" suggested they had held in low regard. Whether in time these two would become serious buyers of Indian art I did not find out, but it seemed to me that they had begun to acquire a taste for a certain kind of game, one that many people play while shopping.

There is much going on at Indian Market that exhibits the characteristics of contemporary primitivism—recent manifestations of the expectation, common among the middle and upper classes throughout much of the last hundred years or so, that societies and things considered "primitive" can provide members of the supposedly more "advanced" societies an antidote for modern anxieties. The antidote includes a sense of wholeness, authenticity, purity, and harmony with nature.[2] To reduce the popularity of Indian Market to primitivist ideology would, however, obscure important connections with other forms of shopping and commodity consumption, as well as more general processes of value construction at work in a society in which many people see consuming activities as a form of amusement, a means of constructing identities, and an opportunity to acquire and exercise knowledge and a sense of personal control and competence. In a competitive, capitalist, and consumer-oriented economy, people are encouraged to devote themselves to self-actualization, "to be all they can be," and to gain a sense of progress from acquiring goods and learning about them (Belk 1995, Brown 1998:51, Lears 1981, 1983). As Mike Featherstone has pointed out, many consumers are motivated by a "desire to be continuously learning and enriching oneself, to pursue ever new values and vocabularies" (1991:48). Like other "hobbies," studying and collecting art can serve as a form of "productive leisure" (Gelber 1999:11).

At the turn of the century Thorstein Veblen mocked such endeavors as a ploy to gain status among the men of the nouveaux riches. The respectability of a "gentleman of leisure" required that a man "discriminate with some nicety between the noble and ignoble in consumable goods" (1899 [1994]:74). Pursuits unconnected to financial gain or practical necessity were the most admirable, inspiring the study of "quasi-scholarly or quasi-artistic accomplishments" and "knowledge of the dead languages and the occult sciences; of correct spelling . . . of the latest proprieties of dress, furniture, and equipage; of games, sports, and fancy-bred animals, such as dogs and race-horses" (45). But the less powerful and privileged also traffic in consumerist categories and values: a study of Generation-x'ers, for example, found that devotion to the specialized vocabularies associated with consumer goods was not reserved for those with university degrees or elevated socioeconomic status (Lury 1996:222). Class, however, influences not just what sort of things people are able to buy, but also what sorts of knowledge and goods seem legitimate to people.

Although in the course of writing this book I have thought much about other people buying Indian art, I myself have very little experience of buying it, nor do I have much experience of buying any other kind of art. It is as a "plant nerd" that I have the most personal familiarity with the sorts of desires and pleasures, for me very private ones, associated with learning "new values and vocabularies" associated with consumption. When I was twenty-three I wondered why in the world, other than to display some kind of superiority, anyone other than a botanist would want to know the Latin names of plants. I am now—to my own surprise—well familiar with the perverse pleasures of plant consumer trivia, pleasures gained from distinguishing, for example, between tiarella and heuchera. At plant nurseries I have even found myself delighted at my ability to recognize the mislabeling of species: *why, that's not monarda, it's veronica* . . . I relish knowing common names too: that monarda is also bee balm, that ajuga is bugleweed. Such categories may seem far removed from Indian art and Indian Market, but other consumers find similar pleasures in recognizing a piece as "Navajo folk art" or "Santa Clara style" pottery or recognizing the work of an individual artist or a particular period of an artist's career.[3]

Much of the knowledge deployed at Indian Market, and other events like it, is reminiscent of that deployed by early twentieth-century anthropology: works can be considered in relation to groups of people ("cultures") and to particular periods. But there is also much attention to individual artists, their careers and reputations. Just as the 1931 Exposition of Indian Tribal Arts (EITA) merged the discourse of art with anthropology, the aesthetic with the ethnographic, Indian Market allows for a similar merging of vocabularies and sensibilities. Drawing on one or both of these realms, consumers make distinctions among artists and objects, including distinctions of value, and they take pleasure in the sense that they "know" what they are looking at.

This chapter surveys something of the contemporary legacy of one institution established by the art patron-philanthropists discussed in the previous chapters. It considers how Indian Market and its sponsoring organization have begun to depart, in some ways but not others, from the more colonial mentalities and practices followed by earlier patrons, while continuing to bring economic rewards to many artists and local businesses. Indian Market provides such opportunities in large part by staging a "tournament of value," a type of periodic event which Arjun Appadurai has defined as one "removed in some culturally well-defined way from the routines of economic life" (1986:21). The tournament aspect, most noticeable in the awarding of prizes, but evident also in the race to purchase favored items, adds drama and spectacle. The outdoor setting around Santa Fe's central plaza encourages a carnival atmosphere, but in the shadow of more sobering museums and art galleries. Thus are potential buyers encouraged at once to spend with abandon (Alfonso Ortiz used to tell me gleefully, "it is a feeding frenzy, as among sharks!") yet also to exercise socially sanctioned, valued and valuable knowledge and taste. Such an event is possible only with the careful creation and maintenance of boundaries—around the event, the objects, the artists. Such boundaries, increasingly contested by artists and patrons alike, encourage a certain degree of confidence about the value of objects and their classification, while also serving as a sort of obstacle course for potential consumers to exercise acquired skills in discrimination. Objects and artists are valued more highly for their positioning within these boundaries in an event that itself, over the years, has gained prestige and value.

From "Indian Fairs" to "Indian Market Week"

Historically, of course, market and place are tightly interwoven. At its origins, a market was both a literal place and a symbolic threshold . . .
—Sharon Zukin, *Landscapes of Power*

Consumers like stability in categories of events as well as of objects. The identity of Indian Market is itself constructed to satisfy this desire. For the last twenty years or so, program guides and press releases have referred to Indian Market with the phrase "since 1922," or with a number in front of the name of the event: it was not just "Indian Market" in 1997, for example, but "the 76th." Such designations suggest, generally without any intention of deceit, that the same event has been occurring year after year. Yet prior to the 1950s there was no such stable identity; the predecessors of the contemporary institution appear in the records of the sponsoring organization to have been more a series of experiments, initiatives, or projects, rather than an institution. As discussed in the two previous chapters, in the 1920s and early 1930s the New Mexico Association on Indian Affairs (NMAIA) and the Southwest Indian Fair Committee sponsored what they called "Indian Fairs," first on an annual basis in Santa Fe, then periodically in nearby pueblos.

In 1936 local patronage of Indian art reached a new peak when Maria Chabot organized weekly "Indian markets" around the Plaza. This seems to have been the first time that such events were termed "markets," but newspapers, archived meeting minutes, and other documents reveal no mention of a singular event with a capital "M." To the wealthy, middle-aged group of patrons and art dealers then heading the NMAIA, Chabot brought a youthful enthusiasm as well as more ambitious plans inspired by a slightly different sort of nostalgia and concern than that motivating the older and wealthier Santa Fe patrons. Whereas the older patrons were perhaps most concerned with the reproduction of certain objects, Chabot displayed more interest in reproducing a kind of *event* and, even more ambitiously, a kind of society. In 1990 Chabot recalled that after living in and near Mexico City, her intention was to create markets "similar to the ones in Old Mexico . . . I wanted it in the public plaza as it would be in any Mexican town."[4] The Association's minutes from 11 June 1936 confirm her recollection. During a period when Chabot was being paid $100 per month to promote Indian art (her salary furnished by Elizabeth White), the minutes recorded her rationale: "Miss Chabot said the market plan had come to her after seeing the markets held in all the little villages in old Mexico on their fiesta days. She said she would like to see an Indian market developed here along the lines of the Mexican markets. She suggested that the Indians be encouraged to come in by offering prizes and that once they got in to town they would undoubtedly sell their pottery. She suggested that Santa Fe should be publicized as a place where there was an open air market where Indian goods could be bought" (SWAIAC, SRCA).

Chabot, not at the time in a position to purchase artwork herself, appears to have been inspired by a vision of a world where markets gave towns distinct identities and brought people from diverse communities together. Though able to relate to her sponsors' more elitist concerns, she seems to have celebrated the boundary-crossing potential of the marketplace. Her plan meshed well with the older patrons' longstanding interests in improving economic conditions in Indian communities, while influencing the work of artists and the tastes of potential buyers. After discussion about whether the local traders would tolerate the potential for competition (according to the minutes, it was agreed that they would, though perhaps with some reservation), the plan was approved; about a month later, the first market was held, with succeeding markets taking place on the following eight Saturdays. Over fifty years later, Maria Chabot recalled that in fact local traders had been more resistant to her idea than the Association minutes reveal. She reported that her success in initiating the event was achieved only after recruiting some of the more "liberal" traders and business owners, men who were, like herself, she recalled, "willing and anxious to help the poor Indian if we could."[5] Chabot remembered that Pueblo potters were especially enthusiastic participants. She mentioned that Maria Martinez of San Ildefonso, who by then had acquired a significant national reputation, "saw great possibility" in the new forum and at the end of the summer told Chabot that as a result of the markets, "'We have made enough money to put in eight houses with running water and bathrooms.'" Chabot provided transportation to and from the city and at noon would take potters into the Laboratory of Anthropology, where they would inspect the collections, pointing out pots they or their relatives had made (this practice of encouraging potters to study the museum's collections dated at least to the early 1920s, when it was started by museum curator Kenneth Chapman and anthropologist Edgar Hewett). Over the next several years, the Association continued to host the weekly markets on summer Saturdays, culminating in a large market held in conjunction with the end-of-summer Fiesta, then the city's biggest event of the year.

By the early 1940s it seems that Pueblo artists had begun to count on the weekly markets, with their monetary awards for prize-winning pieces and opportunities for direct sales to collectors and tourists, rather than relying on traders (Indian art "dealers," in Santa Fe, emerged only in the 1970s [Bernstein 1999:63]). But the Association, headed by Margretta Dietrich, became more preoccupied with providing support for Indian soldiers than with art (members were sending care packages—containing piñon nuts, photos of pueblo plazas, and other such items—to soldiers overseas and were operating a "social club" for the benefit of Indians working in Santa Fe). Consequently, members reluctantly ended their sponsorship of the weekly events. If the Association was not to "lose the good will of the Indians," Dietrich wrote in 1942, they would need to convince them of the urgency of the war effort (SWAIAC, SRCA). Whether or not the artists were convinced, the weekly markets, with their prizes and minimal fanfare, came to an end. Archaeologist Marge Lambert, who began judging at fairs and markets in the 1930s, told me that she remembered prices of Indian art falling during the wartime years. Artists continued to travel regularly to the city plaza to sell their work, but the annual market at Fiesta was the only event in the area with judges, prizes, and significant crowds.

In 1971 Indian Market was established as an annual event separate from Fiesta, which since its inception had centered on a celebration of the city's colonial Hispanic heritage. In fact, officially Fiesta was intended to commemorate the Spanish reconquest following the Pueblo rebellion in 1680, hence it was a particularly odd venue for a celebration of Indian art— though I never had the sense that many local people who participated then, Indian or non-Indian, recognized any particular incongruity. For art patrons, Fiesta was a means of celebrating and consuming "local color," and they gave little thought to the political implications of the event. For Indian artists, Fiesta was primarily a way to sell art and generally a very effective way of doing that, given the crowds. Eventually, both patrons and artists were confident of drawing large crowds for Indian art alone (or, at least, Indian art with dances and other displays).

By the time Indian Market became a wholly separate institution, Dietrich and the other early patrons had died, and the sponsoring organization had changed its name to the Southwestern Association on Indian Affairs (SWAIA). Though the "Affairs" part of the name would not change to "Arts" until 1993, by the late 1970s the organization had become almost exclusively focused on art, ending a period, beginning after the end of World War II, of active concern with legislation, land rights, education, economic conditions, and support for projects such as the return of Blue Lake to Taos Pueblo. When Margretta Dietrich wrote to her Bryn Mawr alumnae magazine in the 1950s, she discussed at length the Association's attempts to protect Indian land rights, mentioning only briefly at the very end that she could show her classmates "a colorful Indian Market where we award prizes for the best in arts and crafts" (Bryn Mawr College Archives, Alumnae Association files).

Some people who were members at that time told me that they felt the shift in the 1970s toward a more specific focus on art resulted from a recognition that an organization composed then almost entirely of non-Indians should leave politics and matters of social policy to Indian leaders. In other words, the organization was moving away from the colonialist paternalism taken for granted by the earlier generation that included Margretta Dietrich and the Whites. But the organization was also becoming more heavily dominated by dealer-collectors (including more men than in previous years). The shift toward an exclusive concern with art reflected a general trend toward greater specialization and compartmentalization of patrons' interests and expertise. Especially after what many described as a boom in the Indian art market in the early 1970s (Bernstein 1993, 1999), Indian art seemed a large enough concern for one organization and many individuals.

In contrast to the earlier periods, from the early 1970s through the 1990s a greater number of the organization's most active members lived and breathed Indian art (particularly Pueblo pottery) in a way that would have seemed somewhat foreign to the earlier patron-philanthropists such as White, Dietrich, or Chabot. Such earlier patrons referred to people "collecting" Indian art, a phenomenon they very much sought to encourage, but they did not define themselves primarily as "collectors." From the 1970s to the early 1990s, people who were more comfortable with being identified as collectors took on especially powerful roles in running the organization.

Since the middle of the century, then, Indian art collecting has expanded in some ways and narrowed in others. There are, on the side of expansion, many more people and institutions involved in collecting and involved, centrally or peripherally, in the market in which Indian art is valued and sold. In the 1920s and even later, the Indian art world had been one into which well-placed newcomers such as White and Dietrich could enter and very quickly establish expertise, authority, and significant public influence. Of course, compared to other art markets in the late twentieth century, such as that in Impressionist painting, the American Indian art market must still seem a small pond of small fish, one less intimidating to newcomers and more open to their influence. Now, however, private collectors of Indian art are more numerous and are joined by many more professionals—curators, arts organization administrators, scholars, as well as art dealers. Moreover, prospective buyers or collectors, while I sense that they still often perceive their tastes as especially progressive, rarely imagine their actions bringing about major changes in popular tastes.

For many early twentieth-century collectors, Indian art collecting was perhaps also more directly linked to wider social and political concerns, including those of the Bryn Mawrters described in chapters 2 and 3. In discussions with collectors, mostly conducted in the early 1990s, I found that patrons who had been involved with SWAIA (whether as board members, donors, volunteers, or in Indian Market judging) were not unsympathetic to such concerns, but they did not see their art collecting as intimately linked to them, nor were they likely to consider themselves to have the expertise to tackle matters not directly related to art. Some of these later collectors indicated that they shared earlier patrons' belief that the art market offered opportunities to aid Indian communities economically and culturally. I often heard for example, the assertion that art production is one way for many Pueblo people to make a living in rural communities and continue to participate in religious life. A few Pueblo artists, and artists from other regions as well, corroborated this assertion with stories of how their artwork allowed them to give up office jobs that they had found more constraining and less satisfying and did indeed allow for more participation in religious events. (On the other hand, I encountered Pueblo artists who had either left traditional communities or were tempted to do so, in part to escape rivalry with other artists—a phenomenon well known to the more experienced collectors.) In my discussions with patrons and collectors involved in Market from the 1970s on, although I heard their approval of the economic opportunities it offered artists, none of them cited economic opportunity for Indians as any sort of motivation for their collecting or their involvement in Indian Market. Instead, with some exceptions, they tended to emphasize the role the Association might play in promoting and encouraging what they considered to be high-quality Indian art—suggesting that art was the raison d'etre of the organization, and Indian Market its primary event. Some also expressed a sense of personal obligation to the artists who depended on Market for sales, contacts, awards, and publicity.

In contrast to the city-of-ladies art patrons of the 1930s, contemporary collectors struck me as much more strongly divided in their tastes. In interviews with Maria Chabot, Marge Lambert, and others concerning Indian art collectors active in the 1920s and 1930s, I found that differences in taste were always minimized. Chabot, for example, in November 1990 insisted that "on art they could agree. There was never any question of taste, never any controversy, that I ever knew . . . We were united against the Maisels of the world. And you had to be. They were out to make a buck—and they didn't care how they did it!" (Maisel was one of the most prominent Indian art traders in Albuquerque, involved in the mass production of silver and turquoise jewelry for the tourist trade.) Rather than assuming that differences among Santa Fe patrons really did not exist (the archives give a more complicated picture), I took Chabot's statement as an indication of a strong sense of a community more conscious of a unity in its tastes and beliefs than of the differences that existed. Earlier patrons' sense of cohesion was enabled by their very clear opposition to people considered to pose problems for Indian art—those thought to lack good taste or those perceived as too directly connected to the world of commerce—and their confidence in their ability to exert and maintain authority.

Moments of solidarity are to be found among more recent patrons, but they are a much larger, more diverse, and fluid group than the earlier Santa

Fe patrons, and I was struck much more often by a sense of rivalry than of solidarity. Of course, rivalry and solidarity are not mutually exclusive (consider, as discussed in chapter 2, Sergeant's depiction of her simultaneous rivalry and bonding with Willa Cather as they traded images of people and places). But, at least to me, more influential collectors seemed to emphasize individual inclinations rather than collective ones, often emphasizing their support for particular artists over those supported by others. I did, however, encounter quite a number of married couples who seemed to use shopping for Indian art as a way of expressing and developing their relationships (a phenomenon Miller describes among couples shopping for more everyday goods in North London [1998]). Apart from couples, I rarely heard collectors refer to themselves in the first person plural as was fairly common among their predecessors.

It is likely that very few collectors now feel the sense of power and control that those sponsoring the early Indian Fairs or the Exposition of Indian Tribal Arts felt. As Indians have moved into positions as judges and curators and the art market has diversified and expanded, collectors are not likely to express the sort of ambition about influencing other buyers and large numbers of artists that patrons commonly expressed in the early and mid-twentieth century. Serious collectors do often feel that they "vote" with their purchases and influence artists they like by buying their work, sometimes assisting their careers in various ways. One patron I met made numerous attempts to help a favorite artist with his career, at times providing him with space to work. But such actions were typically represented to me as individual matters, rather than any sort of movement or collective endeavor.

Analysts of consumption have sometimes described shopping and the acquisition of personal possessions as an ultimately unsatisfying, frustrating affair. A new purchase, long desired, may unleash a host of new desires as it makes older purchases seem shabby in comparison (McCracken 1988:118–20). Indian art collectors surely experience this phenomenon, but there is no ultimate point from which to judge the effects of the games they play, at least on an individual level. At any rate, for many serious collectors, satisfaction may come less from the acquisition of an object than from a sense of development of self and the ever-increasing acquisition of institutionally sanctioned knowledge used in choosing and acquiring a work of art. As Steven Gelber points out in his study of hobbies, "collectors are not

Figure 9 Early on the first morning of Indian Market, a pair of devoted collectors of the work of Gail Bird and Yazzie Johnson decide on a major purchase. Other patrons and spectators look on and applaud when the decision is made. Photograph taken by author.

merely people who accumulate objects, but those who accumulate them in a particular systematic way that necessitates the development of specialized knowledge" (1999:78). If the pursuit of knowledge is what is important to collectors, even purchases later judged "mistakes" are seen as a step in a learning process.

Present-day collectors often participate in the art market as if they are playing a game, planning strategies and sizing up the competition. It is a game without any definite endpoint (unless, as is sometimes the case, they imagine leaving their collections to museums) and often without a clear demarcation between "winners" and "losers." There are certainly moments when they play those roles. Prize-winning pieces at Indian Market are awarded two ribbons, one for the artist, and another which stays with the piece, perhaps encouraging buyers to feel they are winners themselves. Just as people are said to "win" the pieces they buy at auctions, at Indian Market, at daybreak, collectors compete with one another to purchase art, sometimes currying favor with artists or making deals with one another, along the lines of "I'll give you my spot for that piece, if you give me yours for this other one." A crowd gathering at an artist's booth will sometimes burst into applause when a collector, or a husband-and-wife team, buys a highly coveted and particularly expensive item (figure 9). Congratulations to buyers are not uncommon. How much one pays is one part of the game: in 1998, I encountered an experienced collector (and dealer) who explained that he was trying to decide whether to buy a particular piece right then, or take his chances on returning Sunday afternoon when he might get it for a much lower price.

The successes and failures resulting from such decisions are evaluated moment by moment. Collectors will again and again rethink a significant purchase: Do I still like that piece? Is it more valuable than it was when I bought it? Did the artist become better known? Was that the best piece or the best period of an artist's career? Do people admire it (and me for purchasing it)? Or do I know something about this piece now that I wish I had known back then? Small victories and disappointments are also to be found in interactions with other players. Collectors' participation in a market allows them to interact with other consumers as well as with scholars, museum staff, and artists, with whom they seem to enjoy exchanging information, vocabularies, and evaluations. Any sense of community might come as much from the shared experience of playing the game as from particular alliances and bonds that might be formed through shared tastes.[6]

A number of contemporary patrons admitted to me that they could understand how people might perceive them as obsessed—as they showed me pots or paintings stashed in every corner of their houses, eyes lighting up as they cradled the work of favorite artists and periods, explaining distinguishing characteristics and techniques, often recalling personal friendships or encounters with the artists as well as with other patrons. Despite continuing and often quite enthusiastic patronage of younger artists, many patrons (both collectors and dealers, a group with some overlap) spoke nostalgically of earlier periods of Indian art (even if older might mean only the 1960s or whenever it was they first started collecting) and of what they remembered as a less intensely competitive, more easygoing art world, a sentiment echoed by some of the more successful artists.

A number of patrons now or once involved with swaia have, over a period of three or four decades, amassed collections worth fortunes, in their own assessments as well as those of others. Many of these patrons also collected non-Indian art as well. In Santa Fe a number had at least small collections of Spanish Colonial and contemporary Hispanic New Mexican art; some collected modernist painting and sculpture; one longtime SWAIA member displayed Pueblo pots alongside Chinese vases. Perhaps owing to the interest I displayed, only about their Indian art did collectors emphasize dramatic increases in value, though they often remarked that one should never buy any art in the hope of financial reward.

Despite the dramatic changes, I met patrons involved in Markets as far back as the 1930s who seemed to enjoy attending Indian Market into the 1990s, though many were quick to complain about the changes—in atmosphere, organization, or in the art displayed. Dick Howard, a collector and dealer of Pueblo pottery and former National Park Service employee who served on the board of SWAIA for seventeen years, remarked to me in August 1995 that the present-day event was, in many ways, not "the *real* Indian Market." In November 1990, Richard Spivey, also a pottery dealer and a former president and vice-president of SWAIA, told me that in the 1960s, when he first became involved, "pots had soul, feeling—they came alive and spoke to you." ("Soul" was a word I would often hear in discussions of pottery. It was not quite synonymous with authenticity, sometimes suggesting a contrast with the pursuit of technical perfection.) Maria Chabot told me in December 1990 that she had rarely attended since the 1950s; with a bemused expression, she recalled attending one in the 1980s. "I bought one thing," she said gruffly, pointing to a dried, brightly painted devil's claw plant in the shape of a sea horse. "I thought it showed creativity." Chabot gave the example of the extensive packing and mailing operations, with their cardboard boxes and styrofoam peanuts, set up in side streets to explain her alienation from the event: "I was really dumbfounded." Certainly this was a far cry from those "markets in old Mexico," markets that to a young American woman must have suggested something of a celebration of both diversity and a common community identity attached to a particular place. It is likely that it was the control that a relatively small group of white patrons once wielded that explains much of the nostalgia expressed by older collectors, though the changes in the event and the Indian art market as a whole are complex and involve more than the increasing number of Indian people serving in authoritative positions as organizers, judges, and curators of local museums.

The changes include an expansion of commercial activity and a diversification of markets (in the more abstract sense) piggybacking onto Indian

Market. By the late 1980s Santa Feans were making references to "Indian Market Week," encompassing a wide array of additional activities that had sprung up in the days leading up to the official event, designed to appeal to Indian Market crowds: seminars (usually for a steep fee) at the Wheelwright Museum, the Museum of Indian Arts and Culture, and the School of American Research; auctions of antique and contemporary art held by local nonprofit organizations and museums; booksignings (for books having any connection whatsoever to Indians); gallery openings (until recently, predominately for non-Indian artists); and since 1983, a privately sponsored Antique Ethnographic Art Show, featuring "folk, Spanish Colonial, Oriental, African, and other art" offered for sale by dealers (Quick 1997:A1).

These additional events appeal to an overlapping, but not identical, group of consumers. Many are interested, rather exclusively, in either antique or contemporary art. One collector of antique Southwestern pottery, who made a point of attending auctions and sales of antique Indian art during "Indian Market Week," told me he would never think of attending Indian Market because only pots made prior to the twentieth century had "soul" (that word again). Pots made for sale, rather than local use, were, in his view, inherently uninteresting, but they also lacked the patina of age, and often a thrilling story of discovery and salvage. He was especially fond of an eighteenth-century pot excavated in the nineteenth century from what had been a Hopi dwelling—inside were found remnants of peach pits, he exclaimed, awe in his voice. This man seemed to typify the "primitive art" collectors described by Sally Price (1989) and the collectors of African art described in Christopher Steiner's (1994) study of the international trade in African art. For many such collectors, Indian art is valued as a link to an imagined preindustrial world of self-sustaining communities, communities supposedly with little place for individual creativity or genius; consequently, there are collectors who place great value on the anonymity of antique pieces. Of course, nowadays not all antique pieces are anonymous and there are buyers who find the work of known artists of interest as well (recognition of individual artists allows for more distinctions to be made, more knowledge to be acquired and deployed—an aspect many find particularly satisfying). Some buyers find Indian artwork of any era of interest in part because of its perceived connection to "the past": even work that is quite modern in style can be connected to an "American" and, in many cases, a "Western" past, purely by its classification as "Indian."

Other buyers are especially enthusiastic about the idea of supporting contemporary artists they might meet at Market. Knowing something of the artist as a person and following the development of artists' careers is a large part of the appeal of participating in this form of consumption. For such buyers, Indian Market is by far the most interesting event of "Indian Market Week." Nonetheless, some of these buyers are willing to attend a variety of Indian-art related events, sometimes making little distinction between antique and contemporary art. Hotel owners report that many of their guests book the entire week a year in advance, year after year. Indian Market organizers have told me that they found this "Indian Market Week" phenomenon distressing because it takes away from the significance of Indian Market itself and possibly cuts into Indian Market artists' sales, while many of the business owners who profit have proved reluctant to contribute to SWAIA's operating expenses or to work as Indian Market volunteers.[7]

Communities, Indian and White

The SWAIA board of directors first began including Indians in the 1950s (Bernstein 1996:34), but in the 1970s a handful of Indian artists became more substantially involved.[8] Two of the most influential in the 1980s were Ramona Sakiestewa and Gail Bird. Bird recounted her involvement with SWAIA for me on an October morning in 1991 in her living room, in the remodeled farmhouse alongside the Rio Grande that she shares with her partner, Yazzie Johnson. Bird began her story in the early 1970s when she and Johnson sold jewelry in an Indian art gallery in downtown Santa Fe. Her younger brother, Harold Littlebird, she said, graduated from the Institute of American Indian Arts (IAIA) and sold pottery at Indian Market in 1970. Recalling the Markets of the early 1970s, Bird spoke fondly of their haphazard, friendly quality. Indian art galleries closed for the day back then. "There was a feeling," she said, "that this was the day for the Indians to make money." Rules were lax. "Jewelers sold jewelry made by their Anglo girlfriends. No one really cared." Though it was this more casual affair that had first appealed to her and helped inspire and structure her career, in the 1980s Bird would become an important force in developing a much more orderly, professionally run institution, one where people cared very much indeed about the certifiable identities of both objects and artists.

Working in the downtown gallery, Bird and Johnson were well positioned to learn the intricacies of the Indian art world, becoming acquainted with dealers, museum curators, collectors, and producers as well as a wide variety of Southwestern Indian art. They were well positioned in other ways as well. Though Bird was raised in California, her parents were from Santo Domingo and Laguna Pueblos; Johnson is Navajo and grew up in Utah. They had connections, therefore, to multiple Indian communities but, living in Santa Fe, had many white friends and acquaintances as well; probably unlike the majority of Indian Market artists then or now, they not only worked among non-Indian art collectors, dealers, and fellow artists but also socialized with them and often shared many of the same tastes, in matters of food and movies as well as art (or so I gathered from their reminiscences of living as twenty-somethings in Santa Fe). They were the only Indians in the 1970s, Bird noted, working as salespeople in the downtown galleries. Like many artists and collectors I spoke with, Bird recalled a surge of interest in Indian things, "a fad," at that time, and a corresponding expansion of the Indian art market. Whereas she admired some of the older dealers in town for what she saw as a basic integrity and a tremendous amount of knowledge about Indian art, she spoke sarcastically of the new "hippy traders" appearing then, their ignorance, she noted with a laugh, often no hindrance to financial success.[9]

After Yazzie Johnson began making jewelry and sold a piece for $350 in Gail Bird's brother's booth at Indian Market, the two went to study art at the University of Colorado and came back to form a partnership, Bird specializing in design, Johnson in execution. Like that of many of the more successful artists exhibiting, their work could be seen as innovative but also as linked in some way to Navajo and Pueblo traditions. Bird explained that they chose to work with materials that at the time were considered "not very Indian"—copper and brass, later gold, and stones such as jasper. Their work was well received, and in 1978 Bird was asked to join swaia's board of directors. She explained to me that she decided at the time to decline in spite of the fact that she had many ideas about changes that needed to be made (regarding, for example, the award categories and the handling of items submitted for judging). Not yet thirty at the time, she felt she needed more experience and credibility. Her concern seemed to be more about gaining credibility among other artists (who included some of her relatives) than among patrons. I gathered that for a young Pueblo person to cross over the boundary between Indian artists and white patrons was to invite criticism and suspicion from other artists.[10] The concern about such boundary crossing was something I heard from a few other artists as well, though it has surely not been a universal one, and I believe is much less common now with increasing Indian involvement in Indian Market and events like it (since the early 1990s, board members and Market judges have been more often Indian than not, though donors, volunteers, and buyers remain almost entirely non-Indian). After Bird and Johnson received a fellowship from SWAIA and won some of the top awards, including the highly coveted (and valuable) Best of Show in 1981, Bird was asked to join the board again and did, remaining centrally involved in one capacity or another for the next decade, while also serving on the boards of other Indian arts institutions as well. By 1994 she and Johnson were still exhibiting at Indian Market—a commitment Bird spoke of passionately—but they had had numerous disagreements with SWAIA leadership, and despite much recognition elsewhere they had not been winning awards at Indian Market for some years and would soon stop entering their work for judging.[11]

I met Gail Bird and Ramona Sakiestewa while in the midst of research into the activities of the early network of patrons including Margretta Dietrich, Elizabeth White, and, later, Maria Chabot. As professional artists themselves, Bird and Sakiestewa were perhaps more committed than earlier patrons to using the Association to help artists establish successful careers, in ways that went beyond coordinating opportunities for direct sales to consumers and included attention to helping artists develop their artwork and acquire greater knowledge of how to market their own work successfully. They were also more interested than many early patrons had been (as well as some of their contemporary colleagues) in actively encouraging innovation and creativity, thus moving Indian Market art and artists somewhat further in the direction once promised by the "art, not ethnology" slogan of the 1931 Exposition. But when Sakiestewa and Bird (along with some of their colleagues) spoke about their work with Indian Market, they praised the way the institution was capable of embracing both "traditional" and "contemporary" art and artists, with distinct criteria of evaluation for different kinds of work. They contrasted Indian Market with Spanish Market—the event sponsored by the Spanish Colonial Arts Society—and said that Indian Market's relative strength had been its ability to embrace innovation, without displacing or devaluing art and artists more easily considered "traditional." Sakiestewa and Bird took on the task of bridging two boundaries—that between Indian artists and white patrons, but also one between artists with ties to more "mainstream" artworlds and those more connected to localized systems of aesthetic value and production.

Sakiestewa is a Hopi textile artist, with works in many prominent museums and private collections; her weaving suggests a merging of modern art with Hopi and Navajo traditional weaving. Since she was more actively involved in SWAIA in the 1980s, she has served on boards of numerous museums and arts organizations and in 1996 was appointed to the interior design team of the Smithsonian Institution's National Museum of the American Indian. In our discussions of her work with SWAIA and Indian Market (e.g., in August and September of 1990), Sakiestewa, like Bird, expressed an egalitarian sensibility about art that struck me as a departure from that of earlier SWAIA members. I sometimes had the impression that Sakiestewa and Bird thought of art in a manner I associate especially with the 1960s, though I had seen it as well in Julia Lukas's discussions of her work in the 1930s: not the notion of art as a form of political action, but that of art being a good, positive force in people's lives, something akin to vitamins and fresh air, something of which most people (Indian or not) should have more.[12] Though Sakiestewa expressed reverence for the handmade, the carefully crafted work of individual hands, she was critical of notions that artists, including Indian artists, should be urged to affiliate exclusively with the realm of museums and galleries (or Indian Market), avoiding all connections to mass-produced goods and commerce. In her own work, in addition to continuing to produce handwoven textiles, in 1990 she was just beginning what she described then almost as an anti-elitist venture, designing blankets that would be produced by the Dewey Trading Company and Pendleton Woolen Mills for a price more within reach of "ordinary" people, people who would not normally be able to afford the sort of one-of-a-kind, handwoven pieces that she could sell at Indian Market and in galleries.[13]

Yet in the same discussions Sakiestewa expressed sentiments that Margretta Dietrich would have applauded, including concerns about the difficulty of maintaining standards and the reputation of Indian Market as showcase of exemplary Indian art. Even more adamantly than some of the collectors and dealers I spoke with, Bird and Sakiestewa pointed to exclusivity as the only way for Indian Market to continue to serve some of its primary purposes: to give buyers confidence in the value of Indian art, to help them figure out what to buy and what not to buy, and to encourage artists to produce "high quality" work. In 1994, after expressing disapproval with the direction Indian Market was headed (bigger), Gail Bird told journalist Candelora Versace, "At this point, I feel the market is saturated, repetitive and 90 percent of it is bad. There's no originality, no thought in it." Nonetheless, she affirmed her commitment to exhibiting at the event: "You can talk to the people who buy your work and you can pass on your knowledge" (Versace 1994:7).

Like the collectors I interviewed, Bird and Sakiestewa were quick to distinguish also between people with "a good eye" or "people with good taste" and those without or, more generously, those with a lot left to learn. One afternoon in July 1995 I met with Bird and Johnson in Santa Fe, at a shop that sold gifts and fine coffee. As we walked in, Bird praised the good taste of the proprietor, as evidenced by the sort of things she chose to sell (I had often admired them myself, to the point that I had probably been suspected of shoplifting). Of course, I frequently heard comments about people's "taste" in Santa Fe. It is not something one hears much around universities (unless they are talking about *theories* of it), or in the small town where I now live in the Midwest, and it is always a little startling to me, rather like when I first heard Midwesterners offer me bottles of "pop." "Taste" strikes me similarly as an old-fashioned word. I think that people who don't speak of "taste" often use other words to talk about the same thing; though, as I mentioned in my discussion of the "city of ladies," attending carefully to people's aesthetic sensibilities is something that some people take particular pride in and cultivate. In Santa Fe, whenever I heard appraisals of someone's taste (usually from people professionally employed in the art world), I was reminded of the network of art patrons that had included the White sisters, Margretta Dietrich, and Maria Chabot, people who spoke of "taste" frequently and passionately.

Over our cups of dark roast coffee, I told Bird and Johnson that I'd been shocked by the paternalism of some of the earlier patrons, and that students and colleagues reading my work often responded even more strongly and wanted more of an explanation—or condemnation—than I had offered. I gave, as a particularly egregious example, the case of Kenneth Chapman reporting that the quality of objects at a Cochiti fair had been so poor that he gave reprimands instead of prizes (LA, KCC, file KC0.030). This was a tale that had made audiences gasp at anthropology and American Studies conferences (it had made me gasp too, when I first came across it in records at the Laboratory of Anthropology). After a short silence Bird said that in fact she could understand Chapman's frustration. She went on to recount an occasion when she had been in the position of judging jewelry at an Indian art fair smaller than Indian Market, and had not been able to find anything that she felt warranted an award. She had settled, uncomfortably, for awarding a ribbon with a note attached with suggestions for future improvement—not quite a "reprimand," she acknowledged, but probably reflecting similar intentions. This, I knew, was not the sort of answer that would satisfy my audiences.

I explained that in part what seemed so disturbing to people about the Chapman example and, in fact, so much of the early history of Indian arts patronage in the area, was that it was Anglo people who were relative newcomers and outsiders who were doing the judging, telling Indian artists what they should be doing, when the artists were surely the experts. Someone like Chapman, a curator for the Indian Arts Fund and the Museum of New Mexico, as well as a serious scholar of Pueblo pottery, was probably far more knowledgeable than most judges at such fairs, but my audiences, I gathered, almost entirely non-Indian themselves, felt that art should be assessed by members of the communities in which it is made. Chapman was obviously not a member of the community of Cochiti. Bird, clearly not unfamiliar with this line of thought, commented that, as a judge, she would *not* be speaking for an entire community. Although she said she is often expected at museums to represent the people of Santo Domingo, that is something she cannot do: "I can only speak for myself," she stated, noting that she wouldn't want anyone speaking for her. Yazzie Johnson added, with some frustration I sensed, that while he was glad to see the very recent development of Indian people becoming judges at exhibitions such as Indian Market, and becoming curators and art scholars, it seemed a very naive notion that judgment of quality should be left exclusively to the artists or that only Indians should judge the quality of Indian art. It's white people who buy it, he pointed out (echoing Dick Howard, one of the more controversial Indian Market judges, who had told me earlier that day that "buying too is a form of judging").

Bird and Johnson are in fact among the very few Indian artists I have seen actually buying anything from other artists. "We don't have one of these," they said as they purchased one of the styles for which a family of potters had become known.[14] Their house is filled with an eclectic variety of artwork, pieces I inferred they value for many different reasons: craftsmanship, creativity, tradition, a sense of humor, affection for the artist, because something was a gift from a friend, or because they identified it with Northern New Mexico. In their kitchen in 1990 I was surprised to recognize an old photograph of Tsianina Blackstone, the opera singer and "Cherokee Indian princess" whom anthropologist Edgar Hewett had engaged as the star performer at one of the first Fiestas in the 1920s. Bird said she hadn't known who Blackstone was, that she'd found it years ago at a yard sale and thought it was funny.

In 1998, the night before the opening of Indian Market, one of Santa Fe's most prestigious galleries, still unusual for its display of both Indian and non-Indian contemporary art, held an opening reception for a group of Indian artists, including Yazzie Johnson, Gail Bird, and Ramona Sakiestewa. Johnson and Bird would be on the Plaza the next day at daybreak, and by early afternoon most of their pieces at both the gallery and in their booth would all have been sold. During a break in the flow of greetings from familiar collectors, Johnson and I discussed the huge growth in Market, evident even since my first visit. When he remarked that he wouldn't want to be a young artist just starting out, I had the impression he felt extraordinarily fortunate. For Sakiestewa, just back from Washington and on her way to take her son to college, it was the first year in over two decades that she would not be exhibiting on the Plaza. She had enough without Market to keep her more than busy, and she was enthusiastic about her work with the Smithsonian and her new experiments in weaving and lithography. She laughed when I asked her about the claim made by the then-head of SWAIA to be the first Indian leader of SWAIA; yes, she had been the first, she said, and had made a point of telling him so, but added that she couldn't claim to have been "CEO" since they didn't have any such title back then.

Though there are artists who exhibit at Indian Market and achieve rapid success, there are also many who experience little success at all. There are also many who fail, year after year, just in getting their work accepted for exhibition, some never managing to get past the gatekeepers (once a committee of SWAIA volunteers, now SWAIA staff members). Indian Market's popularity and the success of at least some of the participating artists depends on the establishment and maintenance of a boundary, however contested, between legitimate and illegitimate art, between art and "souvenirs" or "trash."

The event's success also depends on maintaining boundaries between Indian and non-Indian people and Indian and non-Indian art. Indian Market authenticates artists and their work as "Indian." Artists' identities and the communities to which they belong are far more complex than the neat boundary constructed in the marketplace (a fact not at all unknown to serious collectors who require institutional "authentication" of the identities of artists and objects but may be quite untroubled by the knowledge that these identities could be constructed quite differently than they are). Artists belong to multiple communities that are not homogeneous in any respect. Taste, moreover—whether in art, food, or language—forms its own communities. Taste separates people from one another, but also unites them, sometimes even across the shifting boundaries of race, class, and region.

Judging Value

In our discussion of reactions to Kenneth Chapman's judging, Johnson remarked that just because judges are Indian doesn't mean they are even from the same community as the artists, and if they are from the same community, that doesn't mean they'll be a good judge of art from that community; in fact, they might be partial to the work of family members or even under pressure to reward their relatives' work.[15] Several other artists I spoke with were quick to recount stories of such judging. In one case, one of the judges so accused claimed with complete sincerity, it seemed to me, that it was just "objectively" true that the best work had been produced by relatives and, if anything, their relationship had encouraged a more critical rather than more generous examination.

One might wonder in response, do people involved in such activities assume that there is such a thing as "objective" judging? Yes and no. Some people I spoke with in the early 1990s suggested that indeed they did think one should and could judge objectively, and they were able to offer specific criteria of evaluation ("specific" in their view, though others might see the same criteria as enormously vague). Many agreed that while judging as a whole might be a subjective process, there were certain aspects of particular pieces, depending on the category, that could be assessed without bias. One Indian artist and judge felt that because other criteria were too "mushy" and "subjective" (subjectivity seeming to disturb her a good deal), the emphasis should be on technical matters—for example, how difficult a piece of art had been to produce, how labor-intensive or time-consuming the process might have been. A white friend who had judged at Indian Market on several occasions reiterated this view, explaining that she hated judging with people who tended to judge on the basis of what they *liked* and that she had most respect for those who could articulate exactly what was good or bad about a piece ("this piece has a bubble in it, that painting is not so precise," she offered as examples of greater clarity). In these discussions, I would often hear calls for greater objectivity or an explicit set of standards (beyond the basic rules about permissible materials and techniques provided by SWAIA). Greater codification of standards would be impossible for any group of artists, collectors, or dealers to agree upon fully, for any length of time. Hence the discussion would often conclude with a statement about how all evaluation of art is subjective, along the lines of the one-man's-meat-is-another's-poison, and there's-no-accounting-for-taste ideas (the sort of ideas that Barbara Herrnstein Smith calls "folk-relativism" [1988:40]).

Sometimes judges seemed so ambivalent about the judging process and the attention paid to the decisions that, if they had not posed such a question already themselves, I had to inquire whether they thought the awards might best be abolished. This is deemed rather an irreverent question (understandably, given the awards' longstanding importance to artists), yet some of the more confident judges seemed to relish advocating such irreverence briefly. Some thought it silly that the awards had such a powerful effect on buyers (artists and experienced collectors and curators are frequently bemused, if not dismayed, at how much more buyers are willing to pay for award-winning items), or they were concerned about the tremendous influence the awards are perceived to have on the direction of artists' work. One non-Indian judge, a prominent artist himself, described the display of ribbons and trophies as "ridiculous—like some kind of dog show." In the end, however, judges, including that one, would find some reason for continuing the awards, whether it was to provide motivation for artists, the raising of prices, or informing buyers about what they should buy. My friend who said she was so much more comfortable with very precise criteria of evaluation said she wasn't sure why the awards were important, but she knew they were: "It seems to help make it more of an art form. It is nice to know that people really take pride in their work and want to win a prize for it, they don't just make things for the money." Her statement might appear ridiculous, because the awards clearly are directly linked to money (and less directly to successful careers, meaning paying careers), but I did speak to artists who spoke reverently of the awards they had won and recalled them as having served as motivation, because they wanted to win, they wanted to "be the best." (The mentality is similar to some of my students' attitudes toward grades; while many students who care about their grades do so purely for their value in achieving other goals, many see them as desirable certification of approval and achievement.) By the time I spoke with them these artists had become quite successful; their ambition had served them well, and they suggested that similar ambition was worth encouraging in the next generation of artists. One artist told me that she no longer needed awards to give her a feeling of accomplishment and had come to see them as at least partly a subjective affair (the judging could, in her view, be done far more objectively), but she wasn't sure that she would ever have achieved what she had if, as a young artist, she had never been motivated by them.

I did encounter one patron and erstwhile Indian Market judge, Sallie Wagner, who was decisive that evaluation could never by objective: absolutely, in her view, judging was subjective, and any attempt to do it objectively was misguided and would likely result in rewarding bad art—"bad," I assume she would acknowledge if pressed, in her opinion and in that of a few artists, curators, and other collectors (in fact, I had met people, including Ramona Sakiestewa and Gail Bird, who had given me reason to think that they shared many of her sensibilities). In particular, she was critical of the idea that degree of technical difficulty should be the measure of value. It is quite possible to like simple things more than intricate ones, she pointed out. Wagner once studied anthropology at the University of Chicago, ran a trading post on the Navajo Reservation in the 1930s, and never revealed any qualms about her attempts to influence weavers (as well as consumers). In a published memoir she recalls how she and her husband "demanded plain stripes" rather than more intricate designs and urged the use of vegetal dyes to produce more subtle hues (Wagner 1997:55).[16]

Though Wagner emphasizes the quirky, individual nature of her tastes, they do conform neatly to longstanding patterns of what Bourdieu calls "bourgeois discretion": "bourgeois discretion signals its presence by a sort of ostentatious discretion, sobriety and understatement, a refusal of everything which is 'showy,' 'flashy' and pretentious, and which devalues itself by the very intention of distinction" (1984:249). The rugs she admires, except for their size, do seem very humble works compared to the intricate designs that became especially popular among Indian Market buyers in the 1980s. There are similar tensions between devotees of the simple and those of the intricate, the subtle and the conspicuous, in relation to other art forms, including pottery and silverwork. In many cases, those on the side of the more intricate and conspicuous would seem to be gaining the upper hand, at least judging by Indian Market awards in the 1980s and 1990s.

I did not encounter many who were so straightforward about evaluation, and Wagner seemed to have no illusion that her views were common, explaining that she felt her ideas and opinions had become increasingly marginalized in recent years. Many might imagine this marginalization to be the result of greater Indian involvement in judging or of an attempt among white patrons to avoid imposing their preferences on Indian artists. It is true that patrons, including curators and collectors, have become more sensitive about such matters and might wince at Wagner's description of her efforts to influence weavers. A white curator known for arrogance about Indian art told me that his entire perspective had been turned upside down by Sally Price's (1989) critique of the Primitive art market. Another white curator's attitudes and ideas were transformed by working with Indian curators and a politicized group of artists affiliated with the Institute of American Indian Arts. But Wagner's sense of marginalization was, I would argue, primarily the result of the increasing power of other white patrons with tastes dramatically opposed to hers.

Though neither Wagner nor anyone else I spoke with explicitly connected such differences in taste to differences in class background (an aspect of individuals not easily discerned or discussed), many artists and collectors, including Bird and Johnson, expressed interest in how patterns of evaluation might be linked to an individual's occupation or other position; whether someone was an artist (whether Indian or non-Indian), museum curator, dealer, or collector often appeared to influence their perceptions of quality. From observing the judging process and from talking to people who had judged, I did get a sense that such patterns existed. The differences are, not surprisingly, a matter of some controversy, and I spoke with a number of people who criticized the judging habits of one group or another (sometimes including the one to which they belonged). Dealers, for example, were apt to be accused of evaluating work more on the basis of what they think they can sell easily rather than on the "actual merits of the piece." According to anthropologist and curator Bruce Bernstein, who has judged Pueblo pottery at Indian Market, dealers have often awarded prizes to the artists they represent, despite the blatant conflict of interest (1993:291). Less often than complaints about dealers I heard criticism of the judging habits of artists (sometimes from other artists), who were said, for example, to place too much emphasis on how difficult a piece had been to produce—that is, to place too much emphasis on technical achievement, sometimes at the expense of other criteria of evaluation. In general, however, none of these positions was thought to guarantee "proper" evaluation in any individual case, and I often heard people (including artists) advocate that judges should probably include a combination of curators, dealers, collectors, and artists. Since the mid-1990s the SWAIA Council of Artists has pushed for artists to have more of a say in the judging process.

Some people involved in judging were more cynical about it than others. The outcome of the judging process is often the result of a process of negotiation among judges, a "tournament of value" in itself in which judges trade ideas about the strengths of one piece, the flaws of another. Some judges seemed to believe that a winning item is chosen only because it "truly deserves" to win, and the judges who speak on its behalf only make other judges see what is in fact true (discussing a debate among judges over Best of Show, a Pueblo potter said that the dealer who argued on behalf of the award-winning piece made her see the beauty that was truly there, that she had overlooked). I inferred that few would assume that the outcome might have more to do with the persuasive powers and reputation of those judging, their confidence, their abilities to deploy the knowledge—whether traditionally associated with art or "culture" or some combination—that might legitimate an award. Though the judging is considered extremely important by many and is a matter of frequent comment and discussion, the list of awards is never accompanied by the list of judges' names; judges are permitted to remain relatively anonymous, though they are required to sign their names on the back of the ribbons they award. It is possible that drawing more attention to judges' identities would encourage buyers to view the awards more skeptically, not because of who the judges might be, but because drawing attention to their names at all might draw attention to the fact that the awards are the result of specific individuals' opinions.[17]

Though many artists, curators, and serious collectors often disagree with the award decisions, the overall respectability of the judging process is seen as important for maintaining the status of the event. As I mentioned at the beginning of this chapter, there are other "Indian markets"; in fact, they have been proliferating in recent years, most of the newer ones directly inspired by the one in Santa Fe. In Northern New Mexico, Santa Fe's Indian Market is most often compared to the Eight Northern Indian Pueblos' Artist and Craftsman Show and the older Gallup Intertribal Ceremonial. Though both of these are well attended, they lack the prestige of the Santa Fe event. I imagine some buyers prefer the Eight Northern show, held at one of the Northern Pueblos, to Indian Market because it is a good deal less crowded, having more room to spread itself out; it is less flashy; and it has a more casual atmosphere. Fewer collectors, however, see the Gallup and Eight Northern shows as important, and fewer of the more established and successful artists are likely to attend. One of the things assumed—by artists and patrons—to make the Santa Fe market superior to the other two events is the judging, including the logistics of receiving and returning objects and the expertise of the judges (the monetary value of the awards is also quite a bit smaller at the other events, making for less incentive for artists to enter and less drama for all).

When I observed judging at all three events in 1991 and 1992, differences in the judging process, the appointment of judges, and the accepted standards of evaluation were readily apparent. In Gallup one of the judges was a journalist from Japan who had been writing about American Indian art for Japanese magazines but was not considered to have any particular knowledge of it; it seemed that inviting her to judge was a way of encouraging her to publicize the event in Japan and perhaps to help her forge connections with local dealers. In the 1920s the Gallup show was started by dealers (or "traders" as they were then known) who wanted to attract tourists to the area.[18] Santa Fe patrons including Margretta Dietrich and Oliver La Farge were occasional judges in Gallup and wrote of attempts to influence the taste of the Gallup dealers—when not attempting to take over the judging from them entirely (SAR, AEWC, NMAIA files; meeting minutes, SRCA, SWAIAC, folder 38). In 1991 it was clear that Gallup was still geared more to serving the interests of dealers, who could even enter pieces for judging (at other markets entries and sales are made only by artists). Throughout the 1980s and 1990s, judges in Gallup were more often dealers. Indicative also of dealers' influence is that, at least in 1991, judges were free to consider price in determining their awards. At the Santa Fe and Eight Northern shows, prices are not meant to be seen by judges, and if judges see them inadvertently, they do not feel free to comment upon them. But in Gallup I heard judges, who were dealers, argue that a particular katchina carving deserved an award because as well as being "spectacular," it had a "reasonable" price on it ($6,000 as opposed to $16,000), one described as "marketable." A Ganado rug was also praised as having a "marketable" price ($16,000). During the discussions, one of the judges mentioned that she had thought it was possible to disqualify a piece because of an "unreasonable" price; the other judges responded that they did not think this was grounds for disqualification but affirmed that it made sense that they take prices into account. Back in Santa Fe, when I related this discussion to people involved in Indian Market, they shook their heads in disapproval and sighed in disgust: the piece alone, in their view, should be judged, not the price, and the price should not be allowed to influence the judges' perceptions of a work's merits.

The show at Eight Northern, started in 1973 by Pueblo leaders, was directly inspired by Indian Market's success. In 1992, when I showed up to work as a volunteer during the judging process, I quickly got the impression that the judging was taken a little less seriously than at Indian Market, where the boundary between volunteers and judges was quite clear. Arriving at San Juan Pueblo with one of the judges, I discussed my research with one of the organizers, who immediately responded that perhaps instead of recording judges' decisions, I would be willing to serve as a judge myself, one of the appointed judges not having shown up as scheduled. My protests that I really didn't know much about the art in question were initially brushed aside (while I suffered a moment of panic) but in the end I was given the task of tabulating results for the painting and graphic arts entries.

Still, the boundary between judging and volunteering seemed less distinct than I had come to expect from experiences at Indian Market and Gallup, the judges at Eight Northern not only welcoming the volunteers to listen in on their discussions but on occasion even inviting our opinions. The judges for this division included David Bradley, a well-known Ojibwa painter, sculptor, and printmaker, with a reputation at that time as a "radical" in the Indian art world, who had been serving on the board of SWAIA. The other three judges were white and middle-aged or older, with some experience as art educators and collectors; one was a photographer. I had the impression that Bradley was looked to by the others as the expert; in part I would guess this was because of his identity as an Indian artist, but their deference was probably even more the result of his assertive display of a professional vocabulary. Bradley was the only one of the group with much familiarity of the materials and techniques, and he pointed out to the others which were wood block prints, which were linotypes, which paint was oil and which acrylic. In the judging of the category of traditional painting, the distinctions included ethnicity: Bradley pointed out that a painting of a Pueblo scene was signed with a name that sounded Navajo; all agreed that it was not traditional for a Navajo to be painting a Pueblo village, and in the end the work was transferred to the "contemporary" category, where such boundary transgressions are considered more acceptable. Most of the group's decisions were either unanimous or something of a compromise. Every so often the group would come to an impasse and look to me and the other volunteer, Bradley asking, "Well, what do you think?" Despite my earlier panic at the thought of judging, I rather enjoyed offering my opinion. When later I told this story to Indian Market veterans—who knew how limited my knowledge of Indian art was—they looked disapproving and spoke of various attempts to improve the judging at the Eight Northern Show, never quite as professional, in their opinion, as it could be.

The Commodification of Knowledge

Indian Market and related events, along with Santa Fe museums, depend on the labor of numerous volunteers. At Indian Market and the Eight Northern show, I met just a handful of Indian volunteers, one of them interested in a career in arts organization management and hoping to gain relevant experience. Of the non-Indian volunteers, most either collected Indian art or were interested in doing so. Their motivation for volunteering was largely to acquire more information about the art and artists, information that they would put to use while shopping.

In Gallup one of my fellow volunteers had just moved to Northern New

Mexico from Pennsylvania. As we wrote down numbers from tags on Navajo rugs she turned to me and exclaimed, "I wish I could have been here yesterday to see how they judge these rugs. That way you'd know what to look for when you go to buy one!" A few lingering judges and the other volunteers were happy to educate her, explaining, for example, "The colors on that one are just too harsh, they should be more subtle." As we examined Navajo dolls, we admired one in particular, until one of the volunteers pointed out that the artist had "messed up on the moccasins." They should have been wrapped leather, she noted, but instead were made of dark colored wool. The volunteer from Pennsylvania and I later returned to a discussion of our own preferences. She was so interested, she said, in learning more about Indian art, which was a new world to her, and eager to learn how to evaluate it. "Of course, with art," she added in a wistful tone, "what really matters is your own personal feeling about a piece and not what you're *supposed* to like." She was right that one was "supposed to" rely at least in part on the "personal": I thought of one of my artist friends in Santa Fe, who worked at a bar downtown, and how she laughed when telling stories of customers from Texas and Oklahoma (ever common targets of derision among Santa Feans) who had asked her what art they should buy.

Knowledge, including knowledge of others' opinions, of course does influence what people like and what they buy. In the Indian art world, people are willing to invest considerable amounts of time and money in obtaining knowledge of experts' standards of value, as well as their vocabularies. In their quest for knowledge, buyers look to lists of awards given out to artists at Indian Market, they read the "buyers' guides" published by SWAIA as well as books and magazines like the glossy *Native Peoples* or the now defunct *Indian Artist;* they attend talks and exhibits at museums and enroll in seminars at the Indian Arts Research Center at the School of American Research or at the Museum of Indian Arts and Culture or other such institutions. While working as volunteers at Indian Market or at museums, they pay close attention to judges, other buyers, and artists.

The sources of knowledge do not just provide implicit and explicit evaluation; they also produce the value of objects, artists, and even institutions such as Indian Market. Indian Market awards usually result in higher prices obtained for award-winning pieces and other work by award-winning artists and, books, museum exhibitions, and lectures have a similar impact. As with art markets generally, many of the more ambitious artists are careful students of this value-making process, many regularly seeking publicity, inclusion in museum exhibitions, and other forms of recognition, whether or not they find such self-promotion enjoyable. At a forum on the future of Santa Fe's Museum of Fine Arts, Ramona Sakiestewa told the audience, "As an artist you might have many shows in galleries, and you can sell, and that's wonderful; but when you have a museum on your resume that has given you the 'Good Housekeeping' seal of approval . . . that provides a very different signal to people who might collect or just buy single pieces of your work. And it's also an incentive for other museums to begin to look at your work" (McDowell 1992:14, 41).

Of course it is not only in the Indian art market that people seek knowledge of goods and their evaluation; this is true for other markets as well, though often information is easier to come by and the stakes for prospective buyers less high than with Indian art, where buyers face the constant threat of inauthenticity. Artists who they think are Indian may not be after all (that is, they are pronounced by some authority not to be); wares may have been produced not in the United States, but in the Philippines or Mexico; what purchasers think is handcoiled pottery just might turn out to be glassware with a painted clay slip over it; what looks like turquoise could be plastic; what is assumed to be expensive "art" might turn out to be worthless "trash." Artists are at least as willing as dealers, collectors, or museum curators to point out, with disapproval, what they see as fraudulent or a "short cut." In 1998 a SWAIA seminar designed for inexperienced buyers of Indian art provided the kind of warnings and advice frequently offered to novice buyers: the audience was warned about the prevalence of "fakes" and encouraged to approach buying a work of Indian art "the way you would a car" (asking lots of questions but also, presumably, looking out for lemons, and getting artists to provide written documentation of materials and techniques). They were also told that what's most important is "how you feel emotionally about a piece."

"How you feel" might seem a very personal, individual affair, but such sensibilities do not exist independently of a social context, including institutionally constructed categories and standards of value. "Feeling" might be presumed a more "natural" response to an object than "knowledge," but in fact one's feelings about an object are subject to dramatic change if what one knows about it changes (it was observed in an article about authenticity in painting, "admiring a fake, it's said, is akin to making love in the dark to someone who turns out to be the wrong person" [Kimmelman 1998]).

Buyers seek not only the knowledge to purchase wisely, but also knowledge that makes their shopping expeditions and their acquisitions a more meaningful project, knowledge that gives them that sense that they "know what they are looking at." Such knowledge usually includes knowledge about the ethnicity and even personality of the artist, the artist's relationship to other artists, and a relationship to "tradition": whether the artist is celebrated more for departing from tradition, recreating it (probably still the most popular relationship to tradition), or some combination of these. As buyers' knowledge of art and artists increases, they gain more confidence in their purchases and also a sense of personal development and enrichment, of self-actualization and progress. A retired schoolteacher— who did not collect Indian art because he lacked the means to do so, but who studied it and volunteered at a museum devoted to Indian art— laughed at the sight of a brightly painted piece of Pueblo pottery. He seemed to be laughing more at a memory of his former self than at the piece: "I can remember when I first came here and didn't know any better. I might have liked that." A woman at Indian Market showed an artist a set of silver button covers, her first Indian Market purchase, made some thirty years before: "I didn't know anything then. Nothing! But I figured I couldn't go too far wrong with these." An Indian Market volunteer was less satisfied with her progress over the years: "I really haven't studied as much as I should have," she said regretfully.

Many artists, as Gail Bird suggested, are aware of buyers' hunger for knowledge and attempt to satisfy that hunger during Indian Market and other events. Robert Tenorio, for example, will avidly discuss his pots' relationship to late nineteenth- or early twentieth-century pots in the collection of the School of American Research or pots in photographs of books he may have on hand about Pueblo pottery, pointing out specific styles of painting and shapes, discussing techniques. Marcus Amerman, with more of a connection to mainstream art worlds, will discuss how his beadwork challenges stereotypes and mass media depictions of Indians. Of course, many artists, especially those blessed with extraordinary patience and tolerance of ignorance (about Indians as well as about art), probably genuinely enjoy such interactions, and the more successful they become, the more selective they can be about responding to queries. At Indian Market, most will spend a lot of time sitting by their booths anyway. But the more charismatic, persuasive, and patient artists often have an advantage over their competition, especially when starting out.

In order to get knowledge about artists and objects, many buyers go shopping for it. Though talking to artists at Indian Market is a way of gaining knowledge without paying for it, information is a valuable commodity. As Appadurai observes in *The Social Life of Things,*

> Knowledge *about* commodities is itself increasingly commodified . . . [T]hough even in the simplest economies there is a complex traffic in things, it is only with increased social, technical, and conceptual differentiation that what we may call a *traffic in criteria* concerning things develops. That is, only in the latter situation does the buying and selling of expertise regarding the technical, social, or aesthetic appropriateness of commodities become widespread. Of course, such a traffic in commodity criteria is not confined to capitalist societies, but there seems to be considerable evidence that it is in such societies that such traffic is most dense. (1986:54–55)

Similarly, in her discussion of "The Value of Value Judgements," Barbara Herrnstein Smith notes that "professional evaluations—of artworks along with anything else consumable, and what isn't?—are themselves commodities of considerable value" (1988:99).

Indian art buyers often are looking for knowledge to apply in their shopping less directly than the Gallup volunteer who wanted to know "what to look for." They don't necessarily want such direct instruction, which might, after all, be considered evidence of naïveté. Also, for those devoted to projects of self-actualization, exercising one's own taste, acting on "how one feels" about a piece—however that might be influenced by others—offers pleasures that a shopping list authored by another would not. So, instead of being told directly "what to buy," many seek background information, histories of artists and their communities, knowledge of museum collections, trends—and a language to use to talk about artists and objects.

The language offered them, by artists as well as others involved in the Indian art world, often combines the discourse associated with anthropological notions of "cultures" with the discourse associated with modern art. In the 1990s, at lecture series and seminars for collectors, the array of speakers would usually include some who emphasize the one or the other. Edmund Ladd, a curator from Zuni, might discuss the complex cultural and historical context of something like katchina carvings; Jerry Brody, an art historian, might review the history of Pueblo painting; artists might talk about techniques and sources of inspiration. At the 1991 "Collectors' Symposium" at the School of American Research's Indian Arts Research Center, the languages of art and anthropology were combined most noticeably by Rick Dillingham, who was a renowned ceramic artist (non-Indian) as well as a scholar and dealer of Pueblo pottery with some academic training in anthropology. To an audience whose members had paid $750 for several days of lectures by artists and scholars just prior to Indian Market, Dillingham emphasized his attachment to the personalities of individual artists: "My collection is sappy and emotional. I look at the individuals who make these pots as well as the cultures who make them." With occasional plugs for the book he was finishing up on Acoma and Laguna pottery (1992), Dillingham attempted to persuade his audience that "it is possible to see a personality and a culture in a pot." He encouraged his audience also to consider "tradition" as an evolving concept and set of styles and techniques, not something static and part of "the past" but rather a "statement" produced in the present. Afterward I heard enthusiastic responses from members of the audience. A couple from Dallas told me that his talk, along with consultations with museum curators and artists, had helped them plan their shopping list for Indian Market, a list that consisted of artists' names used as nouns—"a so-and-so and a so-and-so . . ."—and then the name of a pueblo, one they had decided they wanted a pot from, but they had not yet decided on the artist.[19]

Postcolonial Indian Market?

I have a tendency to respond contemptuously to the sort of list making engaged in by the couple from Dallas. To be honest, my contempt might stem at least in part from envy of the sort of wealth that makes it possible to turn a list like theirs into a collection of pots. Then, too, I have been indoctrinated enough by an ideology emphasizing reliance on "personal" taste to the point that I am a little squeamish about people relying so blatantly on expert advice when it comes to art (cars, I assume, really are a different matter). But I am also uncomfortable with what such list making suggests of the commodification of human beings and their identities.

Rick Hill, a Tuscarora artist, scholar, and museum curator, had some things to say about Indian Market that might be reassuring to people who find the event disconcerting in ways having to do with commodification: "There's a difference between culture and commerce, and Indians understand that really clearly. They understand that the purpose of Indian Market is to put as much of the white man's money into our pockets as possible. It's not to convert them about the truth of our existence, but to make an income. The non-Indian doesn't understand, because they think they are buying Indianness. They don't realize you can't buy that" (Abbot 1994:80).[20]

Leaving aside the question of whether many artists would find meaningful Hill's distinction between "culture" and "commerce," are non-Indians who buy art at Indian Market attempting to buy "Indianness"? They do believe they are buying a piece of "Indian art," a "Santa Clara jar," or a piece of jewelry made by an Indian—and the popularity of Indian Market is based on the event's ability to affirm that belief. More experienced buyers also see themselves as buying "a Margaret Tafoya" or "a Pablita Velarde."

It is true that many buyers of Indian art have ideas about what is or is not appropriately "Indian" (these are ideas subject to change, varying quite considerably among different collectors, and artists, including Rick Hill, have sometimes been successful in changing people's ideas and expectations). Though very few would admit to doing so, some buyers may in fact attempt to influence "Indianness"—that is, Indian people's lives and communities as well as art—through the purchases they make. The fact that they see a connection between Indian identities and Indian art and see themselves as in a position to have influence over both adds to their sense that buying Indian art is a philanthropic endeavor, a public service, rather than a private indulgence. As I have argued, this was very much the role played, at least at times, by earlier patrons including Elizabeth White and the other organizers of the Exposition of Indian Tribal Arts.

But many buyers, I believe, do not have any illusion that they are "buying Indianness" at Indian Market any more than I think that I am buying "plant-ness" when I go shopping at the plant nursery. Indian Market buyers have varying degrees of awareness and concern about the relationship between Indian art and life. They become united, however, in their attempts to master the categories, to distinguish Acoma from San Ildefonso, concha belts from ketohs, David Bradleys from Dan Naminghas. They want to "know what they are looking at" and to go about further acquiring and exercising such knowledge, gaining a sense of personal competence, progress, and self-transformation, along with the objects they consider beautiful or interesting. In many ways, it is better selves they are after.

In 1991 Sylvia Loomis, Margretta Dietrich's former secretary, showed me a photograph of what she thought had been a meeting of the NMAIA, SWAIA's predecessor. She wasn't at all sure of the date, but thought it might have been taken in the late 1940s or early 1950s. The photograph, out of focus and overexposed, was taken under the shade of a cottonwood tree outside Margretta Dietrich's house on Canyon Road. Loomis pointed out Dietrich there, gray haired and a bit stooped, next to Elizabeth White, amid ten other women, sitting in a circle of lawnchairs, all in dresses, many with high heels, hats with ribbons and bows, pocketbooks. Loomis identified a younger, stronger-looking woman at the back of the group as Maria Chabot. Then again, she said she wasn't sure if that was Chabot, or even if this had really been a meeting of the New Mexico Association after all; it might, she mused, have been a meeting of the Garden Club, or the Spanish Colonial Arts Society.

For me that blurred image of the "ladies" in the garden—whether they were discussing gardens or art, of whatever variety—captures a particular version of what anthropologist Nicholas Thomas has called "colonial culture" (1994). As Thomas points out, colonialism was not a unitary process or ideology, though there are fundamental parallels that can be discerned in a wide array of periods and regions. The photograph's colonialism was a very different version than that suggested by the monument in the midst of Santa Fe Plaza, the one erected in the 1860s and dedicated "TO THE HEROES WHO HAVE FALLEN IN THE VARIOUS BATTLES WITH SAVAGE INDIANS IN THE TERRITORY OF NEW MEXICO"; as argued in the previous chapter, if members of the NMAIA perceived some people as savages, their savages were not Indians. But it was still a context in which individuals from metropolitan centers of political and economic power were taking possession of a region where there were significant differences in power and authority between colonizers and colonized. The colonizers were never undivided by gender or class, and my previous chapters have argued, the "ladies" of the

NMAIA championed a revisioning of "art" and "culture" in ways that allowed them new sources of public influence and authority in a context that was not just "colonial," but one where people were increasingly defining themselves in relation to the commodities they consumed, including those produced by the colonized.

The successors of the NMAIA work in a context that has undergone profound change in recent years. Ruth Phillips, a curator and scholar of Native art, has written of a "visible fracture between colonial and postcolonial museum practice" marked by the establishment of the Smithsonian's National Museum of the American Indian, an institution to be directed and managed by Native Americans (1995:98).[21] Increasingly, Indians are gaining control over the way museums represent Indians to non-Indians and are also attempting to make museums and their collections more accessible to Indian audiences. Other indications of fundamental change in the world of Indian art and objects include the 1990 Native American Graves and Repatriation Act, mandating the return of human remains and sacred objects to Native communities. Though not taking place everywhere at the same rate, significant movement away from the policies of a colonial era can be found nationwide, and Santa Fe has been no exception. Beginning in 1997, visitors to Indian Market could also visit a new permanent exhibition at the Museum of Indian Arts and Culture. Titled "Here, Now and Always," the $2.9 million exhibition in a new wing of the museum is billed as "pioneering a new approach to exhibiting Native American arts and culture" and as reflecting the museum's commitment to Native involvement in the representation of Native communities. My friend and colleague Deborah Kanter, a historian of Latin America, returned from the exhibition describing it as "a perfect antidote to the old exhibits of Native people where you would have some white, male anthropologist providing all the documentation." Though never fully the realm of the "white, male anthropologist," SWAIA has undergone similar changes, with a steady increase in the number of Indian people involved in administration and leadership.

In 1981 SWAIA was run entirely by volunteers, with the aid of a part-time secretary. Ten years later the organization had a professional staff and suite of offices, with a non-Indian president and CEO. I spoke with white employees of SWAIA at that time who seemed to feel awkward, at least occasionally, about their position as white employees of an organization that exercised substantial influence on Indian artists and, indirectly, on their communities. In the midst of one conversation, one staff member began speaking very quietly, as if she didn't want anyone to hear, and said that she often felt that there should be an Indian in her position, but—her voice taking on an edge of defensiveness—Indian people with her qualifications were difficult to hire. After Indian representation on the SWAIA board of directors steadily increased, including a younger generation of artists with more activist leanings, by 1994 such discussions had become more public. A group of younger artists organized what they called the "SWAIA Council of Artists" demanding, among other things, greater Indian involvement in SWAIA policy making. That year Paul Rainbird (then going by the name Gonzales) from San Ildefonso was appointed SWAIA's president and CEO. Under Rainbird's direction, a number of changes were introduced, many of them extremely controversial among artists as well as longtime patrons.

Some of the changes, generally not the most controversial ones, marked a definitive departure from the colonialist model of white patrons exhibiting Indians and romanticizing Indians as remnants of premodern authenticity. Though many artists and patrons would argue that SWAIA had long displayed a certain willingness to embrace "innovative" as well as "traditional" work, acceptance of Indian art as modern was made more explicit with sponsorship of a Native film festival, featuring works by Native filmmakers, and the inclusion of photography beginning with the 1997 Indian Market. Also in 1997, the Indian Market "costume contest" was abolished as a result of complaints that it featured ceremonial dress that many Indian community leaders might well find inappropriate for such a context. The event was replaced by a "Contemporary Fashion Showcase," held at the Museum of Fine Arts. Afterward Paul Rainbird remarked to a local journalist, "One of my best quotes was from a lady who I would say is a very avid collector and world traveler. She said the fashion show would stand up to anything she's ever seen in Milan. I loved that comment more than anything" (Soto 1997:A1).

Many Indian Market artists and patrons disagree with the kind of ambition implicit in Rainbird's remark. For the last decade there have been ongoing controversies over the proper focus of SWAIA's activities and to whom the organization should devote allegiance and service. Greater Indian involvement in running SWAIA has not put an end to these disputes. For example, many more artists (about five hundred in 1997 according to SWAIA) would like to exhibit at Market than the thousand to twelve hundred who are admitted, even after their work has been approved by the committee that reviews slides of artists' work and deems the work acceptable for exhibit and sale.[22] With some arguing that "tenured artists" should be required to make way, at least periodically, for newcomers, others see such proposals as a betrayal of people who have counted on the event and in some cases developed lifelong careers around it. One of Rainbird's solutions was to invite a select group of artists to give up their Indian Market booths in exchange for inclusion in more exclusive shows, including a "SWAIA Masters' Show" held in May at one of Santa Fe's luxury hotels and a show at a Manhattan art gallery. Exclusivity, however, does not guarantee prestige, nor the attendance of an established clientele, and many artists were reluctant to participate.

The debates over access to Indian Market booths and the focus of SWAIA's activities are perhaps intensified by the fact that increasingly many of the newcomers clamoring for exhibit space are what artists from communities near Santa Fe, particularly those from the Northern Pueblos, call "out-of-area Indians"—including many artists from the Plains states and some from as far as Alaska, Florida, and New York (beginning in the mid-1990s, Native artists from Bolivia, Siberia, and Australia have also been invited to Market as "guests"). Of course, many of the "out-of-area" artists call Santa Fe home, many drawn, at least initially, by the Institute for American Indian Arts or by the area's reputation as a lively center of the Indian art world. The relationship between the more locally identified artists and those with ties to more distant parts is a complicated one. Artists compete for influence and authority among one another and among non-Indian patrons, drawing on diverse claims to legitimacy. Artists with ties to art schools and elites may have the cultural capital of elite vocabularies and tastes. Others' authority may gain legitimacy from ties to traditional communities, sometimes a more recognizably "Indian" physical appearance. Some have the advantage of a combination of all of these. Influenced by homogenizing notions of "cultures" as entities with clear-cut boundaries, non-Indians without familiarity with contemporary Indians so often think of Indians as speaking with one voice, thinking with one mind, and would be surprised by the heterogeneity that exists, including sharp differences of opinion, even among members and residents of the same pueblo, but especially among people coming from regions with very different histories.

Artists involved in SWAIA report that the most bitter disputes in recent years have been over money, particularly over how to spend it and raise it. While Indian Market has steadily expanded in recent years, in part to include younger and less experienced artists, the organization has also taken on a diverse array of other commitments, including the annual "Master's Show" of work by selected artists in Santa Fe, the show for selected Indian artists in a Manhattan art gallery, an "Indian Market" at the Museum of Civilization in Ottawa, and Indian-art related tours of Santa Fe and the surrounding region geared for Indian art collectors. Though some of these projects are fundraisers, others in the mid-1990s were made possible by a budget of nearly a million dollars coming from individual donations, memberships, and donations from corporations such as USWest and American Express. In late 1997 a large contingent of Indian Market artists responded with outrage when the SWAIA board announced a substantial increase in booth fees for artists. The fees had been steadily increasing since Rainbird's appointment as executive director. Artists showed up to protest at SWAIA board meetings and the fee increase was the focus of a nationally broadcast radio call-in program, "Native America Calling" (Chang 1998). At Indian Market in 1998 artists spoke bitterly of the fee increases and Indian and non-Indian people involved with SWAIA in earlier years also expressed disapproval. Members of the SWAIA board eventually agreed to something of a compromise, but charges of gross financial mismanagement and a lack of concern for artists' interests continued until Rainbird was asked to resign.

In many ways, SWAIA and Santa Fe Indian Market exist in a vastly transformed setting from the one in which Margretta Dietrich, Elizabeth White, and Maria Chabot went "shopping for a better world." Nonetheless, there are many continuities. Like the NMAIA, Santa Fe Indian Market exists in a context marked by the ever-expanding importance of commodities in the lives of consumers, the tendency to use goods to invent and reinvent identities, to differentiate selves from others and to express relationships and attachments. For upper-middle-class consumers who feel compelled to use their "leisure" time to engage in projects of self-transformation, associated with such bastions of respectability as museums, universities, and art galleries, shopping for art seems worthwhile in ways that other forms of consumption do not.

Meanwhile, the value and meaning of commodities is increasingly open to contestation, and individuals and groups struggle for authority to define them—including their worth, their authenticity, their identity. Within this struggle, the concept of culture formed in a colonial era is still used at times as a means of validation and continues to coexist with a notion of culture as "the best," as something to be bought and sold and put on display, and a notion that allows the "genuine" to be differentiated from the "spurious," and "art" from "trash." Prior to his departure from SWAIA, Rainbird stated his ambition for the organization in terms that echoed those of the Exposition of Indian Tribal Arts in 1931: "The role that SWAIA can play for the future is to bring a new consciousness to the non-Indian American public of what value there is in Indian art and culture" (Wheeler 1997).[23] As Rick Hill's comment on Indian Market suggests, this is a notion of culture tailored for the marketplace: if "culture" means an entire way of life or the essence of a group's existence, this is not it.

Indian Market shoppers, however, are likely to remain largely unconcerned about such distinctions: they have enough others with which to keep themselves preoccupied. My acquaintances who first visited Indian Market and complained that they had expected "more opportunities for the Indians to share their culture" no longer seemed to care about that once they acquired from the museum the sense that they could return to the event and "know what [they] were looking at." To call what they are looking at "culture" can, in certain contexts, give it some enhanced legitimacy or prestige. When Rick Dillingham offered to teach his audience how to see both an individual's personality and "a culture" in a piece of pottery, such instruction was valued for its ability to give consumers that sense that they "know" what they are buying. "Culture," with its multiple meanings, including "the best" and the more holistic notion of a way of life or an entire collectivity, gives shopping for such objects particular prestige, if "art" is not prestigious enough. To say, however, that it is "not culture" that they are buying is unlikely to deter shoppers, eager to exercise a host of other categories and distinctions, to choose one thing over another, to acquire goods and a sense of personal accomplishment.

EPILOGUE: IN THE DOG CEMETERY

 At the School of American Research the most memorable high-light of the visitors' tour is probably the Indian Arts Research Center, with its stores of pottery (much of it immense), textiles, silverwork, basketry, carvings, and graphic arts. Also memorable are the terraced gardens and the rambling adobe buildings that once formed the White sisters' abode and now house the School's administration. Visitors are less likely to recall pausing at a spot along a wooded path between the Whites' former dwellings and the more recently constructed art center. It is here that we arrive at the cemetery of the White sisters' dogs. Beneath the fifty-odd small, bright blue wooden crosses lie the Whites' prize-winning Irish wolfhounds and Afghan hounds, their names painted in red: *Penny, Gael, Cucullin, Farouz, Sargon, Finn, Rosaleen* . . . The dog cemetery, so highly personal, festively colored, and seemingly incongruous in this institution devoted to art and scholarship, comes as such a surprise that it is almost possible to miss the formal marble tombstone and bust marking the sisters' own grave, just a few steps away. But for most visitors the attention granted the dogs' graves is momentary, quite likely soon forgotten or chalked up as an example of the sort of eccentric indulgence to be expected of the very wealthy, at any rate an indulgence overshadowed by the significant philanthropic deeds and bequests of the dogs' owners. The dog cemetery plays a role similar to that of the tale of the sisters buying the property after stopping to have their hair done in the middle of a cross-country roadtrip—it is an amusing foil for the School's present purposes.

My own initial response to the dog cemetery was similar to that of most visitors. I had set out to investigate the White sisters' involvement in art and anthropology. Only after learning a good deal about that did I begin to wonder whether the dog cemetery was not a more significant part of the puzzle of these women's lives and of connections among gender, taste, anthropology, commodification, and consumer society. I was aware that the Whites had a kennel and team of show dogs and that Elizabeth had established the Santa Fe Animal Shelter in her sister's memory. I had perused photographs of the Whites with their dogs, scanned records of the kennel among Elizabeth White's papers, and even fingered the large toothmarks adorning the woodwork of the old kennel that now serves as housing for the School of American Research Press. But I tended to assume that the dogs were incidental, or at least a quite different story, despite indications that they had been of considerable importance to the Whites. For example, when I met with Elizabeth White's former nurse and companion, Catherine Rayne, she expressed concern that the dog cemetery be maintained as "Miss E." had wanted. Some of the crosses had recently fallen down, and she was disturbed that they had not been replaced promptly enough. Though White had made it a condition of the bequest of the property that the cemetery be maintained, Rayne sensed that because the dog cemetery had no one to appreciate it the way that Elizabeth White had, it might one day vanish from the landscape—if not from decay, then as a result of being a favorite target of neighborhood kids on Halloween.

Rayne's concerns might well have piqued my interest: inspired in part by Michael Thompson's *Rubbish Theory* (1979), many of my questions about Native American art patronage centered on how some things are deemed worthy of preservation and others not, and how value is produced and reproduced over time. But as Rayne spoke passionately of the dogs and their graves, I was anxious to return to hearing about what I perceived to be matters of greater importance: Elizabeth White's involvement in the campaign for women's suffrage, for example, her turn-of-the-century education at Bryn Mawr, or her patronage of anthropology and American Indian art. Such matters were part of the history shared by other members of her network; the pattern puzzled me. It was not that I was much attached to the notion of art as hallowed realm, and indeed I had no lack of appreciation for dogs. Art, however, like anthropology, I associated with public and rather serious matters; dogs were, in my experience, a matter of private indulgence and affection. It was only much later that I realized my error, at least in understanding the world of Elizabeth White: for White, the dogs, art, and anthropology were all connected.

It was after an encounter with a tarantula that I began to think more seriously about the dogs. One fall evening a friend brought me to a party hosted by two wealthy lesbians who had recently moved from Colorado to one of the comfortable suburbs springing up on the outskirts of Santa Fe, places with large houses on large lots with dramatic views of mountains and mesas. Increasingly, many of these "communities" are gated; this one, more in keeping with the hosts' hippy roots, was not. Guests at the party were offered a tour of the main house, the studio next door, the extensive Xeriscape gardens featuring native plants. One of the women hosting the party was an artist, and the house was filled with paintings and sculpture, much of which expressed a playful sense of humor, a delight found in things many might dismiss as tacky, as kitsch, or just as "odd." Though none of the art or furnishings were Indian, like a lot of the things sold in galleries in Santa Fe, some of it was vaguely "Indian-inspired"; much might be associated one way or another with the West and Southwest. The women who owned the house shared with many of the guests interests in New Age healing and spirituality; in some cases I knew these were pursuits arising from lengthy battles with life-threatening illness. Conversations took up such topics as various forms of "bodywork," traditional Chinese medicine, and the activities of SantaFeCares, an umbrella organization with which I had worked that provided practical and emotional support for people with HIV / AIDS. Because they were so striking, conversation also focused on the resident animals of the house, which included a large white parrot and two very large white dogs, what seemed to me an enormous boa constrictor, and two tarantulas which inhabited cages in the main bedroom. Before the evening was out, I knew what tarantulas feel like when you pet them and when they walk across your fingers and up your arm—soft and furry, gentle, not at all the way I had imagined. Despite my long-standing objections to the keeping of "exotic pets," I was fascinated to find myself beginning to see the tarantulas the way their owners did: as sentient beings, with interesting habits and lives, capable of inspiring affection and curiosity rather than terror or revulsion.

I had spent the previous several days writing about the White sisters' taking up residence in Santa Fe in the 1920s and the elaborate parties they staged at "El Delirio," so it is not surprising that I began to compare the owners of the tarantulas to those earlier newcomers to Santa Fe. I was reminded of how much the Southwest, especially Northern New Mexico, continues to be perceived by many as a place to achieve self-realization and a healing of body and soul—healing aided by traditions perceived as at least slightly mysterious and exotic, nowadays even more often associated with distant parts as well as the local (for many current residents, Santa Fe's identity is as much about the popularity there of "alternative medicine" and New Age spiritual practices as it is about the Sangre de Cristo mountains or regional aesthetic traditions). The "therapeutic ethos" that Lears (1983, 1994) describes as emerging at the turn of the century has flourished especially well in what my Albuquerque friends like to call "Fanta Se." As in the Whites' day, the area continues to be perceived as a relatively tolerant place with regard to gender and sexuality; I had met a number of gay men and lesbians who said they moved to the city at least in part because of its gay community. Another common thread between the past and present arrivals in Santa Fe seemed to me to reside in a preoccupation with the value and revaluing of commodities.

It occurred to me that the tarantula owners collected pets the way Elizabeth White had collected art: they purchased creatures that most people would have considerable difficulty imagining in the "pet" category, creatures outside the usual patterns of consumption—outside in part because they are not domestic but "wild." Such category shifting and revaluing is not altogether different from the way the White sisters promoted the idea that Indian art was "art," and could be treated the same way as other kinds of art, that is, as something to put on display both on the more personal stage of one's home as well as on the more public one of the museum, something to study, something to admire for aesthetic as well as "scientific" reasons. Although the Whites were by no means the first to champion this approach to Native art (and they had plenty of company to support them), it did seem that they saw their sensibilities as unusually progressive. In both cases (tarantulas and dogs), to see value where many others did not represented a powerful affirmation of individuality and freedom from convention. There were differences of course: Elizabeth White's collecting, for example, had transcended the realm of private consumption and offered the promise of significant public influence and authority, legitimated by its association with charity and social benevolence. The tarantula owners, people with careers and somewhat more modest means, seemed to feel few of those Bryn Mawrter ambitions that had so inspired the Whites.

In addition to breeding dogs, Martha White had raised horses on a ranch in Arizona and collected horse-related things, including silver bridles made by Navajo silversmiths. After Martha's death, Elizabeth had established the Santa Fe Animal Shelter in her sister's memory. Had the Whites collected animals the way they collected art? Though I had not come across any other animal breeders among the early art patrons, in a memoir of the Whites' friend, neighbor, and fellow Indian art patron, the painter Dorothy Stewart, there is a story about how she had insisted that she and her sister, Margretta Dietrich, keep ducks around their house, " 'because they are so funny' " (A Book About D.N.S.:1955). I had had the sense, when I first read this line, that the memoir's authors felt that this revaluing and recontextualizing of a commodity—in this case, taking something associated with utilitarian purposes and valuing it for reasons having to do with entertainment and aesthetics—was something considered quite typical of the memoir's subject, and perhaps of the community of which she was a part.

In his study of the international market in African art, Christopher Steiner observes that in constructing the authenticity and value of older works of art, collectors and dealers are apt to draw on terms associated with the controlled reproduction of animals: art objects are said to have "pedigrees" listing their previous owners; objects are "vetted" for authenticity. "The term pedigree," Steiner notes, "neatly captures what might be called the domestication of African art. In its wild, undiscovered state, African art is raw, meaningless, and without value to the Western collector. Tamed, through appropriation and the controlled reproduction of ownership, African art becomes assimilated to the broader category art" (1994:124).

The market for American Indian art maintains many important differences from the African art market Steiner describes. Though the identities of previous owners certainly play a significant role in how dealers and collectors construct the value of Indian art (a phenomenon of which patrons such as the Whites were well aware), for a number of reasons the metaphor of domestication has seemed to me of more limited usefulness in understanding this particular art market, especially in work produced by living artists. However, I have argued here that women such as the Whites were able to use Indian art as part of an effort to transcend their own "domestication." Both art and dogs can be commodities over which people attempt to exert control over boundaries, meanings, value, and reproduction. Art, animals, places: the more distinct their identities, the easier to say, "I want one of those, or some of that," the easier to use as a means of distinction, a means of performing identities, as an exercise of taste and judgment. But how to make the identities of such commodities distinct and keep them that way? As Igor Kopytoff has noted, commodities must not only be "produced materially as things, but also culturally marked as being a certain kind of thing" (1986:64).

When I looked again at material I had gathered during my research on the Whites, I was surprised by the similarities between their art patronage and their dogs, similarities of both method and ideological justification. In both cases there was an emphasis on purchasing as an influential act of evaluation, on the power of display and exhibiting highly valued specimens for actual and potential consumers, and on educating consumers about standards of evaluation, standards to be determined and maintained by experts. Both art patronage and dog breeding merged personal pleasure with public influence. Such activities also merged consumption with production and reproduction, work and leisure.

In a history of Irish wolfhounds in the United States, the Whites are described as having "made breed history" during a period in the 1930s, but they are also mentioned as examples of individuals who made brief forays into an activity more demanding than many people realize (Starbuck 1970:52–53). In the late 1920s Elizabeth and Martha White had marveled at the Irish wolfhounds—the first to be exhibited in the United States—they saw at the Westminster Kennel Club show at Madison Square Garden. Irish wolfhounds are the most giant of dog breeds (and, especially in the 1920s, quite rare in the United States), and the two sisters seemed especially to appreciate the combination of their massive size with "gentleness" and "trustworthiness" (Jones n.d.:9), qualities they are said to have "sensed . . . when looking into the deep, understanding, dark eyes of those specimens at Westminster" (8).

By the early 1930s—probably the peak years of Elizabeth White's efforts to promote American Indian art—they had purchased and bred Irish wolfhounds of their own. In the dog-breeding world, individual dogs help to make the reputation of particular "kennels," which are embued with distinct identities as producers of past and future dogs. The White sisters established "Rathmullan Kennels" (named after a castle they had once visited in Ireland) on their property in Santa Fe, with individual rooms built to wolfhound scale and a full-time manager and professional dog handler, Alex Scott. During the next several years, Scott would show the Whites' dogs at Kennel Club shows throughout the country. After Martha White's death in 1936, Elizabeth began gradually dismantling the project they had

Figure 10 Elizabeth White and her dogs in downtown Santa Fe, ca. 1930. Reprinted, by permission, from *El Delirio: The Santa Fe World of Elizabeth White,* by Gregor Stark and E. Catherine Rayne. © 1998 by the School of American Research, Santa Fe.

started, though she remained involved with the Irish Wolfhound Club of America through the 1940s.

Compared to her dog breeding, Elizabeth White's art patronage—carried out with a network of other patrons—ended up being a more sustained endeavor with far more long-lasting impact. But it seems clear to me now that both dogs and art were in many ways part of the same package. In 1939 they were quite literally part of the same package when the painter John Sloan gave Elizabeth White a scrapbook of newspaper clippings collected during the previous year: one section was devoted to her gifts to art museums throughout the country and another to the prizes her dogs had been awarded in dog shows. Though Sloan mentioned only her donations of art in his inscription (her gifts, he said, "will be lasting memorials to your taste and judgment in art"), it is clear that both dogs and art were seen, at least by White, as a matter of "taste and judgment" and a means of establishing a connection to both past and future (figure 10).

Though dog breeds are in some ways rather modern inventions, since the nineteenth century they have been imagined as relatively pure descendents of ancient varieties (Ritvo 1987:93–94). At the time of the White sisters' involvement, breeders of Irish wolfhounds considered the breed something that they had rescued from the brink of extinction. Though a history of some controversial cross-breeding (with Scottish Deerhounds) was acknowledged as occurring in earlier years, by the 1920s and 1930s American breeders considered the Irish wolfhound a commodity with a firmly established, distinctive identity. Breeders cast themselves as visionary pioneers in developing Americans' appreciation for this commodity—a commodity they saw as still rare and at risk of corruption by uneducated consumers (Starbuck 1970).

The search for "drama, history, and variety" that Sharon Zukin observes among consumers in general (1991:255) can be seen in countless markets, including those for art, dogs, landscapes, therapies, and even tarantulas. Before my reconsideration of the dogs, I had tended to assume that the White sisters were focused almost exclusively in connecting to an *American* past—especially that of the Southwest. But in a promotional pamphlet written about Rathmullan Kennels in the mid-1930s, I see that the Whites' dogs provided a link to a dramatic and ancient past of a different sort: an Irish one. I was aware that the Whites had more than once traveled in Ireland, and I suspected that their interest at least in part stemmed from a lifelong affection for the Irish nanny, Mary Ann Carroll, in charge of raising the sisters after their mother's death. But after I had spent so much time with materials that emphasized their concern with maintaining a purity of local identity in Santa Fe, I was surprised to see this elaborated connection to the dramatic and ancient past of another former colony, Ireland. Elizabeth White is described in the Rathmullan pamphlet as busy with "Indian welfare work" and the secretary of the National Association on Indian Affairs, with a strong interest in Indian art. Then we jump to ancient Ireland: "The breeding and raising of Irish wolfhounds at the Rathmullan Kennels is being done in the finest traditions that have existed since earliest times in Ireland . . . This breed is one that carries a glorious heritage of sport afield, and of royal environment. It was known and revered in Erin long before the Romans swept over Britain, and it is welded inseparably with the folklore of the Irish people" (Jones n.d.:6).

Such connections may have been primarily strategic; the pamphlet seems to have been written to appeal to potential dog buyers. As I have argued here, the American cultural nationalism the Whites emphasized in projects such as the 1931 Exposition of Indian Tribal Arts was similarly strategic, a means of gaining value by association with already legitimated projects and sentiments, similar to the way their erstwhile friend and Bryn Mawr alumna Elizabeth Sergeant in 1923 had marketed New Mexican tourism and support for the Pueblos by appealing to images of "the Orient." Concerns about American national identity likely contributed to the Whites' perceptions of the value of Indian art, but their eagerness to celebrate an imagined Irish past and regional identity suggests the extent to which people like the Whites were drawn to the "exotic" more generally— to a world with distinctive local identities, histories, and aesthetic traditions from which cosmopolitan traveler-consumers could pick and choose what to study, purchase, salvage, and promote.

The Whites' interest in Irish wolfhounds fit with their support of Indian land rights and art in that both interests involved a sort of primitivism, a connection to something imagined as more ancient, mysterious, and authentic than anything "modern." There is also an irony in their particular taste in dog breeds: Spanish conquistadores had traveled with dogs similar to wolfhounds and mastiffs, dogs they used to hunt and kill Native people and to convey imperial power (Schwartz 1997:162–63). The Whites were clearly unaware of this irony, judging from their appearance with the wolfhounds in a historical reenactment of a sixteenth-century hunting party during the Santa Fe Fiesta (Jones, n.d.:20–21).

The Whites would most likely have perceived Native people's dogs as undesirably wild and "impure." As Ayse Caglar (1997) notes in an ethnographic study of dog-owning among German Turks, people often seem to choose dogs as a reflection of how they would like to see themselves. Dogs may reflect their owners' aspirations of upward mobility or assimilation, but they may also be chosen to perform gender identities, and particular personalities: pit bulls or Rottweilers, for example, may be chosen to create a more confident, masculine self. Elizabeth White was ambitious, especially as a philanthropist, but in Santa Fe she is remembered as quite shy and in many ways constrained by class and gender conventions. Such a combination of ambition and inhibition may partly explain her attraction to such large and powerful dogs.

John Borneman (1988) has described the development of horse breeds in the United States as a form of "reverse totemism" in that breeders model types of horses after systems of classifying humans according to race and nationality. Breeders imagine breeds such as Arabians and Quarter Horses as natural categories, the biological purity of which must be maintained by humans. Concerns about racial purity and national identity guided breeding programs supported by Nazis, both with humans and with dogs (Arluke and Sax 1995). As Harriet Ritvo writes in an examination of gender stereotypes in discourse on animal husbandry, "animal-related discourse has often functioned as an extended, if unacknowledged metonymy, offering participants a concealed forum for the expression of opinions and worries imported from the human cultural arena" (Ritvo 1991:70).

The Whites' kennel pamphlet hints at parallels between their perceptions of human and animal kinds as it moves from a discussion of Irish folklore to contrast the Irish wolfhounds with "the wild dogs, of mixed breeds" who share the countryside around Santa Fe. In their art patronage, the Whites and fellow patrons established connections between white elites and the Indians and Indian art that they certified as "pure" and "traditional" in ways that reflected prejudice against working- and middle-class whites. The depiction of the wolfhounds' relationship to other Santa Fe canines suggests a similar bias and a borrowing of human classifications for application to dogs. One tale mentions that Gareth of Ambleside was once attacked by a pack of wild dogs, described as "marauders" known for "harrasing the ranchers, killing cattle, and running down horses"; Gareth, we are told, flung four of them into the air, breaking their backs. The tale is provided as evidence that at Rathmullan, "Irish wolfhounds still live up to the greatest traditions of the breed" and seems to have been an attempt to assert the dogs' usefulness.

The pamphlet concludes by mentioning that although the Whites own other dogs (an elderly Scottie and a prize-winning Afghan hound), these "really are only pets, while the Irish wolfhounds are the fulfillment of a breeding ideal, and exemplars of one of the finest things that has been attempted in the breed" (Jones n.d.:36). In such distinctions I see the main reason for which I was slow to see the connection between the dog cemetery and the Whites' art patronage. I had thought of dogs only as "pets," as a matter of private pleasure, whereas, to the Whites, dogs too could be a *project,* one that like Indian art and anthropology promised connection to imagined pasts and a way of shaping the future.

The Whites and their colleagues in Santa Fe sought to promote "Indian art as art, not ethnology," and I have argued that was in part because aesthetic authority was something they could lay claim to as people, especially as women, without professional careers, who had developed an extraordinary confidence in their aesthetic sensibilities and, as a result of their experience with pageantry, in their ability to stage public performances that would instruct others in how to classify and evaluate objects. They never sought to overthrow the authority of anthropology, however, with its "language of typification" (Thomas 1994:89), its ability to link objects with histories of particular places and communities. Anthropology made the pleasures of consuming Indian art all the richer, with its additional vocabularies and distinctions, its notion of a plurality of cultures each with a specific nature or essence that could be defined much in the way that writers of natural history sought to define and describe the nature of a species (Thomas 1994:81–90). Coupled with the language of modern art, anthropology offered consumers such as the Whites an even stronger sense of knowing "what they were looking at."

In the 1920s, when the Whites bought their first pair of wolfhounds, purebred dogs had long been associated with the idle rich (Ritvo 1987). In 1899 Thorstein Veblen argued that "canine monstrosities," as he termed the dogs of the dog fancy, exemplified conspicuous consumption among the nouveaux riches. As a means of conveying status, purebred dogs, he surmised, were far more effective than cats, who were not only less inclined to demonstrate subservience, but were apt to hunt rodents, thereby suggesting a practicality unflattering to their owners (1899:140–41). Veblen argued also that women of the nouveaux riches were expected to convey status through idleness and triviality (81–85). With their Bryn Mawrter ambitions for public influence, the Whites were especially apt to resist such a role for themselves. Both art and dogs provided the sense that they were doing something important (although the Whites had Scott to perform most of the work associated with the dogs, Elizabeth White worked quite hard to promote Indian art) and linked them to communities of consumers and producers. Domesticated animals, with their pedigrees making clear their distinction from the "wild," allowed the Whites at least partly to escape their own domestication, with no loss of status.

Both dogs and art fit uncomfortably into the category of commodity: dogs because of their role as "man's best friend"; art because it is a realm in large part defined as a refuge from commerce. At the School of American Research the potential of dogs and art to serve as commodities is especially obscured: in the vaults of the Indian Arts Research Center, art is the object of scholarly study and venerated as a link to the past and as a model to inspire contemporary artists. The dog cemetery is considered an odd but amusing relic from the estate's past life as a private residence. But the two collections, that of art and that of dogs, are linked by more than a footpath. Although the art has maintained value in ways the dogs have not, for the Whites, the value of both art and dogs was less in individual creatures or objects than in the endeavors surrounding them.

ABBREVIATIONS

AEWC   Amelia Elizabeth White Collection

BIA   Bureau of Indian Affairs

EAIA   Eastern Association on Indian Affairs

EITA   Exposition of Indian Tribal Arts

ESS   Elizabeth Shepley Sergeant Papers

IACB   Indian Arts and Crafts Board

IARC   Indian Arts Research Center

KCC   Kenneth Chapman Collection

LA   Laboratory of Anthropology

MDLC   Mabel Dodge Luhan Collection

NA   National Archives

NMAIA   New Mexico Association on Indian Affairs

RIACB   Records of the Indian Arts and Crafts Board

SAR   School of American Research

SWAIA   Southwestern Association on Indian Affairs (changed, in 1993, to the "Southwestern Association for Indian Arts")

SWAIAC   Southwestern Association on Indian Affairs Collection

SRCA   State Records Center and Archives

WM   Wheelwright Museum

YCAL   Yale Collection of American Literature

NOTES

Preface

1 For related discussions of the concept of culture, including its history and recent critique, see, e.g., Brown (1998), Di Leonardo (1998), Hegeman (1999), Kuper (1999), Marcus and Myers (1995), Michaels (1995), Ortner (1999), Segal and Handler (1995), Stocking (1989), and Wallerstein (1990).

2 For discussion of ethnographic research into "art worlds," see Becker (1982) and Marcus and Myers (1995).

Chapter One Culture and Cultures

1 For a more thorough discussion of Austin's relationship to feminism, see Jacobs (1999).

2 Leah Dilworth provides a thorough discussion of Austin and *The American Rhythm* and documents the connection between Austin's cultural nationalism and her anti-Semitism (1996:173–210).

3 Susan Hegeman has analyzed Waldo Frank's notions of culture in relation to American modernism. Waldo Frank, she notes, imagined *Our America* as "a kind of guidebook to what he perceived to be the important cultural sites, and actors, in the United States" (1999:105).

4 On connections among artists and other intellectuals in the U.S. and in Mexico in the early twentieth century, see Oles, who reports that for many American artists, Mexico was "an almost natural extension of their experience in the Southwest. Mexico was 'older,' its ruins grander, its mountains higher. And unlike the Southwest, tourism and modernity had not yet overwhelmed it" (1993:147).

5 In Edith Wharton's novels, wealthy women in nineteenth-century New York turned themselves into objets d'art for men to desire (Montgomery 1998:71). Montgomery notes, however, that in Wharton's world once such women married they played the role of curator within their homes.

6 As George Marcus notes in an interesting discussion of eccentricity and class, eccentricity is a class-bound concept and is "predominately associated with the lavishly powerful, wealthy, and famous" (1998:167). Although the Whites were, on a national level, hardly all that tremendously wealthy or famous, in Santa Fe they were certainly among the wealthiest of the city's early twentieth-century residents and therefore suitable targets for accusations of nonconformity.

7   Linda Davis's biography of Katharine White is a good source of additional infor-
     mation about the Sergeant family and their history; the Sergeants' ancestors
     included the Reverend John Sergeant, Yale scholar and missionary to the Indians
     of Stockbridge, Massachusetts (1987:14). In Brookline, the Sergeant sisters grew
     up in an 8,800 square-foot Georgian house (18); their father was remembered by
     E. B. White, Katharine's husband, as "a typical Boston capitalist home man" (21).
     Concerning Elizabeth Sergeant, see archivist Diane J. Ducharme's excellent
     description of her papers in the Beinecke Library (ESS, YCAL MSS 3).

8   Sergeant occasionally suggests that she found it difficult to reconcile her gender
     identity and her public ambitions—a conflict she tried to elaborate more fully in
     an autobiographical novel which she never published (ESS Papers, Beinecke
     Library, Yale). When struggling to write her first book in 1911, Cather came to
     visit her where she was living with family in Brookline. Sergeant recalled in her
     memoir that she felt Cather empathized with her alienation from her family:
     "We exchanged comprehending looks, la famille, la famille, sounding out of the
     darkening skies. Single women making their way to individual destinies—who
     in the home circle understands them? If they try to share what they have found
     in their further reach, who wants it?" (1963:61).

     In Linda Davis's biography of Elizabeth Sergeant's sister, Katharine White,
     Elizabeth is described as "a lonely, troubled woman" suffering from unspecified
     psychological problems (1987:26).

9   Bryn Mawr entrance requirements included a knowledge of three of four
     languages—Latin, Greek, French, and German, languages that students were
     required to continue studying at Bryn Mawr (Davis 1987:34). In the foreword to
     her memoir of Cather, Elizabeth Sergeant illustrated the Eurocentric nature of
     the Bryn Mawr curriculum with a recollection of how, some fifteen years after
     her graduation, one of her former professors scoffed at her admiration of
     Cather's novels, the professor finding it impossible to imagine that a novel set in
     rural America and written by a woman could be worthy of the category of
     literature. Sergeant recalled that if she and her classmates read any American
     literature at all, it would have been that of expatriates like Henry James or Edith
     Wharton, but even those texts they would never have been assigned as part of a
     college course, but would instead have considered them a temporary diversion
     from more serious studies. Sergeant writes that in a course in descriptive writing
     she was given passages of *Madame Bovary* to imitate. Her friend Cather, as a
     young instructor at the University of Nebraska at the turn of the century, also
     urged her students to study Flaubert, deeming *Madame Bovary* worthy of memo-
     rization (Sergeant 1963:10).

Chapter Two Elizabeth Sergeant, Buying and Selling the Southwest

1   Elizabeth Sergeant to Mrs. Brewer, 16 November 1922, John Collier papers,
     microfilm reel 5.

2   Concerning the connection between such women's careers and the exercise of
     taste, Nancy Franklin describes a similar blending of taste and ambition in an

article about Sergeant's sister, Katharine White, former editor at *The New Yorker*. Franklin, who started working at the magazine not long after White's death in 1977, recalls that White was often described as "aristocratic" (in addition to "formidable" and "forbidding") and that she "stood out in her beautifully tailored clothes and Sally Victor hats" (1996:174–75). Franklin offers an interesting explanation of her own surprise, while studying White's papers and correspondence, to learn of the very ambitious and creative role White had played as editor: "Having grown up with the idea that good taste was not something you exercised so much as it was something you didn't violate, I had assumed that Katharine White's much lauded good taste in editorial matters was reined-in and backward-looking, more concerned with what the magazine shouldn't be doing rather than with what it could be doing" (181).

3 The title of *O Pioneers!* derives from Whitman. Sharon O'Brien offers an interesting discussion of the book's complex relationship to Whitman's work: "In associating her novel with Whitman's poetry, Cather was claiming an affiliation with America's epic and prophetic writer and associating herself with the heir of Emerson, the nineteenth-century progenitor of the Adamic myth" (1987:433). Yet at the same time Cather was using her heroine, Alexandra Bergson, to break down the nationalist myth's masculinist quality.

4 Despite her Eurocentric literary interests, Cather had long been interested in the Southwest, and particularly in cliff dwellings. As children, she and her brothers had been intrigued by stories of Mesa Verde. "The cliff-dwellings were one of the native myths of the Southwest," Edith Lewis recalled in her biography of Cather, and "children knew about them before they were conscious of knowing about them" (quoted in O'Brien 1987:405).

5 As Sharon O'Brien and others have pointed out, the wilderness has often been used to represent an American essence. When the wilderness—or farmland—is constructed as masculine space, women are excluded from the national identity. By making the outdoors a home for her heroines, Cather reimagined the gendered landscape of the national identity (see O'Brien 1987:432–33).

6 Sergeant mentioned, in a letter to John Collier, that she received more than $1400—a sum which seemed satisfactory to her—for the four parts of "The Journal of a Mud House" (30 November 1922, John Collier Papers, microfilm reel 4).

7 It is likely Sergeant is referring to Curtis's famous 1904 photograph *Cañon de Chelly—Navaho,* but she seems to have been confused about her dates. She writes of a Curtis photograph having been given to her as a child, but Curtis only began making such photographs after Sergeant's graduation from Bryn Mawr.

8 On the Bursum Bill and the campaign against it, see Kelly (1983) and Dauber (1993:117–24).

9 Sergeant seems to have wrestled with ambivalent feelings about many of her most salient identities—those pertaining to nation, region, ethnicity, and gender. Her fellow Bryn Mawrters evidently found such identities less nettlesome. For example, although after the late 1920s Elizabeth White spent most of the remaining part of her life in Santa Fe, she continued to retain an ethnic identity rooted

confidently in colonial New England, as evidenced by her 1948 application (including family tree), and acceptance, to the National Society of Colonial Dames of New York (AEWC, SAR [uncatalogued]).

10   See, e.g., Dozier to Sergeant, 18 November 1949, John Collier Papers, microfilm reel 17.

Chapter Three   Shopping for a Better World in a City of Ladies

1   Stark and Rayne report that after their father's death, Elizabeth and Martha White had an annual income of $55,000 each (1998:47) and that at the time of her death Elizabeth White's trust was worth nearly three million dollars (10).

2   White named her shop "Ishauu." While she may have chosen the name because it could sound "Indian" to her clientele, in fact it was her family nickname, a toddler's pronunciation of "Elizabeth."

3   Elizabeth White's patronage of Indian art is discussed in more detail in chapter 4; see also Stark and Rayne (1998), Brody (1971, 1997), Swenson (1983), Rushing (1995), and McGreevy (1993).

4   Judging from formal and informal interviews with her contemporaries, it seems that both Pueblo Indians and white colleagues shared ambivalent feelings about Dietrich (though artists tend to emphasize gratitude for her patronage of their art). While valuing her energy and commitment, many saw her as ruthlessly single-minded and arrogant. Yet on her death in 1961 Dietrich was glowingly eulogized during a "Pueblo Indian Hour" on a local radio station. The eulogy is revealing of an outward acceptance of white paternalism, but also of the respect Dietrich had gained: "She saw and experienced many changes and progress in her Pueblo people. We consider her a part of our people's progress and wonderful results" (1 / 15 / 61, Margretta S. Dietrich Papers, SRCA).

5   For an analysis of similar conceptions of the Southwest among pioneer women in the region, see Kolodny (1984).

6   Michael Thompson similarly describes women as dominating an early phase of collecting English "Stevengraphs" (Victorian woven silk pictures originally sold as souvenirs). Women were the first collectors, but once the market became more established and profitable, it became dominated by men; early collections were gradually bought by men from women and men began writing the authoritative texts and selling the pictures at prestigious auctions. "[T]here does appear," Thompson remarks, "to be a shift from women to men as the Stevengraph goes from rubbish to durable" (Thompson 1979:33).

7   Similar appeals to connections among taste, morality, and national identity were made by proponents of the Arts and Crafts movement, a movement especially appealing to women (see, e.g., Boris 1986, Lears 1981).

8   In a fascinating study of the way that consumer behavior influenced early twentieth-century anthropologists and the curator Stewart Culin, Eliza McFeely has emphasized that there were men such as Culin who also reveled in the pleasures of domestic consumption. When collecting material for museums, they were in effect taking advantage of an opportunity to indulge in the "femi-

nine" behavior of shopping, while "wearing the soberly masculine garb of the scientist and curator" (McFeely 1996:327).

9   In a recent biography, the Pueblo painter Geronima Montoya, who began painting and teaching art during the same period, is quoted as saying that "Margretta was always purchasing paintings. She was interested in Indians in general" (Shutes and Mellick 1996:60). Dietrich however, was capable of thwarting artists' careers as well as aiding them: I suspect that Pop Chalee never knew that in 1944 Dietrich urged that she be dismissed from her teaching position at the Santa Fe Indian School, asserting that morally and artistically, Chalee was a poor role model for young Indian students (Cesa 1997:111).

10 For additional discussion of Peña, her paintings, and her relationship with Hewett and other Santa Fe patrons, see Brody (1997, especially pp. 113–19), Jacobs (1999), and Jantzer-White (1994).

11 On white women's involvement in both suppressing and protecting Pueblo religion in the early twentieth century, see Jacobs (1999). Several of the Bryn Mawrters and their associates in Santa Fe found that their interests in spirituality meshed well with their interests in Jungian psychology. By collecting objects connected with Indian and Hispanic spiritual beliefs, and by compiling ethnographic information, Elizabeth Sergeant, Mabel Dodge Luhan, and Elizabeth White's close friend, Mary Cabot Wheelwright, were able to participate in a search for universal truths about human spirituality—an endeavor which also can be seen as an attempt to bridge public and private spheres of influence. Carl Jung made several trips to Santa Fe during this period and was reportedly impressed by local collections of Pueblo pottery and Navajo weaving and sand-painting. One of the collections Jung visited was that of Mary Cabot Wheelwright, who founded a museum in Santa Fe which she originally called the "House of Navajo Religion." In recalling her years of collecting objects and ethnographic information, Wheelwright expressed ambitions of both a universal and nationalist nature: "As I recorded myth after myth I felt so strongly that the material had a universal application that during ten years, beginning about 1928, I felt compelled to collect all that I could of this extraordinary material, which had come out of our own soil" (n.d.:39).

12 Erna Fergusson, who became a highly successful travel writer in the 1930s, was connected with this network and was also active in marketing the Southwest during the 1920s, but through a more commercial enterprise. In 1922 Fergusson and her friend Ethel Hickey opened a "sight-seeing business," called "Koshare Tours," offering personally guided tours through Northern New Mexico from their base in Albuquerque, often taking in ceremonial dances at the Pueblos. "Koshare Tours" was so successful that it was eventually bought out by the Fred Harvey Company and renamed "Indian Detours" (which continued the tradition of "girl guides" by employing only young women as "couriers"). Fergusson and Hickey marketed a sort of domesticity in the desert to tourists, as Fergusson explained to *The Woman's Home Companion*: "we act as hostesses, and as such on a long, dry trip in the afternoon we often stop in some cool canyon, or in the shade of some overhanging bluff, and have tea. The personal touch means a lot,

and we treat our guests on the road as we would guests in our home. That is why I think a business as ours is more successfully conducted by women than by men. Women make much more of the little things that mean so much, than men do" (Hurt 1928). Similar articles about Koshare tours during the same period announced: "Girls Explain Trails in West," and "You Can Live Among Apaches or Navajos as One of the Family—if Miss Erna Fergusson of Albuquerque Vouches For You" (see Erna Fergusson Collection, University of New Mexico Special Collections, scrapbook 75).

13   Chabot and Lukas's 1936 field notes are housed in the National Archives (NA), Records of the Indian Arts and Crafts Board, record group 435, box 1.

14   "Urgent Navajo Problems," 1940, SWAIAC, SRCA.

15   For a more abstract consideration of relationships between women and taste (or in Erving Goffman's terms, "impression management"), see Randall Collins (1992).

Chapter Four   The Patronage of Difference: Making Indian Art "Art, Not Ethnology"

This chapter is a revised version of an article which originally appeared in *Cultural Anthropology* (Mullin 1992) and later in Marcus and Myers (1995). An early draft was presented at the annual meeting of the American Ethnological Society in Charleston, South Carolina, on 15 March 1991.

1   1931, Exposition of Indian Tribal Arts (EITA), brochure, School of American Research (SAR), Amelia Elizabeth White Collection (AEWC), EITA file.

2   As Barbara Herrnstein Smith notes in her study of theories of value and evaluation, "The labels 'art' and 'literature' are, of course, commonly signs of membership in distinctly honorific categories" (1988:43). The content of these categories is continually open to contestation and change; this chapter aims to illuminate the processes by which "Indian art" came to be accepted as "art."

3   Although there are important differences, the movement discussed here bears resemblance to a slightly earlier movement to encourage the production of American handicrafts as studied by Lears (1981) and Boris (1986), among others. Lears argues that the Arts and Crafts Movement was also a response to a "crisis of cultural authority" perceived by the late-Victorian bourgeoisie in relation to mass production and consumption. His description of Victorian and turn-of-the-century "anti-modernism" would also apply to the movement discussed here: "it was meanspirited and largehearted, suffused with upper-class forebodings and utopian aspirations" (1981:60).

4   According to a biographer, "No undertaking of Abby Aldrich Rockefeller more clearly demonstrates her pride in America and in its cultural history than her collection of folk art which now hangs in the Ludwell-Paradise House in Colonial Williamsburg . . . it records those years in American history when, after the baffling problems of a new world had been solved by the colonists and after the War of the Revolution had finally shattered an earlier dependence upon the culture and learning of England, a new American people began for the first time to stand alone, to work out its own destiny as a nation" (Chase 1950:147—48).

5 Something of an analogy can be found in Marquis's argument that in the 1930s the organizers of the Museum of Modern Art waged a campaign to improve popular tastes by redefining the boundaries of art: "By broadening the definition of art to include a mass of intrinsically valueless items—movies, photographs, advertisements, packages, furniture, articles of daily use—the museum . . . taught the public that it could exercise connoisseurship in a purchase as humble as a potato masher or a soup plate" (Marquis 1986:184, see also chapter 4, " . . . But is it Art?"). Marquis also provides a general discussion of controversies during the 1930s surrounding the relationship between "culture" and "mass culture."

6 For a much more reactionary construction of culture as the province of the upper middle class, serving particular economic interests (and lacking appeals to cultural nationalism), see Debora Silverman's study of connections between Bloomingdale's, the Metropolitan Museum, and the Reagan White House (1986).

7 On modernist painters in Santa Fe, see Udall (1984), Rushing (1995), and Brody (1997).

8 Chris Wilson's study of architecture and the invention of a regional style in Santa Fe (1997) is a source of much relevant information concerning the influence of individuals such as Hewett and Lummis.

9 M. McKittrick to A. E. White, 15 September 1931, SAR, AEWC; Wheelwright, Mary Cabot, "Journey Towards Understanding," n.d., 62–63, Wheelwright Museum, Santa Fe, New Mexico.

10 For an additional examination of New Yorkers' patronage of Indian art, see Rushing (1995).

11 On Indians and the marketing of tourism in the early to mid-twentieth-century Southwest, see also Babcock and Weigle (1996), Dilworth (1996), and Jojola (1998).

12 Anthropologists had long been concerned about the lack of concern for authenticity in the Indian souvenir trade. W. H. Holmes, for example, in the *American Anthropologist* in 1889 denounced the clay figurines being made among the Pueblos. "The country is being flooded," he warned, "with cheap and, scientifically speaking, worthless earthenware made by the Pueblo Indians to supply the tourist trade . . . Only those who happen to be familiar with the refined and artistic wares of the ancient Pueblos can appreciate the debasement brought about by contact with the whites" (1889:320). Babcock, Monthan and Monthan (1986) provide information about how the figurines in question eventually became accepted as a legitimate(d) "folk art."

13 My understanding of the view of patron-philanthropists (White, Dietrich, et al.) has been influenced greatly by discussions with contemporary Indian art patrons, who represented their concerns and efforts in a similar fashion, seeing themselves as not fostering "alien" influence, but rather counteracting it with more authentic and "more truly Indian" standards of value. This was not a perspective exclusive to non-Indians; I spoke with many artists and patrons who were themselves Indian who represented their concerns similarly. My under-

standing was also influenced by discussions with individuals who worked with White, Dietrich, and their associates in the 1930s. Interviews with Maria Chabot (20 Nov. 1990; 7 Dec. 1990), Moris Burge (30 Ap. 1991), and Julia Lukas (10 May 1991) were especially helpful.

14 The artists were accompanied on their trip to New York by Moris Burge and Margaret McKittrick. McKittrick married the much younger Burge while working for the NMAIA and EAIA. Burge, originally from England, had attended the Art Institute of Chicago in the late 1920s before coming to Santa Fe, where he first found work with the NMAIA and EAIA, coloring photographs of Navajo textiles at the Laboratory of Anthropology. The idea, he told me in April 1991, was to use the photographs as models for weavers, counteracting the influence of traders. Burge recalled that the artists he brought to New York for the Exposition in 1931 thoroughly enjoyed their trip, despite the fact that few spoke much English. In addition to being treated as celebrities, Burge recalled, they visited the top of the Empire State Building and Jones Beach, where they filled containers with sea water to bring home with them. Burge, who went on to work for the BIA, remembered his work with artists fondly (noting especially their sense of humor) but said he recognized that he and other art patrons were naive: "We were well-meaning, but paternalistic."

15 Brody (1997:182) reports that museums were not always supportive of the idea that Pueblo paintings belonged in art museums: the Art Institute of Chicago and New York's Metropolitan Museum of Art rejected gifts of Pueblo paintings offered them by Elizabeth White, stating that the paintings would be more appropriate in museums of anthropology or natural history.

16 Hewett seems to have envisioned the Fiestas as a mini–World's Fair, a type of event with which he had previous experience, having been director of exhibits for the 1915 Panama-California Exposition in San Diego (which celebrated the completion of the Panama Canal). On Hewett and his role in the Fiestas and the San Diego Exposition, see Chauvenet (1983), who touches on differences between Hewett and other Indian art patrons in Santa Fe. Also, on the early history of Indian Fairs in the Southwest, including a number of projects not covered here (such as the Hopi Craftsman Show), see Wade (1985). Wade analyzes the Fairs as an element of a struggle for power in the Indian art market between factions composed of philanthropists and traders. As I argue here, however, many philanthropists saw tourists and other "uneducated" consumers as a more important threat than traders, among whom they sometimes found allies. Stocking (1982) provides additional information about Hewett and his relationship to other anthropologists and patrons of anthropology.

In 1926 writer and literary critic Yvor Winters published a scathing critique of Hewett's management of the Santa Fe Fiesta and his patronage of "pseudo-Indian" performers: "I had the pleasure last evening of attending the opening of the Santa Fe Fiesta, which was directed by Cadman, the fake Indian musician, at the instigation of Edgar Hewett, Santa Fe's fake archaeologist, who sits on top of a good job, like a lady spider in her web, while a lot of lean scholars roam around the hills and do the dirty work for him. And starve, of course. Hewett was everywhere in evidence, in white ducks with a pink sash around his naturally florid tummy, looking like a eunuch who couldn't find his scimitar" (Winters 1926:32).

Winters went on to note his delight in observing that the Pueblo Indians in attendance appeared to find Hewett's performers—singers Oskenonton, Tsianina Blackstone, and "a nice girl called Te Ata, who may be part Indian, and who calls herself . . . a Chickasaw princess"—hysterically amusing in their pseudo-Indianness. "The Taos delegation," he claimed, "wrapped their heads in their sheets and tried to strangle themselves, and one fell over backwards. One, in tears, pulled out a handkerchief, but had to give it up for his sheet. Mothers from Tesuque and San Ildefonso tried to smother their infants, and all the little girls from the Santa Fe Indian school were lolling on one another's laps and shoulders from exhaustion. The old men from Tesuque, dressed up for the bow and arrow dance, almost ruined their make-up before they came on" (1926:32–33).

17 In 1934 the Southwest Indian Fair Committee was absorbed into the New Mexico Association on Indian Affairs (NMAIA), the organization formed in Santa Fe in 1922 by Elizabeth Sergeant and other Anglo-Americans to protect Indian land rights and religious freedom as well as to improve health and economic conditions among nearby Indians. The NMAIA today is known as the Southwestern Association on Indian Arts (SWAIA). For additional historical information on these groups, see Bernstein (1993 and 1996) and Mayhew (1984).

18 For a very interesting analysis of the effects of patronage and the growth of the market for Pueblo pottery on Santa Clara and San Ildefonso, see Dauber (1993:275–336), who draws on surveys conducted by the Soil Conservation Service during the 1930s.

19 Among members of Pueblo communities, it is possible that people who were not artists were likely to be more critical of the actions of white patrons. Alfonso Ortiz told me that as a young man at San Juan Pueblo he resented some of the patrons discussed here who "thought they knew everything about Indians." That resentment, he surmised, was part of what inspired him to pursue a career as an anthropologist.

20 It seems that Santa Clara Indians took quite the opposite approach in 1936 and asked Santa Fe patrons, including Amelia Elizabeth White, if they would serve as judges for their Fair and provide prize money (Sophie Aberle to A. E. White, SAR, AEWC, "misc.").

21 In his 1924 article promoting the Indian Fair, Kenneth Chapman mentioned that one potter at San Ildefonso, presumably Maria Martinez, was "capable" of earning $300 per month from pottery, whereas the cash return on farm products for the entire Pueblo during the previous year was only $3,300 (Chapman 1924:224). Though Chapman seems to have remained unconcerned about the social consequences of such individual success, this was precisely the sort of division and social transformation that Elizabeth Sergeant expressed concerns about in her report on San Ildefonso in 1935. Sergeant had no alternative to propose, but she argued that patrons should at least take into consideration the sort of *changes* they were fostering in the name of "tradition." I believe that Sergeant was quite

correct in her assertion that very few of the more influential patrons gave such matters any significant thought.

22 This information concerning the immediate impact of awards on collectors was provided in personal interviews conducted in 1990 and 1991 with Marjorie Lambert (14 Feb. 1991), Letta Wofford (25 Feb. 1991), and Sallie Wagner (12 Sept. 1990), who served as judges during the Indian Markets of the 1930s and 1940s. As discussed in the following chapter, in the contemporary Indian Market, entries are judged before they can be exhibited and sold, and many buyers especially seek to buy award-winning pieces (which often are sold for greatly increased prices as a result of having won an award). Lambert made a point of stating that Elizabeth White had never served as a judge, though I know from archival records that in fact she did. Lambert's explanation, however, echoed some of the other descriptions I heard of White's personality: Lambert said she couldn't imagine White mixing with the "hoi polloi—the tourists" in an atmosphere she described as similar to that of a carnival.

23 For a history of the Indian Arts Fund, which was funded partly by John D. Rockefeller Jr., see Dauber (1990, 1993); Stocking (1982) also discusses the Indian Arts Fund and Rockefeller's role as an important patron of anthropology in the region.

24 In a letter to Mary-Russell Colton at the Museum of Northern Arizona, Kenneth Chapman, who was a special consultant to the Indian Arts and Crafts Board (IACB), explained that such designs were not accepted "since the prevailing opinion is that all these [designs] have been suggested by traders or by other whites" (KCC, LA, 1938, file 89KCo.005). Along with their concern about protecting Indian arts as an important source of Indian income, the IACB made it clear that they were concerned about "these products as art, and as part of the art heritage of the American people as well as of the Indian" (KCC, LA, 1934, file KCo.020). On the history and policies of the IACB, see Schrader (1983).

25 The anthropological assumption of cultures as discrete entities, now less prevalent after two decades of substantial critique, probably encouraged patrons to consider "Indian" and "Hispanic" as unrelated, even oppositional, identities. Studies by John Chávez (1984) and Ramón Gutiérrez (1990), among others, have emphasized that neat divisions between "Indian" and "Hispanic" obscure the historical fluidity of these populations.

26 Charles Briggs has produced an extensive study of how the patronage of Hispanic New Mexican woodcarving has led to tremendous social changes in artists' communities, despite patron's intentions of fostering the "revival" of tradition (1989).

27 A common reaction to the sort of hothouse flowering of tradition presented here is to praise the more "avant-garde" of Indian artists (see, e.g., Wade [1985] and Babock [1990])—those who stress innovation and experiment with "European" traditions, those who speak the language of art schools, or those who resist popular stereotypes—as if these were *really* the authentic and creative artists. But what of the many "traditional" artists who say they have never felt

"forced" in their traditionalism (despite all the awards for it)—who are proud of their "culture," and "heritage," however profitable it may be? As Bourdieu (1984) and many other analysts of taste have shown, there is as much mystification and essentialism in "Western" art traditions.

28 Kathy M'Closkey's work on the history of Navajo textile market is especially important for its attention to the profits being made by dealers, especially in the early twentieth century, when most Navajo textiles were being purchased by the pound and transported by the bale (M'Closkey 1994, 1996).

29 For an overview of debates concerning "mass culture" (or, more sympathetically, "popular culture"), see Brantlinger (1990). Barnard (1995) examines such debates among intellectuals in the context of the 1930s.

30 Chase's *Men and Machines,* published in 1929, is filled with similar lists, e.g., in his discussion of whether to consider modernity a process of standardization or diversification: "Look at the fads which follow one after another in crazy procession—bicycle riding, ping pong, golf, bridge, mah-jong, jazz, crossword puzzles, bobbed hair, antiques, prohibition cocktails" (271). On the practice of listing senselessly diverse commodities in American writing during the 1930s, see Barnard (1995), who also provides a relevant discussion of Nathanael West's use of Indians in his critique of consumer capitalism (1990:279–85).

Chapter Five Culture and Value at Indian Market

1 *Albuquerque Tribune* reporter Shonda Novak (1997) wrote an article on anti–Indian Market sentiment in which she describes the affair as "a monied Mardi Gras with a native twist." While living in Santa Fe in the early 1990s, I sensed that the term "Indian Markup" was not always simply a means of denigrating the event or what it seemed to represent. When used by my Hispanic hairdresser, for example, who had friends among the artists and enjoyed attending when he could, it seemed a way of drawing a boundary between insider and outsider knowledge, local people and tourists. The idea, I gathered, was that local people would know better than to buy their Indian art at Indian Market, rather than some other time of the year when it could be had for a good deal less money. In fact, though, I met many local people, including some quite knowledgeable about Indian art, who *did* buy pieces at Market. In some cases, that might well have been the only occasion the desired pieces could be purchased; and, unlike my hairdresser, many of these people were not very much concerned with getting any kind of bargain. Sometimes, too, it seemed that collectors bought pieces almost as a way of commemorating the event: at least, they appeared to enjoy saying, "Now, that piece I bought at Indian Market in such and such a year . . ."

2 Thomas (1994) uses the term "contemporary primitivism" to discuss such phenomena as the movie *Dances With Wolves.* See also Torgovnick (1997 and 1990) and Price (1989). On primitivism in the Southwest, see Dilworth (1996). The realm of "art"—of whatever sort—has also often been constructed in opposition

to the more troublesome qualities associated with modern life. As Clifford writes, "expectations of wholeness, continuity, and essence have long been built into the linked Western ideas of culture and art" (1988:233).

3   In his 1995 novel, *High Fidelity,* Nick Hornby provides a relevant fictional analysis of a consumer's obsession with esoteric distinctions regarding popular music: shaken by a lack of success in his career and in living up to expectations of masculinity, his main character uses an extensive knowledge of trivia to shore up his self-esteem and distract himself from his problems. As a connoisseur, his character finds a sense of control lacking in the rest of his life. Many would argue that Indian art is less "trivial" than popular music (or gardening), but I believe consumers of many sorts of commodities are similarly motivated by desires to boost self-esteem (not reducible to class status) and for distraction.

4   Chabot's remarks were made during a presentation she gave at a seminar at the Museum of Indian Arts and Culture in Santa Fe, 20 October 1990.

5   In a subsequent interview in November 1990, Chabot told me that the more reluctant traders were readily won over after the markets' first year, when they realized that the events only increased their business. Presumably their change of heart resulted from increased numbers of people with an interest in Indian objects coming to the downtown, but it is also possible that the traders saw more indirect encouragement of their businesses by the legitimation of Indian art.

6   Collecting as game playing is explored briefly in Susan Pearce's examination of contemporary collectors (not just of art, but anything) in Britain (1998; see chapter 3, "Work and Play," and chapter 8, "Contemporary Collecting"). Russell Belk (1995) provides an extensive examination of the relationship between object collecting and consumer society. After interviewing some 200 collectors, Belk concluded that they were most often motivated by "a feeling of mastery, competence, or success" achieved in their collecting activities (87). Other rewards included the sense of an "enlarged self" and the "thrill of the hunt" (89, 92–93).

7   In 1997 SWAIA sent an announcement to its members that "Indian Market" was a registered trade name that could be used only with SWAIA's permission and that because "not all activities advertised as being connected with 'Santa Fe Indian Market' are sanctioned by SWAIA," the organization is "taking steps to address this unauthorized use of our name."

8   In the 1950s Margretta Dietrich mentioned in a letter to Bryn Mawr alumnae, "All Indians are welcome to attend our meetings, but do not pay dues. They do sometimes contribute" (Bryn Mawr College Archives, Alumnae Association files).

9   Bernstein points out that before the early 1970s there were no "galleries" of Indian art in Santa Fe, only "shops." Bernstein also notes that an indication (as well as source of momentum) of the expanding market for Indian art in the 1970s was the appearance of *American Indian Art* magazine in 1975 (1993:231; 253–54). For his discussion of the impact of the IAIA on the Indian Market of the 1970s and early 1980s, see pp. 267–71.

10   This boundary is a visible one when items are turned in for judging prior to the event's opening. Artists wait in long lines to be received by a cadre of volunteers

and the occasional paid staff member. To be on the receiving end suggests an ability to scrutinize work outside the presence of the artist, as well as to hear judges' and others' assessments of it—information of considerable value. One artist confided to me that before serving as a judge herself, she had never before felt free to examine other artists' work closely except in magazines and books, and sometimes in store windows. To have such freedom she saw as a rare privilege, but perhaps also something of a guilty pleasure. I don't know how representative her perspective was; I met others who seemed to share none of her inhibition. Pueblo potters commonly report a sense of intense competition among the potters in their communities, competition that makes artists guarded about sharing knowledge of their work and concerned about other artists appropriating designs or techniques, or merely envying or deriding their skill (for discussions of competition among communities of potters, see Bruce Bernstein's dissertation on Indian Market's relationship to Pueblo pottery [1993]; Rick Dillingham's *Acoma and Laguna Pottery* (1992, especially chapter 8 on "Native Artists and the Marketplace"); and the work of Santa Clara sociologist and potter Tessie Naranjo [1996]. Such rivalry is not surprising, given what is at stake and how much depends on reputation and the creation and maintenance of a unique identity for the artists and their work. I had the sense that relatively successful artists often feel that their profession's satisfactions and economic rewards more than outweigh such burdens.

11 Bird and Johnson's work is held in a number of museum collections, including the Heard Museum in Phoenix. In 1995 one of their belt buckles ("Tourism / Route 66") was included in the Heard Museum's exhibition "Inventing the Southwest: The Fred Harvey Company and Native American Art."

12 In a forum at Santa Fe's Museum of Fine Arts in 1992, Sakiestewa expressed such an egalitarian sensibility and spoke passionately about the need for public funding for art education, with reference to her own experiences growing up in Albuquerque and traveling to Santa Fe to visit museums. "Showing real art in places like Las Cruces, Grants, and Portales," Sakiestewa argued, "is one of the most basic ways we can keep the kids from being sucked away from the arts by satellite dishes" (McDowell 1992:46).

13 Sakiestewa's initiative has been successful, and other Native artists, including Wendy Ponca, Arthur Amiotte, George Hunt Jr., and Tony Abeyta have also designed blankets for production in "limited" and "open" editions. For a history of such ventures, see Lohrmann (1998).

14 Bird did not seem to think their purchasing at all unusual, but other people involved with the Indian art market contended that such purchases among artists were quite the exception. Nancy Mitchell writes in her study of Indian artists in Santa Fe, "There is practically no market for the internal consumption of contemporary Indian art" (1993:53). I have encountered artists, from Kansas and Oklahoma, at Indian Market and the Eight Northern Indian Pueblos Artist and Craftsman Show who indicated that they would like to buy work exhibited at those events but could not afford to do so. I also encountered a few artists, including Pueblo potters, who reported trading work with other artists.

15 Bruce Bernstein mentions that he was told by Maria Chabot that her initial plan in 1936 was to have Indian artists serve as judges. But when she approached Maria Martinez of San Ildefonso, Tonita Peña of Cochiti, and Severa Tafoya from Santa Clara, they all refused, stating that it would be inappropriate for them to judge members of their own communities (Bernstein 1993:195–96).

16 In her memoir Wagner writes that when she and her husband arrived at the trading post at Wide Ruins in 1938, "the Navajos in the area were making very poor rugs, the kind that were sold from knocked-together stands along Highway 66. The wool was not well cleaned or well spun. The bordered designs were the kind that had originated in Oriental rugs or were crossed arrows and swastikas, and the colors were red, black, and white—the designs and colors usually thought of as 'Indian' " (50). She goes on to relate how she and her husband set out to improve the quality by influencing both weavers and potential buyers. In blatant disregard for prevailing norms of discourse among contemporary Indian Market judges, norms which tend to steer clear of purely personal preference, Wagner writes, "We would not tolerate borders, principally because of a personal reaction of mine that makes me want to jump from bordered rug to bordered rug when I encounter them on the floor" (55).

17 In his doctoral dissertation on Indian Market and its relationship to Pueblo pottery, Bruce Bernstein provides a discussion of the judging process, drawing on his personal experience as a judge as well as conversations with artists and judges (1993:282–98).

18 For a brief history of the Gallup Intertribal Ceremonial, with a focus on the impact on Pueblo pottery and potters, see Bernstein (1993:65–66).

19 Dillingham's book (1992) provides a useful analysis of the system of patronage and value making in the Pueblo pottery market, including information about some of the pressures and constraints on potters. His analysis was clearly informed by his own experience as an artist as well as his years of working with Pueblo potters as a dealer, scholar, and museum curator. In keeping with his taste for irony, Dillingham reflected critically on his own role as tastemaker. Though as passionate about pottery and potters as I can imagine one could be, Dillingham did not portray the social forces surrounding its production in romantic terms.

20 In a recent novel, Isleta / San Juan Pueblo author Evelina Zuni Lucero offers a different view of the relationship between Pueblo pottery and "culture" in her description of an artist pricing her wares: "I wondered whether I was asking too much, perhaps too little. I thought about who might buy it, then hike up the price, resell a piece of Indian culture, a piece of my soul." (2000 15).

21 Ruth Phillips discusses the shift from colonial to postcolonial museum practices in relation to her own experience as a museum curator trained as an art historian, specializing in collections of Native art from Northeastern North America. Phillips explains that in earlier years she did not question her habit of seeking out "the rare and the old, the 'authentic' and the unacculturated for presentation in teaching, exhibitions, and written texts." She writes that, following her disciplinary training and scholarly and curatorial conventions, she at first felt only "side-

tracked" by the "tourist art" she came across, "beaded tea cosies" or "glove boxes of birchbark and porcupine quills," objects that evoked images of "innumerable small meetings across cultural boundaries." She now critiques the exclusion of "tourist art" as the product of a colonial museum practice that insisted on a "representation of Native Americans as other, as marginalized and as premodern" (1995:99–100). Of course, even art that has long been considered authentic, fitting neatly into clear categories, offending no authority's taste or standards of quality, can also be considered the product of "meetings across cultural boundaries."

22   Beginning in the 1980s, artists who apply for exhibit space are required to produce a copy of tribal enrollment or a "Certificate of Indian Blood" (one-quarter considered acceptable); slides of their work are then examined by a committee which decides whether it meets Indian Market standards.

23   Quoted in Wheeler (1997).

REFERENCES

Archival References

Amelia Elizabeth White Collection (AEWC), Catherine McElvain Library, School of American Research (SAR), Santa Fe, New Mexico.

Bryn Mawr College Archives, Mariam Coffin Canaday Library, Bryn Mawr College, Bryn Mawr, Pennsylvania.

Elizabeth Shepley Sergeant Papers (ESS). Yale Collection of American Literature (YCAL). Beinecke Rare Book and Manuscript Library, Yale University, New Haven, Connecticut.

Erna Fergusson Collection, scrapbook 75, University of New Mexico Special Collections, Albuquerque, New Mexico.

Indian Arts Research Center Archives, Indian Arts Research Center (IARC), School of American Research, Santa Fe.

John Collier Papers, 1922–1968. Yale University Library, New Haven, Connecticut.

Kenneth Chapman Collection (KCC), Laboratory of Anthropology (LA), Santa Fe, New Mexico.

Mabel Dodge Luhan Collection (MDLC), Beinecke Rare Book and Manuscript Library, Yale University, New Haven, Connecticut.

Margretta S. Dietrich Papers, 1915–1961. State Records Center and Archives (SRCA), Santa Fe, New Mexico.

Records of the Indian Arts and Crafts Board (RIACB), Record Group 435, National Archives (NA), Washington, D.C.

Sallie Wagner Collection, State Records Center and Archives (SRCA), Santa Fe, New Mexico.

Southwestern Association on Indian Affairs Collection (SWAIAC), State Records Center and Archives (SRCA), Santa Fe, New Mexico.

Wheelwright, Mary Cabot. n.d. "Memoirs: Journey Towards Understanding." Wheelwright Museum (WM), Santa Fe, New Mexico.

Interview References

Bird, Gail, and Yazzie Johnson. Interviews with author, October 2, 1990, July 17, 1995.

Buchanan, Jean. Interview with author, December 11, 1990.

Burge, Moris. Interview with author, April 30, 1991.

Chabot, Maria. Interviews with author and Kenneth Dauber, November 13, 1990, and December 7, 1990.

Chalee, Pop. Interview with author, May 2, 1991.

Howard, Dick. Interview with author, July 17, 1995.

Lambert, Marjorie. Interview with author and Kenneth Dauber, February 14, 1991.

Loomis, Sylvia. Interviews with author, January 17, 1991, February 11, 1991, February 27, 1991, April 1, 1991.

Lukas, Julia. Interview with author, May 10, 1991.

Rayne, Catherine. Interview with author, February 19, 1991.

Sakiestewa, Ramona. Interviews with author, August 29, 1990, September, 1990.

Spivey, Richard. Interview with author, November 20, 1990.

Wagner, Sallie. Interview with author, September 12, 1990.

Wofford, Letta. Interview with author, February 25, 1991.

Published Sources

Abbott, Lawrence, ed. 1994. *I Stand in the Center of the Good: Interviews with Contemporary Native American Artists.* Lincoln: University of Nebraska Press.

Abu-Lughod, Lila. 1991. "Writing Against Culture." In *Recapturing Anthropology: Working in the Present.* Richard G. Fox, ed. Santa Fe: School of American Research Press.

Alarcón, Daniel Cooper. 1997. *The Aztec Palimpsest: Mexico in the Modern Imagination.* Tucson: University of Arizona Press.

Alexander, Charles. 1980. *Here the Country Lies: Nationalism and the Arts in Twentieth-Century America.* Bloomington: Indiana University Press.

Alexander, Stephen. 1935. "Design for a Parasite Class." *New Masses.* January 8, p. 28.

Appadurai, Arjun, ed. 1986. *The Social Life of Things: Commodities in Cultural Perspective.* Cambridge: Cambridge University Press.

Arluke, Arnold J. and Boria Sax. 1995. "The Nazi Treatment of Animals and People." In *Reinventing Biology: Respect for Life and the Creation of Knowledge.* Linda Birke and Ruth Hubbard, eds. Bloomington: Indiana University Press.

Auslander, Leora. 1996. *Taste and Power: Furnishing Modern France.* Berkeley: University of California Press.

Austin, Mary. 1920. *No. 26 Jayne Street.* Boston: Houghton Mifflin.

——. 1926. "The Town that Doesn't Want a Chautauqua." *The New Republic.* (7 July):195–97.

——. 1932. *Earth Horizon.* Boston: Houghton Mifflin.

——. 1933 [1929]. "Regional Culture in the Southwest." In *America in the Southwest: A Regional Anthology.* T. M. Pierce and T. Hendon, eds. Albuquerque: University Press.

——. 1970 [1923]. *The American Rhythm.* New York: Cooper Square Publishers.

Babcock, Barbara. 1990. "'A New Mexican Rebecca': Imaging Pueblo Women." *Journal of the Southwest* 32(4):400–37.

Babcock, Barbara, Guy Monthan, and Doris Monthan. 1988. *The Pueblo Storyteller: Development of a Figurative Ceramic Tradition.* Tucson: University of Arizona Press.

Babcock, Barbara A. and Marta Weigle. 1996. *The Great Southwest of the Fred Harvey Company and the Santa Fe Railway.* Phoenix: The Heard Museum.

Barker, Ruth Laughlin. 1926. "Interview with Dr. Lummis." *El Palacio* 21 (12):319–25.

Barnard, Rita. 1995. *The Great Depression and the Culture of Abundance: Kenneth Fearing, Nathaniel West, and Mass Culture in the 1930s.* Cambridge: Cambridge University Press.

Barrett, Stanley R. 1996. *Anthropology: A Student's Guide to Theory and Method.* Toronto: University of Toronto Press.

Baumann, Gustave. 1989 [1972]. "Concerning a Small Untroubled World." In *The Collector's El Palacio.* Santa Fe: Museum of New Mexico Foundation.

Becker, Howard. 1982. *Art Worlds.* Berkeley: University of California Press.

Becker, Jane Stewart. 1998. *Selling Tradition: Appalachia and the Construction of an American Folk, 1930–1940.* Chapel Hill: University of North Carolina Press.

Belk, Russell W. 1995. *Collecting in a Consumer Society.* London: Routledge.

Bell-Villada, Gene H. 1996. *Art for Art's Sake and Literary Life: How Politics and Markets Helped Shape the Ideology and Culture of Aestheticism, 1790–1990.* Lincoln: University of Nebraska Press.

Bernstein, Bruce David. 1993. "The Marketing of Culture: Pottery and Santa Fe's Indian Market." Ph.D. dissertation, University of New Mexico.

———. 1996. "Celebrating 75 Years: The History of SWAIA and Indian Market." *Indian Market: Official Program of the 1996 Santa Fe Indian Market.* Pp. 29–34.

———. 1999. "Contexts for the Growth and Development of the Indian Art World in the 1960s and 1970s." In *Native American Art in the Twentieth Century.* W. Jackson Rushing III, ed. London: Routledge.

Blake, Casey Nelson. 1990. *Beloved Community: The Cultural Criticism of Randoph Bourne, Van Wyck Brooks, and Lewis Mumford.* Chapel Hill: University of North Carolina Press.

Boris, Eileen. 1986. *Art and Labor: Ruskin, Morris, and the Craftsman Ideal in America.* Philadelphia: Temple University Press.

———. 1991. "From Parlor to Politics: Women and Reform in America, 1890–1925." *Radical History Review* 50 (Spring):191–203.

Borneman, John. 1988. "Race, Ethnicity, Species, Breed: Totemism and Horse-breed Classification in America." *Comparative Studies in Society and History* 30(1):25–51.

Bourdieu, Pierre. 1984. *Distinction: A Social Critique of the Judgement of Taste.* Trans. Richard Nice. Cambridge: Harvard University Press.

Brantlinger, Patrick. 1990. *Crusoe's Footprints: Cultural Studies in Britain and America.* New York: Routledge.

Briggs, Charles L. 1989. *The Wood Carvers of Cordova, New Mexico: Social Dimensions of an Artistic "Revival."* Albuquerque: University of New Mexico Press.

Brody, J. J. 1971. *Indian Painters and White Patrons.* Albuquerque: University of New Mexico Press.

———. 1997. *Pueblo Indian Painting: Tradition and Modernism in New Mexico, 1900–1930.* Santa Fe: School of American Research Press.

Brown, Doug. 1998. "Be All You Can Be: Invidious Self-Development and its Social Imperative." In *Thorstein Veblen in the Twenty-First Century: A Commemoration of "The Theory of the Leisure Class," 1899–1999.* Doug Brown, ed. Northampton, MA: Edward Elgar.

Brown, Michael F. 1998. "Can Culture Be Copyrighted?" *Current Anthropology* 39(2):193–222.

Bynner, Witter. 1979 [1936]. "Designs for Beauty. In *The Works of Witter Bynner*. James Kraft, ed. Pp. 336–42. New York: Farrar, Straus, and Giroux.

Caffrey, Margaret M. 1989. *Ruth Benedict: Stranger in This Land*. Austin: University of Texas Press.

Caglar, Ayse S. 1997. " 'Go Go Dog!' And German Turks' Demand for Pet Dogs." *Journal of Material Culture* 2(1):77–94.

Capote, Truman. 1987. [1976]. *Answered Prayers: The Unfinished Novel*. New York: Random House.

Case, Virginia and Robert Ormond Case. 1948. *We Called it Culture: The Story of Chatauqua*. Garden City, NY: Doubleday.

Cather, Willa. 1913. *O Pioneers!* Boston: Houghton Mifflin.

——. 1991 [1915]. *The Song of the Lark*. New York: Bantam.

Cesa, Margaret. 1997. *The World of Flower Blue: Pop Challee: An Artistic Biography*. Santa Fe: Red Crane Books.

Chapman, Kenneth. 1924. "The Indian Fair." *Art and Archaeology* 18(5–6).

Chase, Mary Ellen. 1950. *Abby Aldrich Rockefeller*. New York: Macmillan.

Chase, Stuart. 1929. *Men and Machines*. New York: Macmillan.

——. 1931. *Mexico: A Study of Two Americas*. New York: Macmillan.

Chang, Richard. 1998. "Indian Market Fees Rankle Artists." *New Mexican*, 8 January B-1.

Chauvenet, Beatrice. 1983. *Hewett and Friends: A Biography of Santa Fe's Vibrant Era*. Santa Fe: Museum of New Mexico Press.

Chávez, John R. 1984. *The Lost Land: The Chicano Image of the Southwest*. Albuquerque: University of New Mexico Press.

Clifford, James. 1988. *The Predicament of Culture: Twentieth-Century Ethnography, Literature, and Art*. Cambridge: Harvard University Press.

Collins, Randall. 1992. "Women and the Production of Status Cultures." In *Cultivating Differences: Symbolic Boundaries and the Making of Inequality*. Michéle Lamont and Marcel Fournier, eds. Pp. 213–31. Chicago: Chicago University Press.

Council on Economic Priorities. 1990. *Shopping For a Better World*. New York: Ballantine.

Curtis, Edward S. 1907–1930. *The North American Indian: Being a Series of Volumes Picturing and Describing the Indians of the United States, and Alaska*. Frederick W. Hodge, ed. 20 volumes. Seattle: E. S. Curtis.

Curtis, Natalie. 1922. "Pueblo Poetry." *El Palacio* 12(7):95–99.

Dauber, Kenneth. 1990. "Pueblo Pottery and the Politics of Regional Identity." *Journal of the Southwest* 32(4):576–96.

——. 1993. "Shaping the Clay: Pueblo Pottery, Cultural Sponsorship and Regional Identity in New Mexico." Ph.D. dissertation, University of Arizona.

Davis, Linda H. 1987. *Onward and Upward: A Biography of Katharine S. White*. New York: Harper & Row.

De Grazia, Victoria. 1996. Introduction to "Part II: Establishing the Modern Consumer Household." *The Sex of Things: Gender and Consumption in Historical Per-*

spective. Victoria de Grazia and Ellen Furlough, eds. Berkeley: University of California Press.

De Grazia, Victoria and Ellen Furlough, eds. 1996. *The Sex of Things: Gender and Consumption in Historical Perspective.* Berkeley: University of California Press.

Deloria, Philip J. 1998. *Playing Indian.* New Haven: Yale University Press.

Dietrich, Margretta Stewart. 1930. "The Indian Fair." *El Palacio* 29(3).

——. n.d. "Nebraska Recollections." Unpublished ms. New Mexico State Library.

——. 1936. "Old Art in New Forms." *New Mexico Magazine* 14(9):26–27, 56.

——. 1959. "New Mexico Recollections: Part I." New Mexico State Library, Santa Fe, New Mexico.

——. 1961. *New Mexico Recollections: Part II.* Santa Fe: Vegara Printing.

Di Leonardo, Michaela. 1998. *Exotics at Home: Anthropologists, Others, American Modernity.* Chicago: University of Chicago Press.

Dillingham, Rick. 1992. *Acoma and Laguna Pottery.* Santa Fe: School of American Research Press.

Dilworth, Leah. 1996. *Imagining Indians in the Southwest: Persistent Visions of a Primitive Past.* Washington: Smithsonian Institution Press.

Doll, Charles. 1926. "Cultural Center of the Southwest." *El Palacio* 20(9):171–81.

Dominguez, Virginia R. 1994. "Invoking Culture: The Messy Side of 'Cultural Politics.'" In *Eloquent Obsessions: Writing Cultural Criticism.* Marianna Torgovnick, ed. Durham, NC: Duke University Press.

Drinnon, Richard. 1980. *Facing West: The Metaphysics of Indian-Hating and Empire-Building.* Minneapolis: University of Minnesota Press.

El Palacio. 1921. "Mary Austin and Feminism." 11(4).

——. 1922a. "Prizes for Indian Handicraft." 12(6):81.

——. 1922b. "The Santa Fe Fiesta and Centenary of the Santa Fe Trail." 13(2):15–17.

——. 1926. "Southwest Indian Fair." 20(10):204–12.

Evans, Clay. 1992. "Gays in Santa Fe." *Santa Fe Reporter,* 11 March, 17–19.

Evans, Sara. 1989. *Born for Liberty: A History of Women in America.* New York: Free Press.

Fauntleroy, Gussie. 1992. "Surveying Indian Art as Culture, Not as Collectible Pieces of Work." *Pasatiempo* (14 August):31.

Featherstone, Mike. 1991. *Consumer Culture and Postmodernism.* London: Sage.

Finnegan, Margaret. 1999. *Selling Suffrage: Consumer Culture and Votes for Women.* New York: Columbia University Press.

Fox, Richard G., ed. 1991. *Recapturing Anthropology: Working in the Present.* Santa Fe: School of American Research Press.

Fox, Richard Wightman. 1983. "Epitaph for Middletown: Robert S. Lynd and the Analysis of Consumer Culture." In *The Culture of Consumption: Critical Essays in American History, 1880–1980.* Richard Wightman Fox and T. J. Jackson Lears, eds. New York: Pantheon.

Frake, C. O. 1972 [1964]. "How To Ask For a Drink in Subanun." In *Language and Social Context.* Pier Paolo Giglioli, ed. New York: Penguin.

Frank, Waldo. 1919. *Our America.* New York: Boni and Liveright.

Franklin, Nancy. 1996. "Lady With A Pencil." *The New Yorker.* 26 February: 172–84.

Friedman, Jonathan. 1990. "Being in the World: Globalization and Localization." In *Global Culture: Nationalism, Globalization and Modernity.* Mike Featherstone, ed. London: Sage.

Frisby, David and Mike Featherstone, eds. 1997. *Simmel on Culture: Selected Writings.* London: Sage.

Frow, John. 1991. "Tourism and the Semiotics of Nostalgia." *October* 57:123–51.

Fryer, Judith. 1987. "Desert, Rock, Shelter, Legend: Willa Cather's Novels of the Southwest." In *The Desert is No Lady: Southwestern Landscapes in Women's Writing and Art.* Vera Norwood and Janice Monk, eds. New Haven: Yale University Press.

Gelber, Steven M. 1999. *Hobbies: Leisure and the Culture of Work in America.* New York: Columbia University Press.

Ginzburg, Lori. 1990. *Women and the Work of Benevolence.* New Haven: Yale University Press.

Givens, Douglas R. 1992. *Alfred Vincent Kidder and the Development of Americanist Archaeology.* Albuquerque: University of New Mexico Press.

Gold, Michael. 1936. "Mabel Luhan's Slums." *The New Masses,* 1 September, 11–13.

Goodwin, Neva R. 1997. Introduction. *The Consumer Society.* Neva R. Goodwin, Frank Ackerman, and David Kiron, eds. Pp. xxvii–xxxv. Washington, D.C.: Island Press.

Gordon, Linda. 1976. *Woman's Body, Woman's Right: A Social History of Birth Control in America.* New York: Grossman.

Gordon-McCutchan, R. C. 1991. *The Taos Indians and the Battle for Blue Lake.* Santa Fe: Red Crane Books.

Green, Rayna. 1988. "The Tribe Called Wannabee: Playing Indian in America and Europe." *Folklore* 99:30–55.

Greenberg, Clement. 1957 [1939]. "Avant-Garde and Kitsch." In *Mass Culture: The Popular Arts in America.* Bernard Rosenberg and David Manning White, eds. Glencoe, IL: The Free Press.

Gupta, Akhil and James Ferguson. 1992. "Beyond 'Culture': Space, Identity, and the Politics of Difference." *Cultural Anthropology* 7:6–23.

Gutiérrez, Ramón A. 1990. *When Jesus Came, the Corn Mothers Went Away: Marriage, Sexuality and Power in New Mexico, 1500–1846.* Stanford: Stanford University Press.

Handler, Richard. 1991. "Ruth Benedict and Modernist Sensibility." In *Modernist Anthropology: From Fieldwork to Text.* Marc Manganaro, ed. Princeton: Princeton University Press.

Hannerz, Ulf. 1990. "Cosmopolitans and Locals in World Culture." In *Global Culture: Nationalism, Globalization and Modernity.* Mike Featherstone, ed. London: Sage.

Harvey, David. 1989. *The Condition of Postmodernity: An Enquiry into the Origins of Cultural Change.* Oxford: Basil Blackwell.

Hegeman, Susan. 1999. *Patterns for America: Modernism and the Concept of Culture.* Princeton: Princeton University Press.

Hemenway, Robert E. 1977. *Zora Neale Hurston: A Literary Biography.* Urbana: University of Illinois Press.

Hewett, Edgar Lee. 1922. "The Art of the Earliest Americans." *El Palacio* 13(1).

Hinsley, Curtis M. 1991. "The World as Marketplace: Commodification of the Exotic at the World's Columbian Exposition, Chicago, 1893." In *Exhibiting Cultures: The*

Poetics and Politics of Museum Display. Ivan Karp and Steven Lavine, eds. Washington: Smithsonian Institution Press.

Holmes, W. H. 1889. "Debasement of Pueblo Art." *American Anthropologist* 2:320.

Horowitz, Helen Lefkowitz. 1994. *The Power and Passion of M. Carey Thomas.* Urbana: University of Illinois Press.

Hornby, Nick. 1995. *High Fidelity.* New York, New York: Riverhead Books.

Hufford, Mary. 1991. "American Folklife: A Commonwealth of Cultures." Publications of the American Folklife Center, no. 17, Library of Congress, Washington.

Hurt, Amy. 1928. "The Koshare Tours: Two Women Run a Sight-Seeing Business." *Woman's Home Companion* (May), n.p.

Jacobs, Margaret D. 1999. *Engendered Encounters: Feminism and Pueblo Cultures, 1879–1934.* Lincoln: University of Nebraska Press.

Jantzer-White, Marilee. 1994. "Tonita Peña (Quah Ah), Pueblo Painter: Asserting Identity Through Continuity and Change." *American Indian Quarterly* 18(3):369–82.

Jojola, Theodore. 1998. "On Revision and Revisionism: American Indian Representations in New Mexico." In *Natives and Academics: Researching and Writing about American Indians.* Devon A. Mihesuah, ed. Pp. 172–80. Lincoln: University of Nebraska Press.

Jones, Arthur Frederick. n.d. "Erin's Famous Hound Finding Greater Glory at Rathmullan." Amelia Elizabeth White Collection, School of American Research, Santa Fe, New Mexico.

Kahn, Joel S. 1989. "Culture, Demise or Resurrection?" *Critique of Anthropology* 9(2):5–25.

Kelly, Lawrence C. 1983. *The Assault on Assimilation: John Collier and the Origins of Indian Reform.* Albuquerque: University of New Mexico Press.

Kimmelman, Michael. 1999. "Comparing the Fake and the Great." *New York Times,* 28 May.

Kolodny, Annette. 1984. *The Land Before Her: Fantasy and Experience of the American Frontiers, 1630–1860.* Chapel Hill: University of North Carolina Press.

Kopytoff, Igor. 1986. "The Cultural Biography of Things: Commoditization as Process." In *The Social Life of Things: Commodities in Cultural Perspective.* Arjun Appadurai, ed. Cambridge: Cambridge University Press.

Kuper, Adam. 1999. *Culture: The Anthropologists' Account.* Cambridge: Harvard University Press.

La Farge, Oliver. 1929. *Laughing Boy.* Boston: Houghton Mifflin.

La Farge, Oliver and John Sloan. 1931. "Introduction to American Indian Art." Exposition of Indian Tribal Arts, Inc. (1970 reprint also available: Glorieta, NM: Rio Grande Press.)

Laermans, Rudi. 1993. "Learning to Consume: Early Department Stores and the Shaping of the Modern Consumer Culture (1800–1914)." *Theory, Culture, and Society* 10(4):79–102.

Landsman, Gail H. 1992. "The 'Other' as Political Symbol: Images of Indians in the Woman Suffrage Movement." *Ethnohistory* 39(3):247–84.

Langness, L. L. 1987. *The Study of Culture.* Novato, California: Chandler and Sharp.

Lears, T. J. Jackson. 1981. *No Place of Grace: Antimodernism and the Transformation of American Culture, 1880–1920*. New York: Pantheon.

———. 1983. "From Salvation to Self-Realization: Advertising and the Therapeutic Roots of American Culture." In *The Culture of Consumption: Critical Essays in American History, 1880–1980*. Richard Wightman Fox and T. J. Jackson Lears, eds. New York: Pantheon.

———. 1994. *Fables of Abundance: A Cultural History of Advertising in America*. New York: Basic Books.

Levenstein, Harvey. 1998. *Seductive Journey: American Tourists in France from Jefferson to the Jazz Age*. Chicago: University of Chicago Press.

Lewis, Sinclair. 1947 [1929]. *Dodsworth*. New York: Random House.

Lohrmann, Charles J. 1998. "Frame Those Blankets: Weaving New Traditions." *Native Peoples* 11(3):26–32.

Lucero, Evelina Luni. 2000. *Night Sky, Morning Star*. Tucson: University of Arizona Press.

Luhan, Mabel Dodge. 1935. *European Experiences: Volume Two of Intimate Memories*. New York: Harcourt Brace and Company.

———. 1987 [1937]. *Edge of Taos Desert: An Escape to Reality*. Albuquerque: University of New Mexico Press.

Lummis, Charles F. 1925. *Mesa, Cañon and Pueblo*. New York: The Century Company.

Lury, Celia. 1996. *Consumer Culture*. New Brunswick, NJ: Rutgers University Press.

Lyman, Christopher. 1982. *The Vanishing Race and Other Illusions: Photographs of Indians by Edward S. Curtis*. New York: Pantheon / Smithsonian Institution Press.

Lynes, Russell. 1954 [1949]. *The Tastemakers*. New York: Grosset & Dunlap.

Main Line Times. 1970. "Miss Gertrude Ely Dies; Humanitarian, Civic Leader." 29 October.

Marchand, Roland. 1985. *Advertising the American Dream: Making Way for Modernity, 1920–1940*. Berkeley: University of California Press.

Marcus, George E. 1998. *Ethnography Through Thick and Thin*. Princeton, NJ: Princeton University Press.

Marcus, George E. and Fred R. Myers. 1995. "The Traffic in Art and Culture: An Introduction." *The Traffic in Culture: Refiguring Art and Anthropology*. George E. Marcus and Fred R. Myers, eds. Berkeley: University of California Press.

Mark, Joan. 1988. *A Stranger in her Native Land: Alice Fletcher and the American Indians*. Lincoln: University of Nebraska Press.

Marquis, Alice G. 1986. *Hopes and Ashes: The Birth of Modern Times, 1929–1939*. New York: The Free Press.

Mayhew, Robert William. 1984. "The New Mexico Association on Indian Affairs, 1922–1958." Master's thesis, University of New Mexico.

McCarthy, Kathleen D. 1991. *Women's Culture: American Philanthropy and Art, 1830–1930*. Chicago: University of Chicago Press.

McCracken, Grant. 1988. *Culture and Consumption: New Approaches to the Symbolic Character of Consumer Goods and Activities*. Bloomington: Indiana University Press.

McDowell, Steve. 1992. "Don't Look Back: On the Museum of Fine Art's 75th Anniversary, New Mexicans Eminent in the Art World Ponder the Future of America's Art Museums." *El Palacio* 98(1:11–14, 41–46).

McFeely, Eliza. 1996. "Palimpsest of American Identity: Zuni, Anthropology and American Identity at the Turn of the Century." Ph.D. dissertation, New York University.

McGreevy, Susan Brown. 1993. "Daughters of Affluence: Wealth, Collecting, and Southwestern Institutions." In *Hidden Scholars: Women Anthropologists and the Native American Southwest.* Nancy J. Parezo, ed. Albuquerque: University of New Mexico Press.

M'Closkey, Kathy. 1994. "Marketing Multiple Myths: The Hidden History of Navajo Weaving." *Journal of the Southwest* 36(3):185–222.

———. 1996. "Myths, Markets and Metaphors: Navajo Weaving as Commodity and Communicative Form." Ph.D. dissertation, York University.

McLuhan, T. C. 1985. *Dream Tracks: The Railroad and the American Indian 1890–1930.* New York: Abrams.

Michaels, Walter Benn. 1995. "Race Into Culture: A Critical Genealogy of Cultural Identity." In *Identities.* Kwame Anthony Appiah and Henry Louis Gates, Jr., eds. Chicago: University of Chicago Press.

Miller, Daniel. 1995. "Consumption and Commodities." *Annual Review of Anthropology* 24:141–61.

———. 1998. *A Theory of Shopping.* Ithaca: Cornell University Press.

Mitchell, Nancy Marie. 1993. "The Negotiated Role of Contemporary American Indian Artists: A Study in Marginality." Ph.D. dissertation, Stanford University.

Moi, Toril. 1991. "Appropriating Bourdieu: Feminist Theory and Pierre Bourdieu's Sociology of Culture." *New Literary History* 22:1017–49.

Montgomery, Maureen E. 1998. *Displaying Women: Spectacles of Leisure in Edith Wharton's New York.* New York: Routledge.

Mullin, Molly H. 1992. "The Patronage of Difference: Making Indian Art 'Art, Not Ethnology." *Cultural Anthropology* 7(4):395–424. Reprinted in *The Traffic in Culture: Refiguring Art and Anthropology* (1995). George E. Marcus and Fred R. Myers, eds. Berkeley: University of California Press.

Museum of New Mexico. 1989. *Window on the West: The Collector's El Palacio.* Santa Fe: Museum of New Mexico Foundation.

Myers, Fred. 1991. "The Production of Discourse(s) for Aboriginal Acrylic Paintings." *Cultural Anthropology* 6(1):26–62.

Naranjo, Tessie. 1996. "Cultural Changes: The Effect of Foreign Systems at Santa Clara Pueblo." In *The Great Southwest of the Fred Harvey Company and the Santa Fe Railway.* Marta Weigle and Barbara A. Babcock, eds. Phoenix: The Heard Museum.

Newcomer, Mabel and Evelyn S. Gibson. 1924. "Vital Statistics from Vassar College." *American Journal of Sociology* 29(4).

Novak, Shonda. 1997. "Indian Market Not Popular with Everyone." *Albuquerque Tribune,* 23 August: A1.

O'Brien, Sharon. 1987. *Willa Cather: The Emerging Voice.* New York: Ballantine.

Oles, James. 1993. *South of the Border: Mexico in the American Imagination, 1914–1947*. Washington: Smithsonian Institution Press.

Ortner, Sherry. 1974. "Is Female to Male as Nature is to Culture?" In *Women, Culture, and Society*. Michelle Z. Rosaldo and Louise Lamphere, eds. Stanford: Stanford University Press.

——, ed. 1999. *The Fate of 'Culture': Geertz and Beyond*. Berkeley: University of California Press.

Pach, Walter. 1931. "The Indian Tribal Arts: A Critic's View of a Unique American Asset." *New York Times*, 22 November, section VIII, p. 13.

Parezo, Nancy J., and Karl Hoerig. 1999. "Collecting to Educate: Ernest Thompson Seton and Mary Cabot Wheelwright." In *Collecting Native America, 1870–1960*. Shepard Krech III and Barbara A. Hail, eds. Pp. 203–31. Washington, D.C.: Smithsonian Institution Press.

Pearce, Susan M. 1998. *Collecting in Contemporary Practice*. London: Sage.

Pearce, T. M. 1945. "Ina Sizer Cassidy: A Tribute." University of New Mexico Special Collections (Cassidy file).

Phillips, Ruth B. 1995. "Why Not Tourist Art? Significant Silences in Native American Museum Representations." In *After Colonialism: Imperial Histories and Postcolonial Displacements*. Gyan Prakash, ed. Princeton: Princeton University Press.

Price, Sally. 1989. *Primitive Art in Civilized Places*. Chicago: Chicago University Press.

Providence Sunday Journal. 1933. "She Learned from the Corn, the Rain and the Buffalo." 27 August.

——, 1997. "Novices Run the Shows." *New Mexican*, 5 August, D-1.

Riley, Denise. 1988. *"Am I That Name?": Feminism and the Category of "Women" in History*. Minneapolis: University of Minnesota Press.

Riley, Michael James. 1993. "Picturing the Southwest Re-Framed: An American Cultural Landscape and the Social Negotiation of Art, Ethnicity, and Place." Ph.D. dissertation, University of Texas at Austin.

Ritvo, Harriet. 1987. *The Animal Estate: The English and Other Creatures in the Victorian Age*. Cambridge: Harvard University Press.

——. 1991. "The Animal Connection." In *The Boundaries of Humanity*. James J. Sheehan and Morton Sosna, eds. Pp. 68–84. Berkeley: University of California Press.

Rivera, Diego. 1924. "The Guild Spirit in Mexican Art." *Survey Graphic* 5(2):174–76.

Rodriguez, Sylvia. 1989. "Art, Tourism, and Race Relations in Taos: Toward a Sociology of the Art Colony." *Journal of Anthropological Research* 45(1):77–97.

Rolt-Wheeler, Francis W. 1909. *The Science-History of the Universe: Anthropology*. New York: Current Literature Publishing Company.

Rudnick, Lois Palken. 1984. *Mabel Dodge Luhan: New Woman, New Worlds*. Albuquerque: University of New Mexico Press.

——. 1987. "Re-naming the Land: Anglo Expatriate Women in the Southwest." In *The Desert is No Lady: Southwestern Landscapes in Women's Writing and Art*. Vera Norwood and Janice Monk, eds. New Haven: Yale University Press.

——. 1996. *Utopian Vistas: The Mabel Dodge Luhan House and the American Counterculture*. Albuquerque: University of New Mexico Press.

Rushing, W. Jackson. 1992. "Marketing the Affinity of the Primitive and the Modern:

René d'Harnoncourt and 'Indian Art of the United States.'" In *The Early Years of Native American Art History: The Politics of Scholarship and Collecting.* Janet Catherine Berlo, ed. Seattle: University of Washington Press.

——. 1995. *Native American Art and the New York Avant-Garde: A History of Cultural Primitivism.* Austin: University of Texas Press.

Sapir, Edward. 1924. "Culture, Genuine and Spurious." *American Journal of Sociology* 29(4):401–29.

Schrader, Robert F. 1983. *The Indian Arts and Crafts Board: An Aspect of New Deal Indian Policy.* Albuquerque: University of New Mexico Press.

Schulte-Sasse, Jochen. 1989. "The Prestige of the Artist under Conditions of Modernity." *Cultural Critique* 12:83–100.

Shutes, Jeanne and Jill Mellick. 1996. *The Worlds of P'otsúnú: Geronima Cruz Montoya of San Juan Pueblo.* Albuquerque: University of New Mexico Press.

Schwartz, Marion. 1997. *A History of Dogs in the Early Americas.* New Haven: Yale University Press.

Segal, Daniel and Richard Handler. 1995. "U.S. Multiculturalism and the Concept of Culture." *Identities* 1(4):391–407.

Seinfel, Ruth. 1931. "Indian Art Exposition Aided by Woman's Intelligence." *New York Evening Post,* 1 December, E-2.

Sergeant, Elizabeth Shepley. 1910. "Toilers of the Tenements: Where the Beautiful Things of the Great Shops are Made." *McClure's Magazine* (July) 35:231–48.

——. 1920. *Shadow-Shapes: The Journal of a Wounded Woman.* Boston: Houghton Mifflin.

——. 1922. "The Journal of a Mud House." *Harper's Magazine* (March, April, May, June): 409–22, 585–98, 774–82, 56–67.

——. 1923. "The Plight of the Pueblos." *New Republic* 37:473.

——. 1923. "New Mexico: A Relic of Ancient America." *The Nation* (21 November):577–79.

——. 1934. "The Santa Fe Group." *Saturday Review of Literature* (8 December):351–54.

——. 1935. "Notes on a Changing Culture, as Affected by Indian Art." Typescript. John Collier Papers. Manuscripts and Archives. Yale University. Microfilm edition, reel 28.

——. 1963 [1953]. *Willa Cather: A Memoir.* Lincoln: University of Nebraska Press.

Seymour, Tryntje Van Ness. 1988. *When the Rainbow Touches Down: The Artists and Stories Behind the Apache, Navajo, Rio Grande Pueblo, and Hopi Paintings in the William and Leslie Van Ness Denman Collection.* Phoenix: The Heard Museum.

Silverman, Debora. 1986. *Selling Culture: Bloomingdale's, Diana Vreeland, and the New Aristocracy of Taste in Reagan's America.* New York: Pantheon.

Smith, Barbara Herrnstein. 1988. *Contingencies of Value: Alternative Perspectives for Critical Theory.* Cambridge: Harvard University Press.

Smith, Mark C. 1979. "Robert Lynd and Consumerism in the 1930s." *Journal of the History of Sociology* 2:99–119.

Smith-Rosenberg, Carroll. 1985. "The New Woman as Androgyne: Social Disorder and the Gender Crisis, 1870–1936." In *Disorderly Conduct: Visions of Gender in Victorian America.* Carroll Smith-Rosenberg, ed. New York: Oxford University Press.

Soto, Monica. 1997. "Artists Report Big Success." *New Mexican,* 25 August, A1).

Starbuck, Alma J. 1970. *The Complete Irish Wolfhound.* New York: Howell Book House.

Stark, Gregor and E. Catherine Rayne. 1998. *El Delirio: The Santa Fe World of Elizabeth White.* Santa Fe: School of American Research Press.

Steedly, Mary Margaret. 1996. "What is Culture? Does it Matter?" In *Fieldwork: Sites in Literary and Cultural Studies.* Marjorie Garber, Rebecca L. Walkowitz, and Paul B. Franklin, eds. New York: Routledge.

Steiner, Christopher B. 1994. *African Art in Transit.* Cambridge: Cambridge University Press.

Stocking, George Jr. 1982. "The Santa Fe Style in American Anthropology: Regional Interest, Academic Initiative, and Philanthropic Policy in the First Two Decades of the Laboratory of Anthropology, Inc." *Journal of the History of the Behavioral Sciences* 18:3–19.

———. 1989. "The Ethnographic Sensibility of the 1920s and the Dualism of the Anthropological Tradition." In *Romantic Motives: Essays on Anthropological Sensibility.* George Stocking, ed. Madison: University of Wisconsin Press.

Susman, Warren, ed. 1973. *Culture and Commitment, 1919–1945.* New York: George Braziller.

Susman, Warren. 1984. *Culture as History: The Transformation of American Society in the Twentieth Century.* New York: Pantheon.

Swiencicki, Mark A. 1999. "Consuming Brotherhood: Men's Culture, Style, and Recreation as Consumer Culture, 1880–1930." In *Consumer Society in American History: A Reader.* Lawrence B. Glickman, ed. Ithaca, NY: Cornell University Press.

Swenson, Sonja. 1983. "Miss Amelia Elizabeth White's Patronage of Native American Art." Master's thesis, Arizona State University.

Teale, Tamara. 1998. "Lawrence and Beauvoir at Tua-Tah: European Views of the Heart of the World." In *Travel Culture: What Makes Us Go.* Carol Traynor Williams, ed. Westport, CT: Praeger.

Thomas, Nicholas. 1994. *Colonialism's Culture: Anthropology, Travel, and Government.* Princeton: Princeton University Press.

Thompson, Michael. 1979. *Rubbish Theory: The Creation and Destruction of Value.* New York: Oxford University Press.

Tompkins, Jane. 1992. *West of Everything: The Inner Life of Westerns.* New York: Oxford University Press.

Torgovnick, Marianna. 1990. *Gone Primitive: Savage Intellects, Modern Lives.* Chicago: University of Chicago Press.

———. 1997. *Primitive Passions: Men, Women, and the Quest for Ecstasy.* New York: Knopf.

Trachtenberg, Alan. 1982. *The Incorporation of America: Culture and Society in the Gilded Age.* New York: Hill and Wang.

Trouillot, Michel-Rolph. 1991. "Anthropology and the Savage Slot: The Poetics and Politics of Otherness." In *Recapturing Anthropology: Working in the Present.* Richard G. Fox, ed. Santa Fe: School of American Research Press.

Turner, Frederick. 1987. "On the Revision of Monuments." In *The American Indian and the Problem of History*. Calvin Martin, ed. New York: Oxford University Press.

Turner, Terence. 1994. "Anthropology and Multiculturalism: What is Anthropology that Multiculturalists Should be Mindful of It?" In *Multiculturalism: A Critical Reader*. David Theo Goldberg, ed. Cambridge, MA: Basil Blackwell.

Udall, Sharyn R. 1984. *Modernist Painting in New Mexico, 1913–1935*. Albuquerque: University of New Mexico Press.

Urry, John. 1990. *The Tourist Gaze: Leisure and Travel in Contemporary Societies*. London: Sage.

Veblen, Thorstein. 1994 [1899]. *The Theory of the Leisure Class*. New York: Random House.

Versace, Candelora. 1994. "The More Things Change, The More They Stay the Same." *Pasatiempo* (July 8): 6–7.

Wade, Edwin L. 1985. "The Ethnic Art Market in the American Southwest, 1880–1980." In *Objects and Others: Essays on Museums and Material Culture*. George Stocking, Jr., ed. Madison: University of Wisconsin Press.

Wade, Edwin L. and Katherin L. Chase. 1996. "A Personal Passion and Profitable Pursuit: The Katherine Harvey Collection of Native American Fine Art." In *The Great Southwest of the Fred Harvey Company and the Santa Fe Railway*. Marta Weigle and Barbara A. Babcock, eds. Phoenix: The Heard Museum.

Wagner, Roy. 1981. *The Invention of Culture*. Chicago: University of Chicago Press.

Wagner, Sallie. 1997. *Wide Ruins: Memories From a Navajo Trading Post*. Albuquerque: University of New Mexico Press.

Wallerstein, Immanuel. 1990. "Culture as the Ideological Battleground of the Modern World-System." In *Global Culture: Nationalism, Globalization and Modernity*. Mike Featherstone, ed. London: Sage.

Wallis, Brian. 1991. "Selling Nations." *Art in America* 79(9):84–92.

Weigle, Marta. 1983. "The First Twenty-five Years of the Spanish Colonial Arts Society." In *Hispanic Arts and Ethnohistory in the Southwest*. Marta Weigle, Claudia Larcombe, and Samuel Larcombe, eds. Santa Fe: Ancient City Press.

——. 1989. "From Desert to Disney World: The Santa Fe Railway and the Fred Harvey Company Display the Indian Southwest." *Journal of Anthropological Research* 45(1):115–37.

Weigle, Marta and Kyle Fiore. 1982. *Santa Fe and Taos: The Writer's Era, 1916–1941*. Santa Fe: Ancient City Press.

Wheeler, Erica. 1997. "SWAIA: With An Eye On Its Origin." Masters of Indian Market Exhibition Guide, a special supplement to the *New Mexican*, May 22, 4.

Whisnant, David. 1983. *All That is Native and Fine: The Politics of Culture in an American Region*. Chapel Hill: University of North Carolina Press.

Williams, Raymond. 1976. *Keywords: A Vocabulary of Culture and Society*. London: Croom Helm.

Wilson, Chris. 1997. *The Myth of Santa Fe: Creating a Modern Regional Tradition*. Albuquerque: University of New Mexico Press.

Winters, Ivor. 1975 [1926]. "Open Letter to the Editors of *This Quarter*." In *Yvor*

Winters: Uncollected Essays and Reviews. Francis Murphy, ed. Chicago: University of Chicago Press.

Wolf, Eric R. 1982. *Europe and the People Without History.* Berkeley: University of California Press.

———. 1999. *Envisioning Power: Ideologies of Dominance and Crisis.* Berkeley: University of California Press.

Zukin, Sharon. 1991. *Landscapes of Power: From Detroit to Disney World.* Berkeley: University of California Press.

INDEX

Abeyta, Tony, 199 n.13
Abu-Lughod, Lila, 2
African Americans, 26, 27
Alaska, 63
Albuquerque (New Mexico), 53, 67, 84, 88, 100, 140
Alexander, Charles, 15, 94
Ambitions (of women art patrons), 33–36, 40, 42, 43, 49, 62, 90, 183. *See also* Philanthropy; Reform
American Anthropological Association, 67
American Ethnological Society, 1
American Express, 171
American Hospital (Paris), 46, 58
American Indian Art, 198 n.9
American Museum of Natural History, 67
American Rhythm, The (Austin), 26
"Americans," 47–48. *See also* National identity
Amerman, Marcus, 163
Amiotte, Arthur, 199 n.13
Anasazi pottery, 43–45, 55, 77, 79, 94. *See also* Cliff-dwellings
Angell, Hildegarde, 66
Answered Prayers (Capote), 73–74
Anthropologists: as evaluators of Indian art, 6–7, 108, 111, 116; as promoters of Indian art, 77, 79, 108, 112, 113; shared interests of, with art patrons, 92, 96, 97–99, 103, 115, 123–24, 134, 174; vs. tourists, 1. *See also* Anthropology; *specific anthropologists*
Anthropology: popularity of, 1–2, 29, 36, 37, 97–100; rise of, as discipline,

92–93, 99–100; Sergeant's interest in, 44–45; Elizabeth White's interest in, 63, 64, 67, 183. *See also* Archaeology
Antigua, 64
Antique Ethnographic Art Show, 145
Anti-Semitism, 26, 35, 187 n.1
Appadurai, Arjun, 134, 164
Appalachian art, 94–95
Arbuckle, Fatty, 18
Archaeologists: "hard-boiled," 45, 55, 79, 92; as Indian Fair judges, 115–16, 137, 196 n.22. *See also* Archaeology
Archaeology, 36, 55, 65–67, 99, 101. *See also* Anasazi pottery; Archaeologists; Cliff-dwellings
Arizona, 41–44, 46, 176
Armenta Spanish Land Grant, 65
Art: Cather's and Sergeant's views about, 39; as commodity, 91–92, 128–84; and concept of culture, 3; definition of, 91; economic effects of patronage of, 57, 114–15, 122–23, 128–29, 134, 146, 155, 195 nn.18, 21; as gifts, 61; as honorific category, 91, 192 n.2; as investment, 116, 144; vs. mass production, 123–27, 149, 192 n.3, 199 n.13; parallels between dog breeding and collecting of, 177–84; as a positive force in people's lives, 76, 86, 149. *See also* Artists (Indian); Art patrons (women, in New Mexico); Culture; Indian art; Interior decoration and fashion; Spanish colonial art; Taste; Value
Art Institute of Chicago, 194 n.15
Artists (Indian): art patrons' influence on, 113–19, 121–23, 136, 141, 146, 155,

Molly Mullin is Assistant Professor of Anthropology at Albion College.

Library of Congress Cataloging-in-Publication Data
Mullin, Molly H., 1960–
Culture in the marketplace : gender, art, and value in the
American Southwest / Molly H. Mullin.
p. cm.
Includes index.
ISBN 0-8223-2610-8 (hardcover) —ISBN 0-8223-2618-3 (pbk.)
1. Indian art—Southwest, New.   2. Women art patrons—New
Mexico—Santa Fe.   3. Indian art—Southwest, New—Marketing.
4. Culture.   5. Santa Fe (N.M.)—History.   I. Title.
E78.S7 M85 2001
306.4'7'08997078—dc21   00-010681